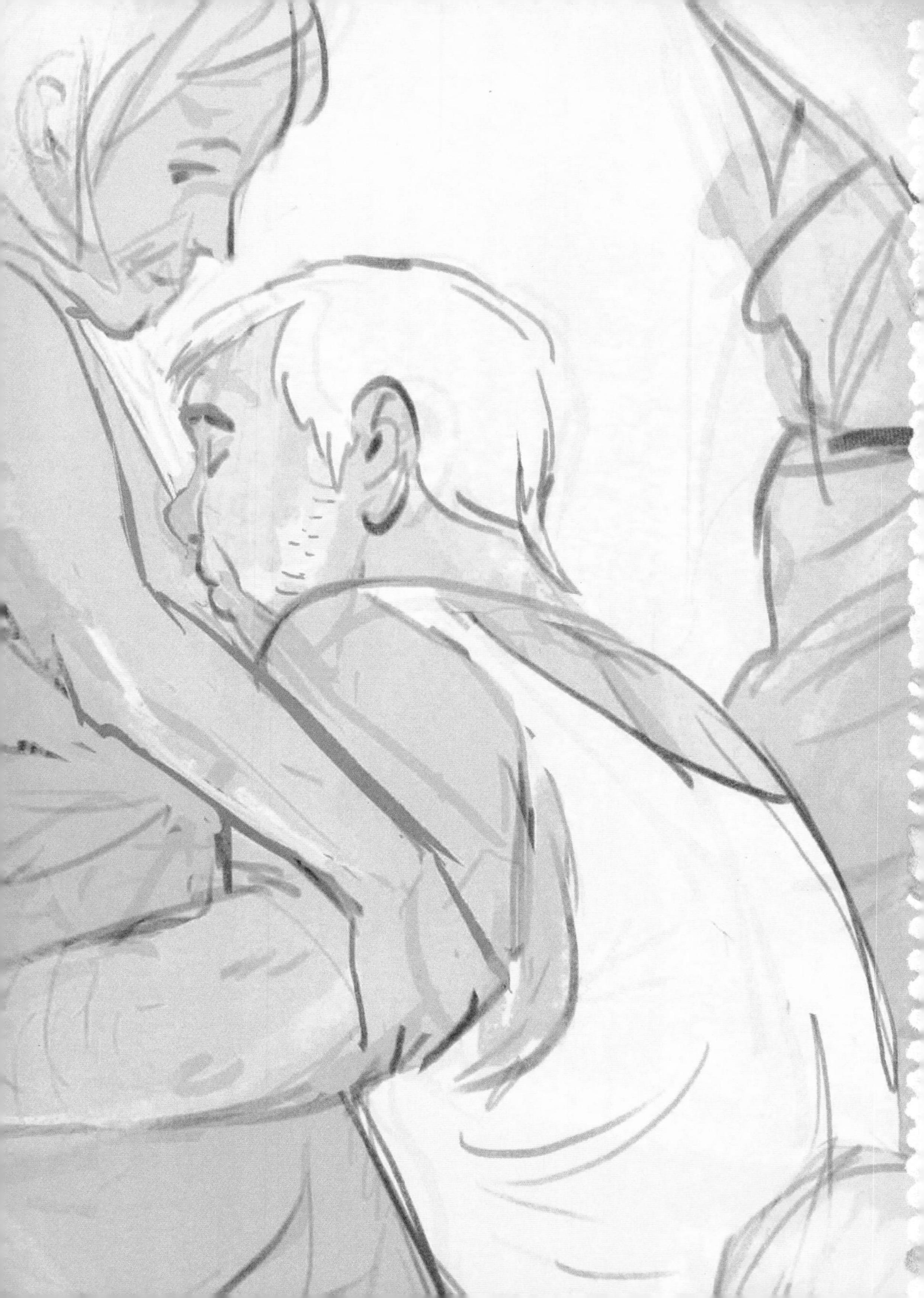

Blossoms in Autumn

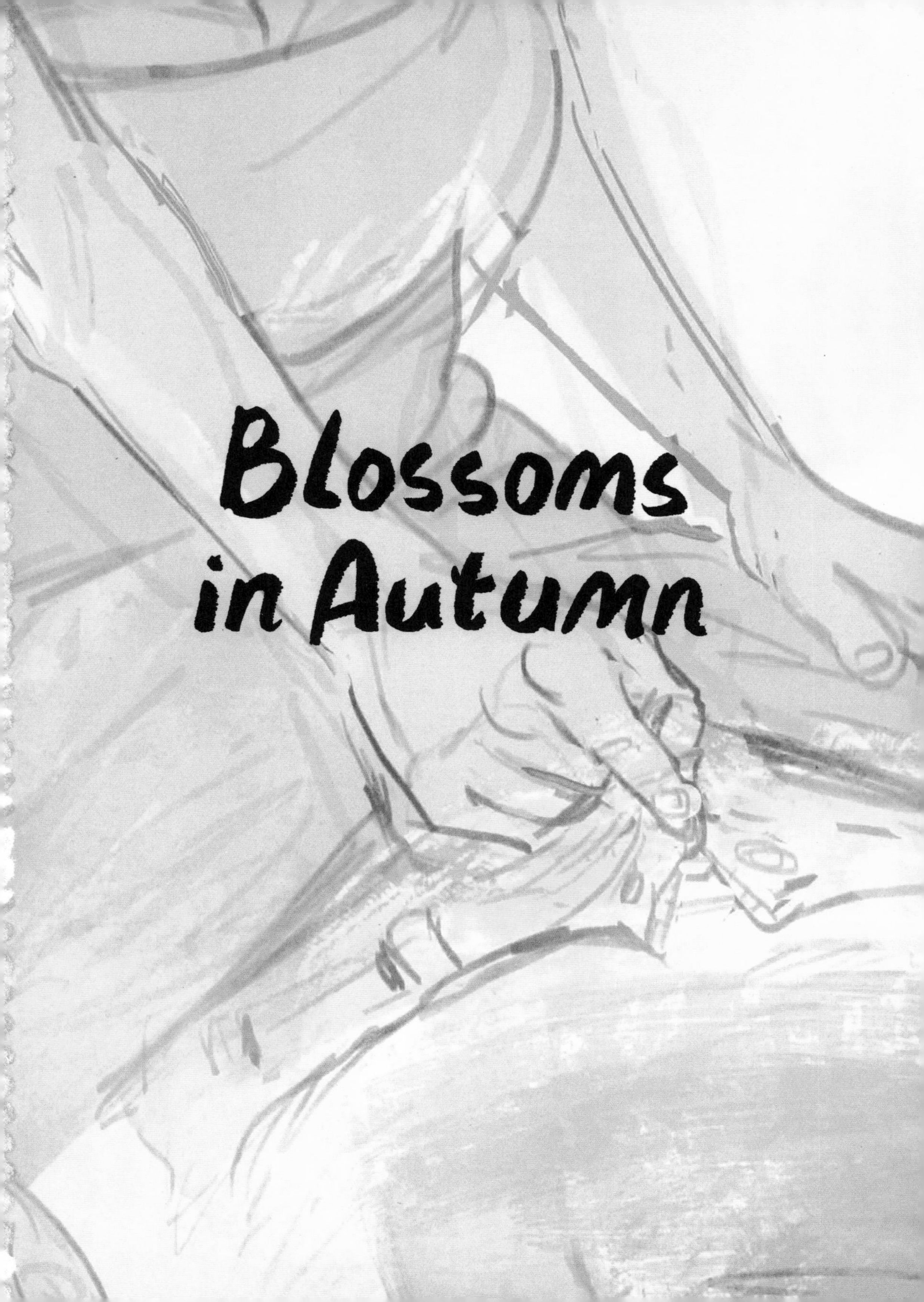

First published in English in 2019
by SelfMadeHero
139-141 Pancras Road
London NW1 1UN
www.selfmadehero.com

English translation © 2019 SelfMadeHero

Words by Zidrou
Art by Aimée de Jongh
Translated by Matt Madden

Publishing Director: Emma Hayley
Sales & Marketing Manager: Sam Humphrey
Editorial & Production Manager: Guillaume Rater
UK Publicist: Paul Smith
Designer: Txabi Jones
With thanks to: Dan Lockwood and Edward Gauvin

First published in French by Dargaud in 2018 as
L'Obsolescence programmée de nos sentiments
© DARGAUD BENELUX (Dargaud-Lombard S.A.) 2018,
by Zidrou, de Jongh
www.dargaud.com
All rights reserved

A CIP record for this book is available from the British Library

ISBN: 978-1-910593-62-2

10 9 8 7 6 5 4 3 2 1

Printed and bound in Slovenia

Words by
Art by

ZIDROU & AiMÉE DE JONGH

Blossoms in Autumn

FRAGILE

SELF
MADE
HERO

Sarah pulls at her dress.
Sarah, Sarah naked.
Sarah whispers:
"My lap weeps ripe cherries."

Sarah,
From every woman comes,
Like bad and good
Like grief and weather,
Now and then, a bit of blood.

– Herman van Veen

1.

The monster in the mirror

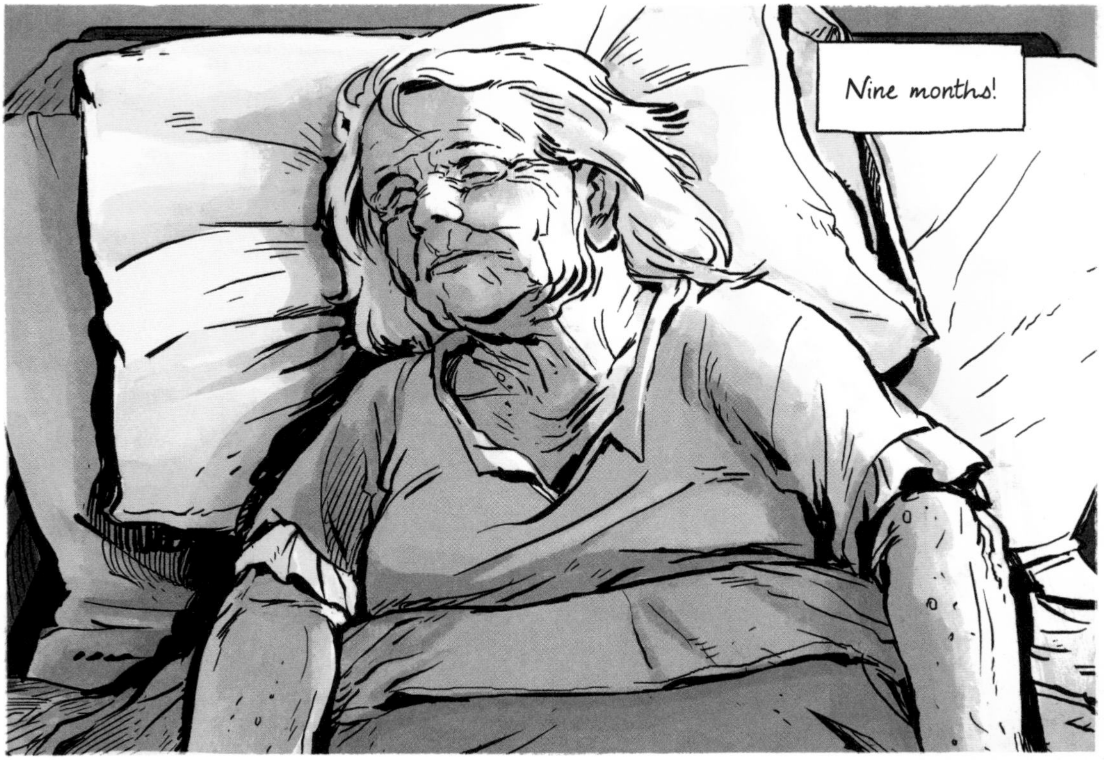
Nine months!

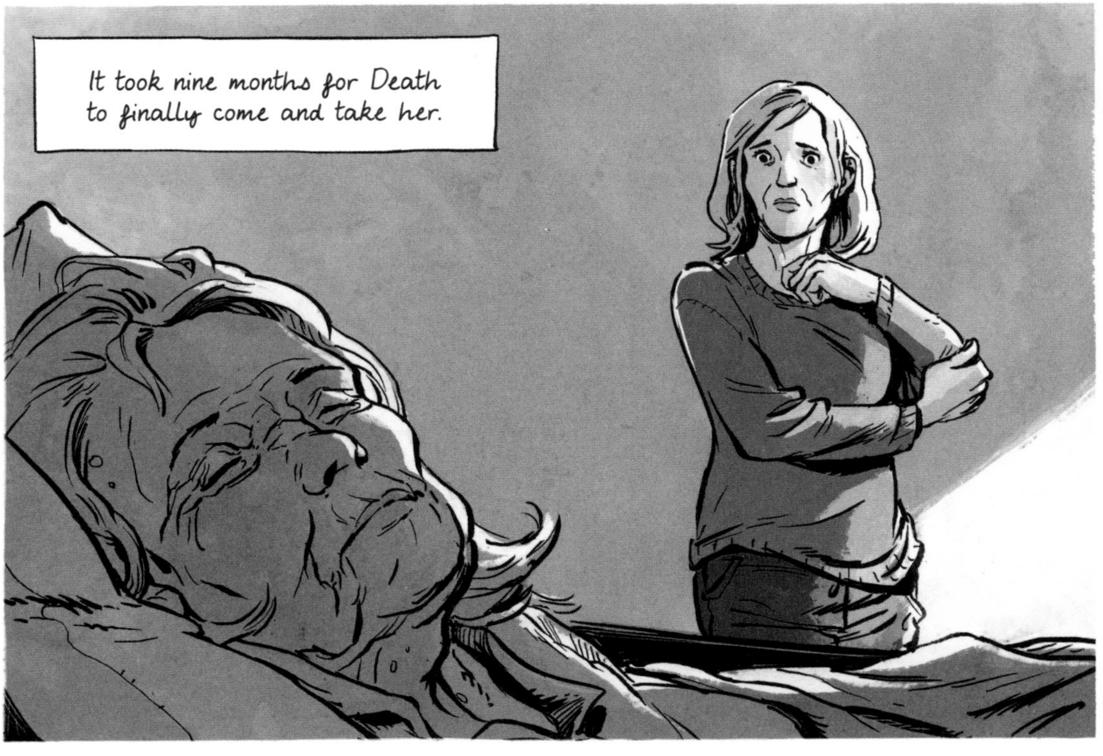
It took nine months for Death to finally come and take her.

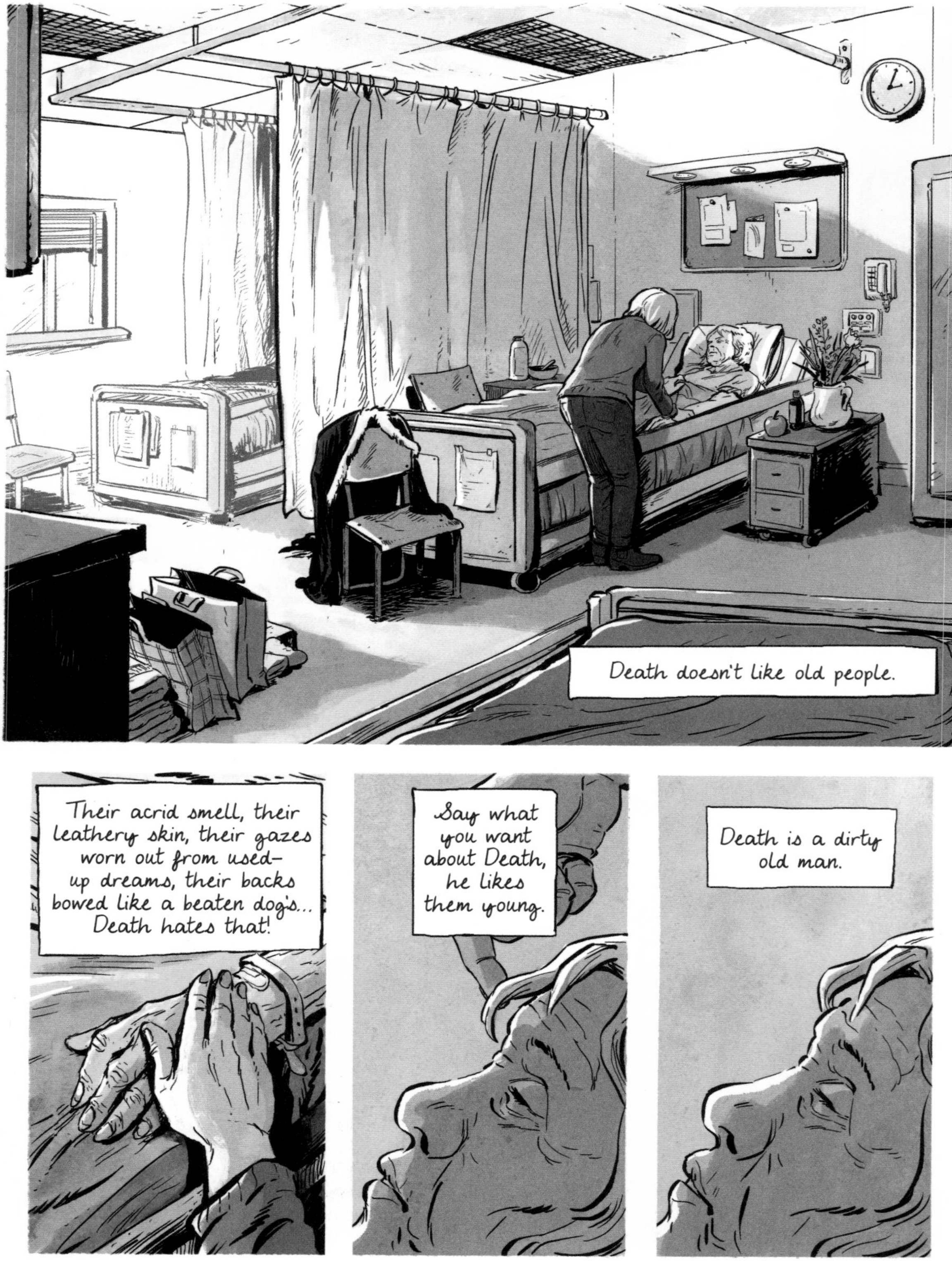
Death doesn't like old people.
Their acrid smell, their leathery skin, their gazes worn out from used-up dreams, their backs bowed like a beaten dog's... Death hates that!
Say what you want about Death, he likes them young.
Death is a dirty old man.

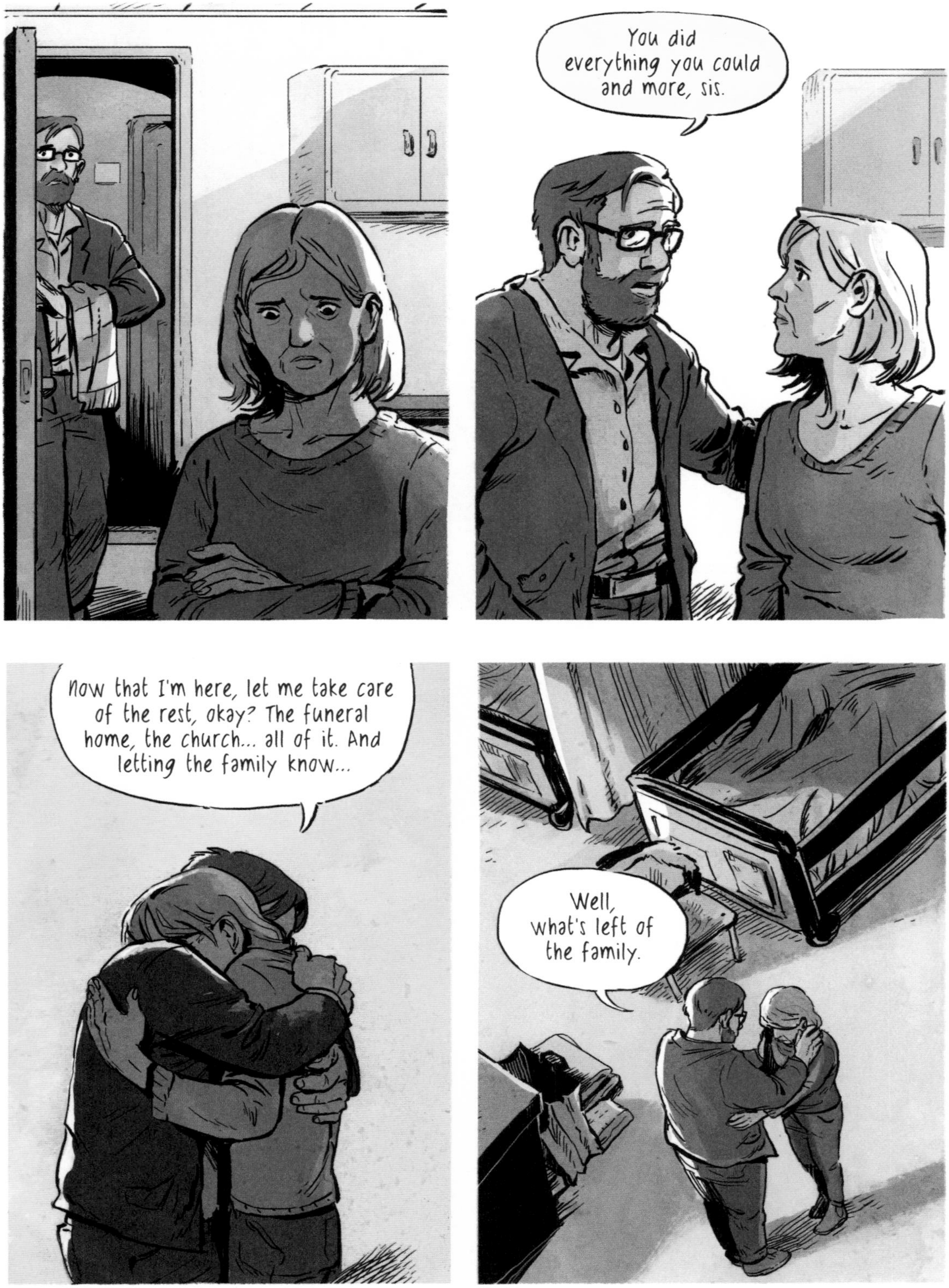
You did everything you could and more, sis.
Now that I'm here, let me take care of the rest, okay? The funeral home, the church... all of it. And letting the family know...
Well, what's left of the family.

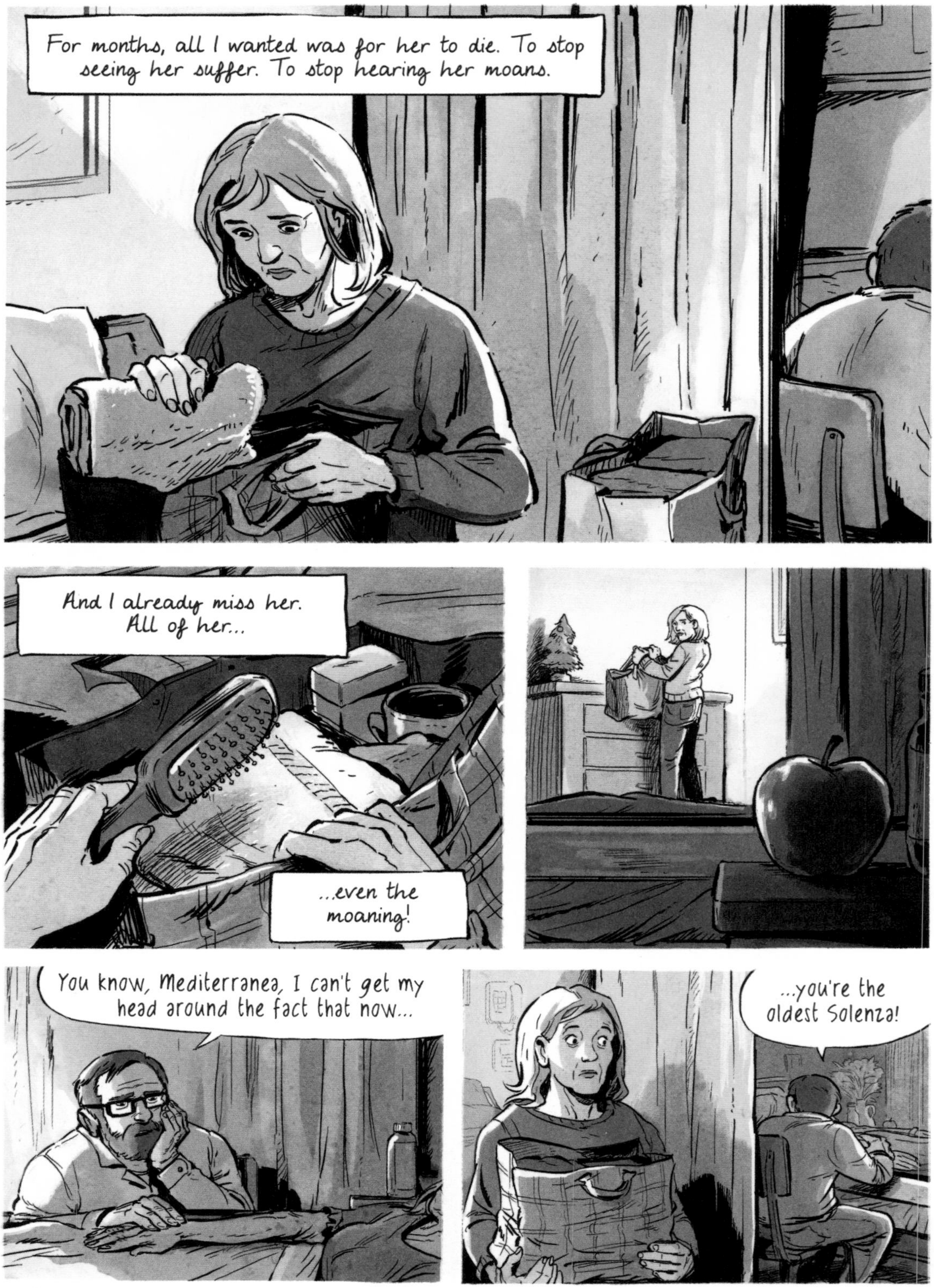
For months, all I wanted was for her to die. To stop seeing her suffer. To stop hearing her moans.
And I already miss her. All of her...
...even the moaning!
You know, Mediterranea, I can't get my head around the fact that now...
...you're the oldest Solenza!

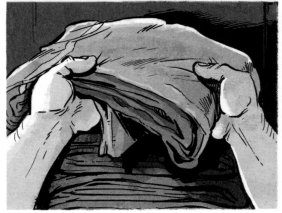

So, this is retirement?

This empty feeling?

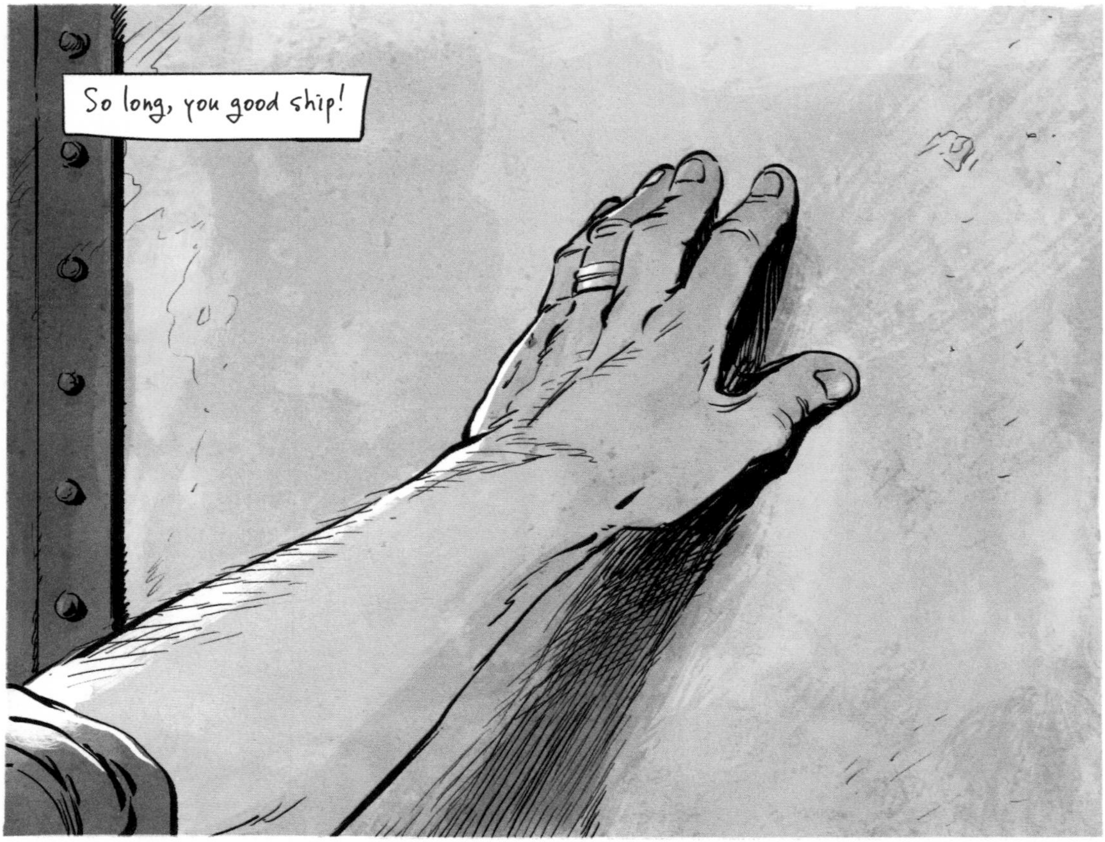
So long, you good ship!

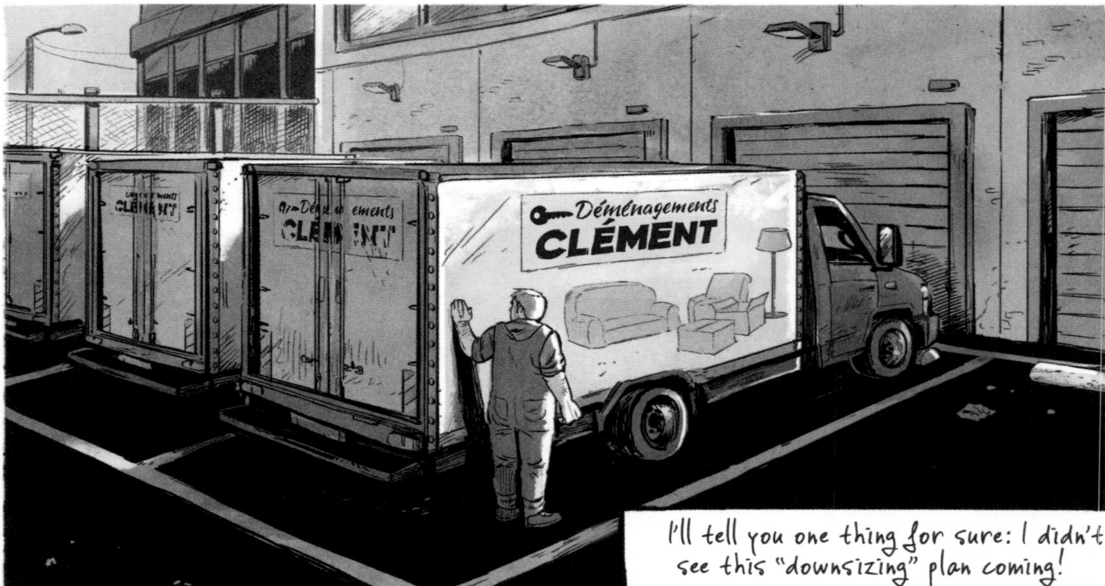
Déménagements
CLÉMENT
I'll tell you one thing for sure: I didn't see this "downsizing" plan coming!

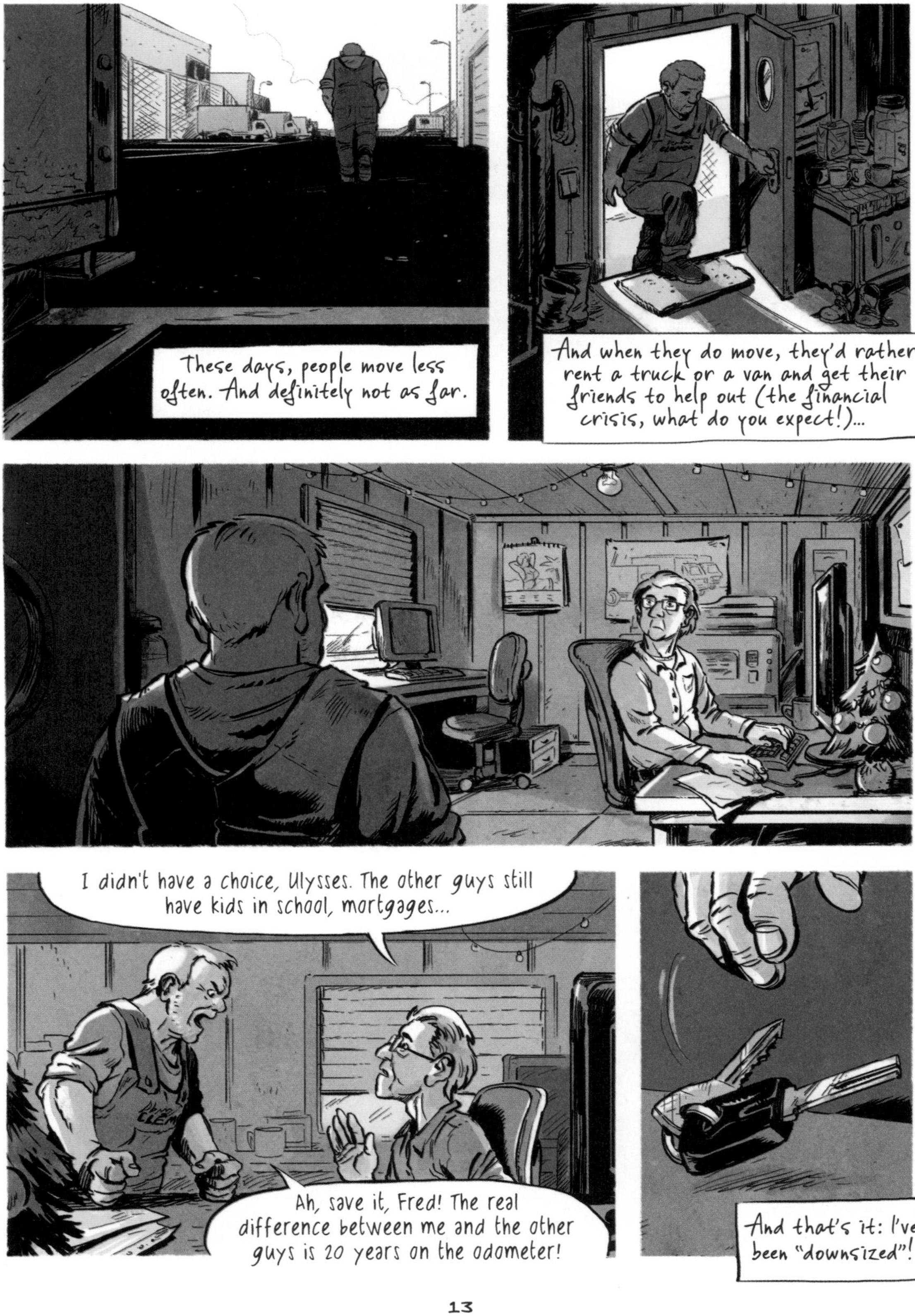
These days, people move less often. And definitely not as far.
And when they do move, they'd rather rent a truck or a van and get their friends to help out (the financial crisis, what do you expect!)...
I didn't have a choice, Ulysses. The other guys still have kids in school, mortgages...
Ah, save it, Fred! The real difference between me and the other guys is 20 years on the odometer!
And that's it: I've been "downsized"!

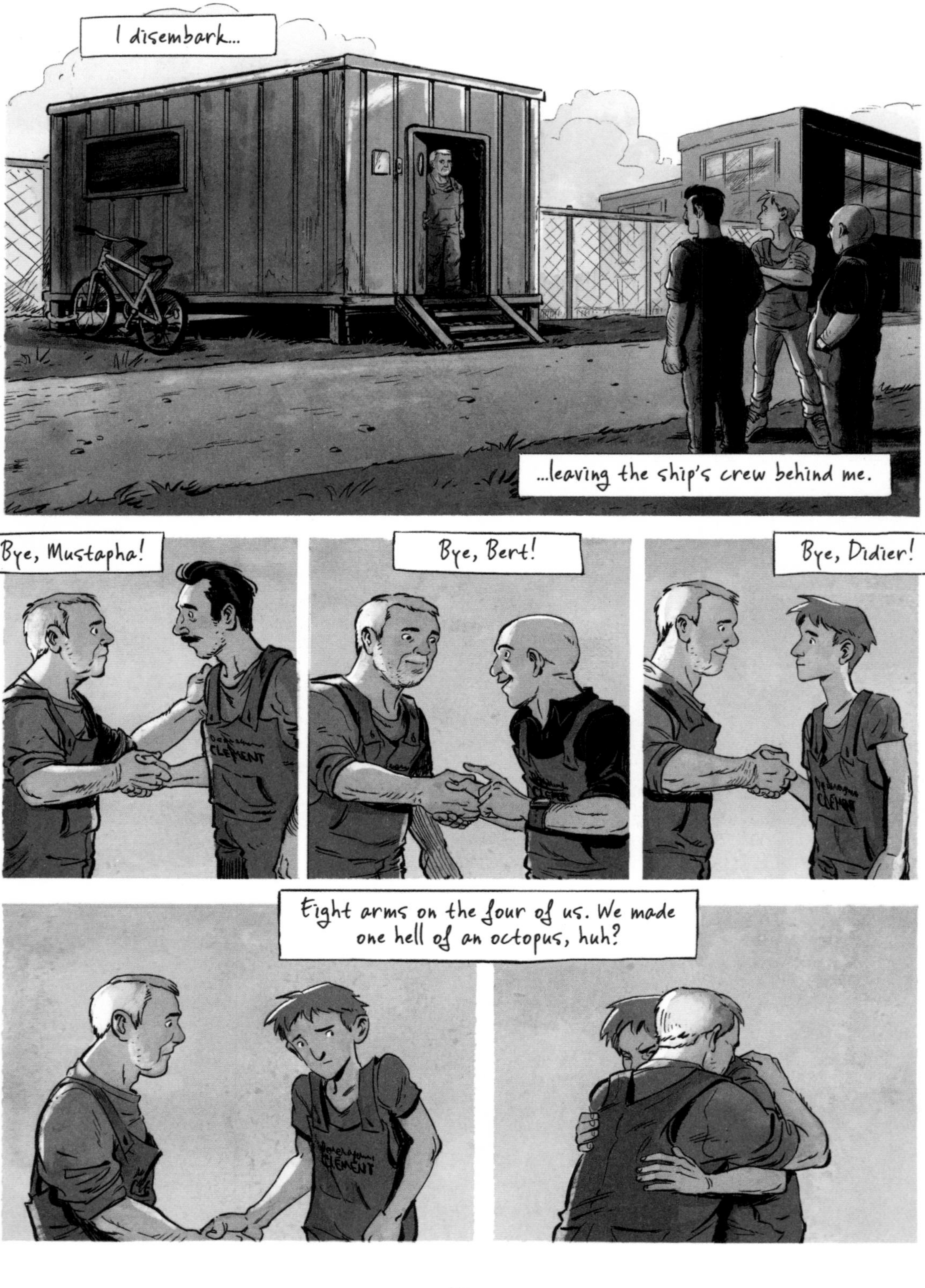
I disembark...
...leaving the ship's crew behind me.
Bye, Mustapha!
Bye, Bert!
Bye, Didier!
Eight arms on the four of us. We made one hell of an octopus, huh?

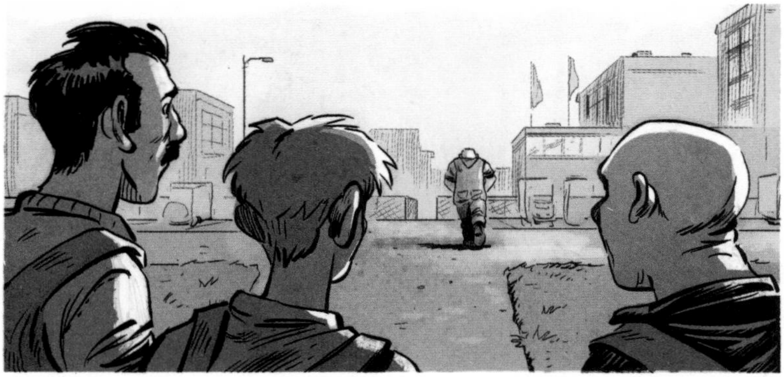

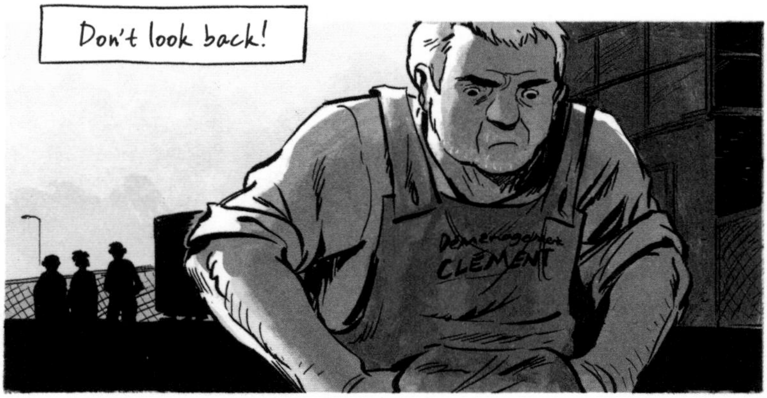
Don't look back!
CLÉMENT

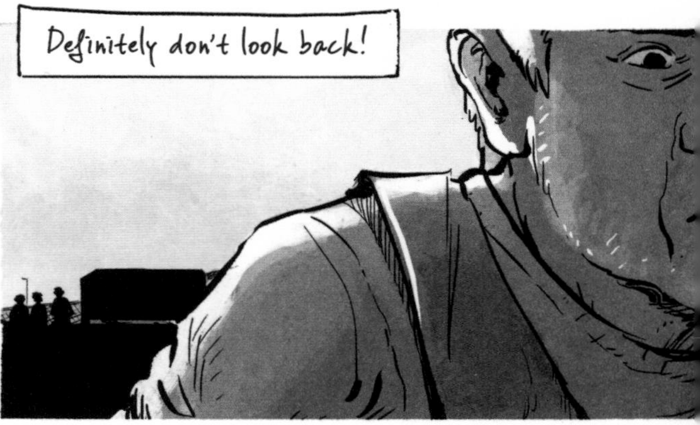
Definitely don't look back!

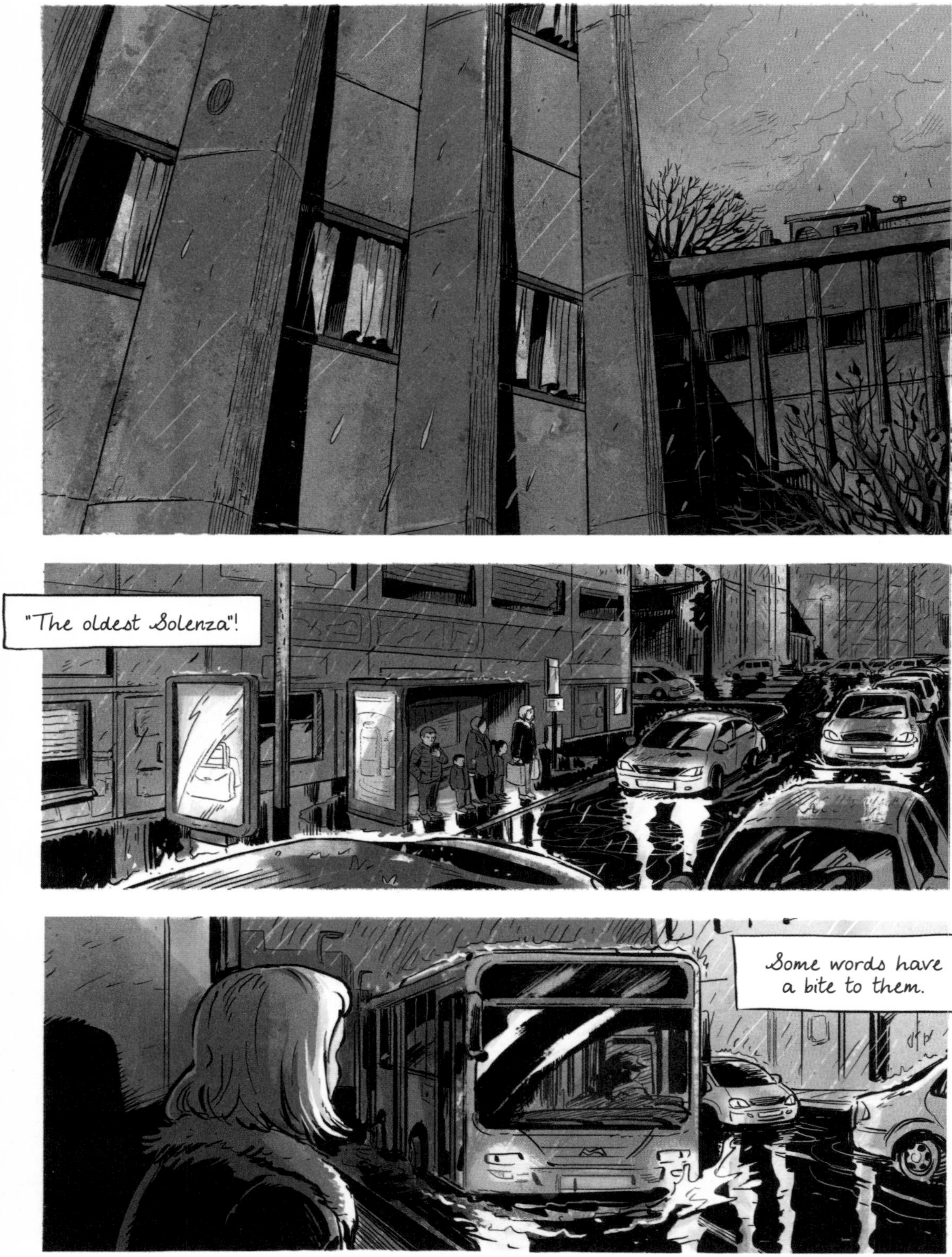
"The oldest Solenza"!
Some words have a bite to them.

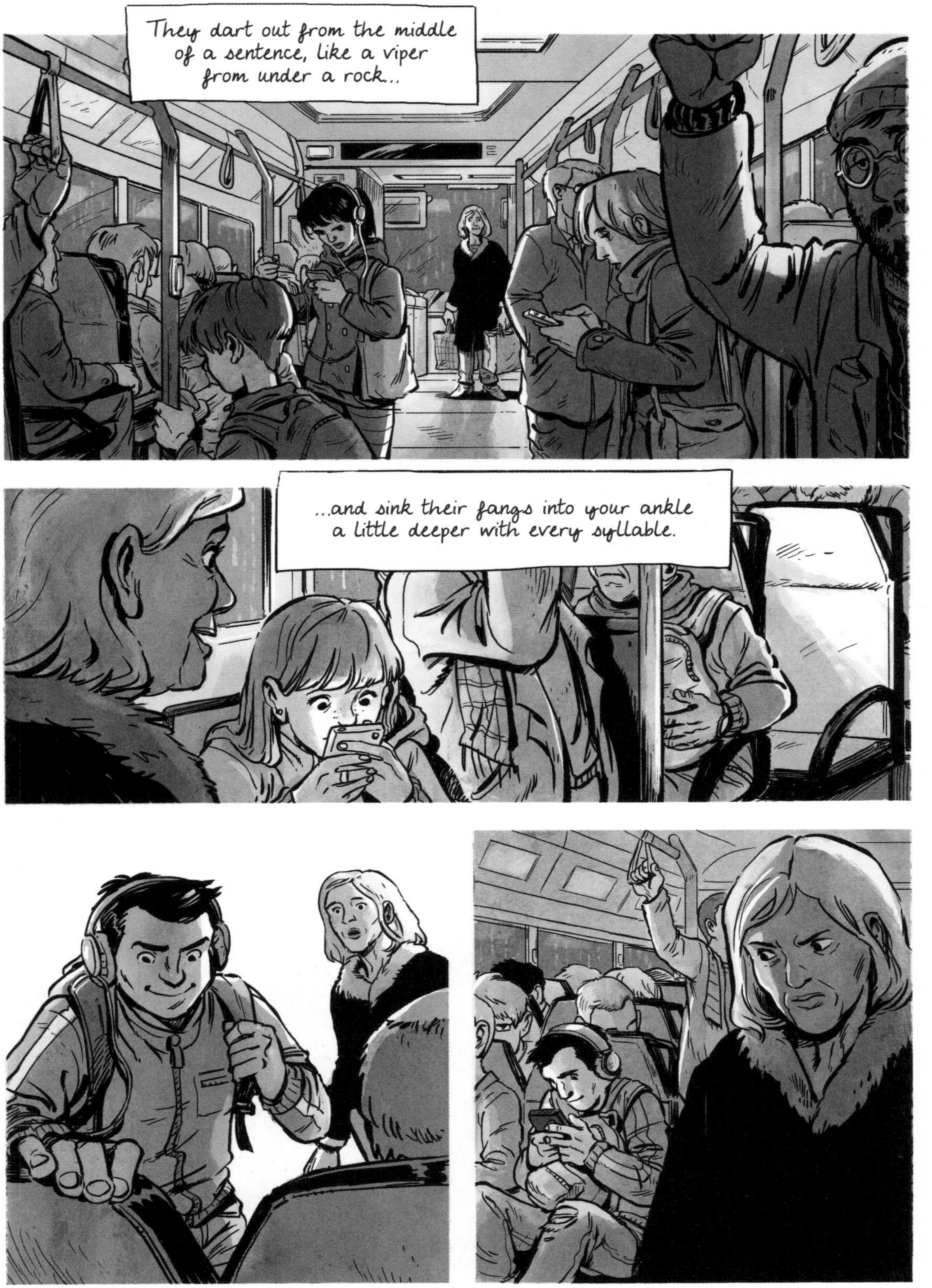
They dart out from the middle of a sentence, like a viper from under a rock...
...and sink their fangs into your ankle a little deeper with every syllable.

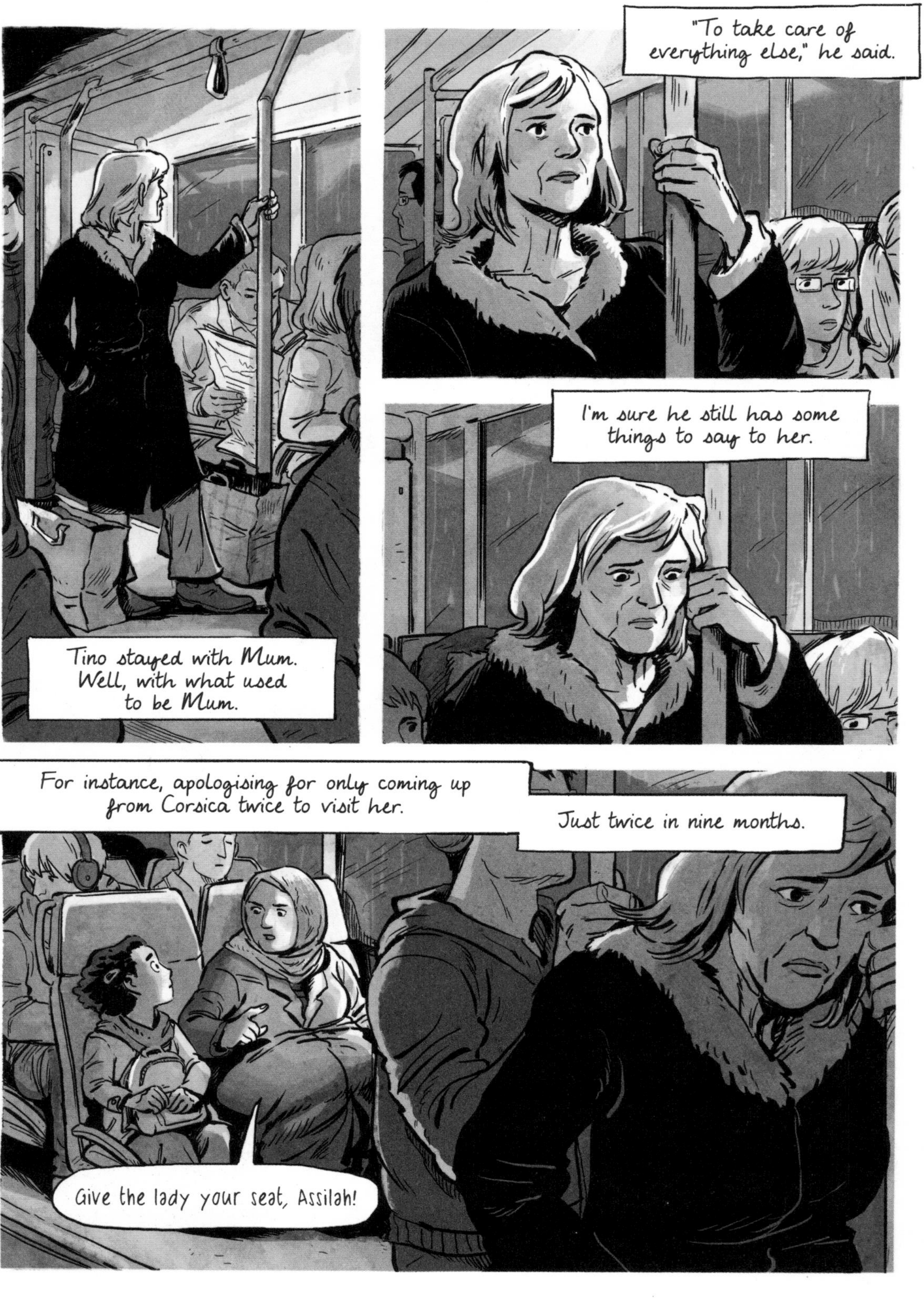

Tino stayed with Mum. Well, with what used to be Mum.
"To take care of everything else," he said.
I'm sure he still has some things to say to her.
For instance, apologising for only coming up from Corsica twice to visit her.
Just twice in nine months.
Give the lady your seat, Assilah!

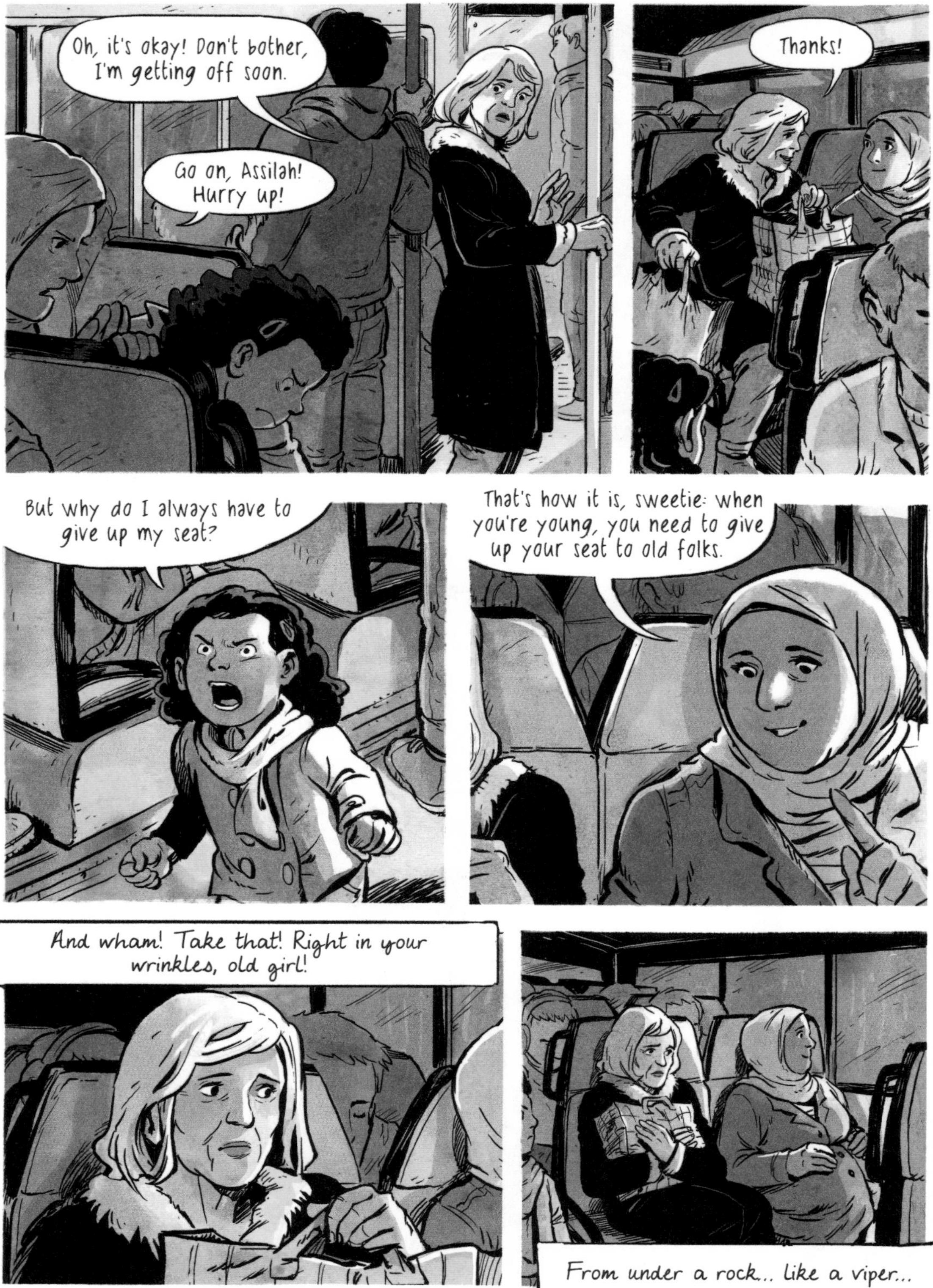

Oh, it's okay! Don't bother, I'm getting off soon.
Go on, Assilah! Hurry up!
Thanks!
But why do I always have to give up my seat?
That's how it is, sweetie: when you're young, you need to give up your seat to old folks.
And wham! Take that! Right in your wrinkles, old girl!
From under a rock... like a viper...

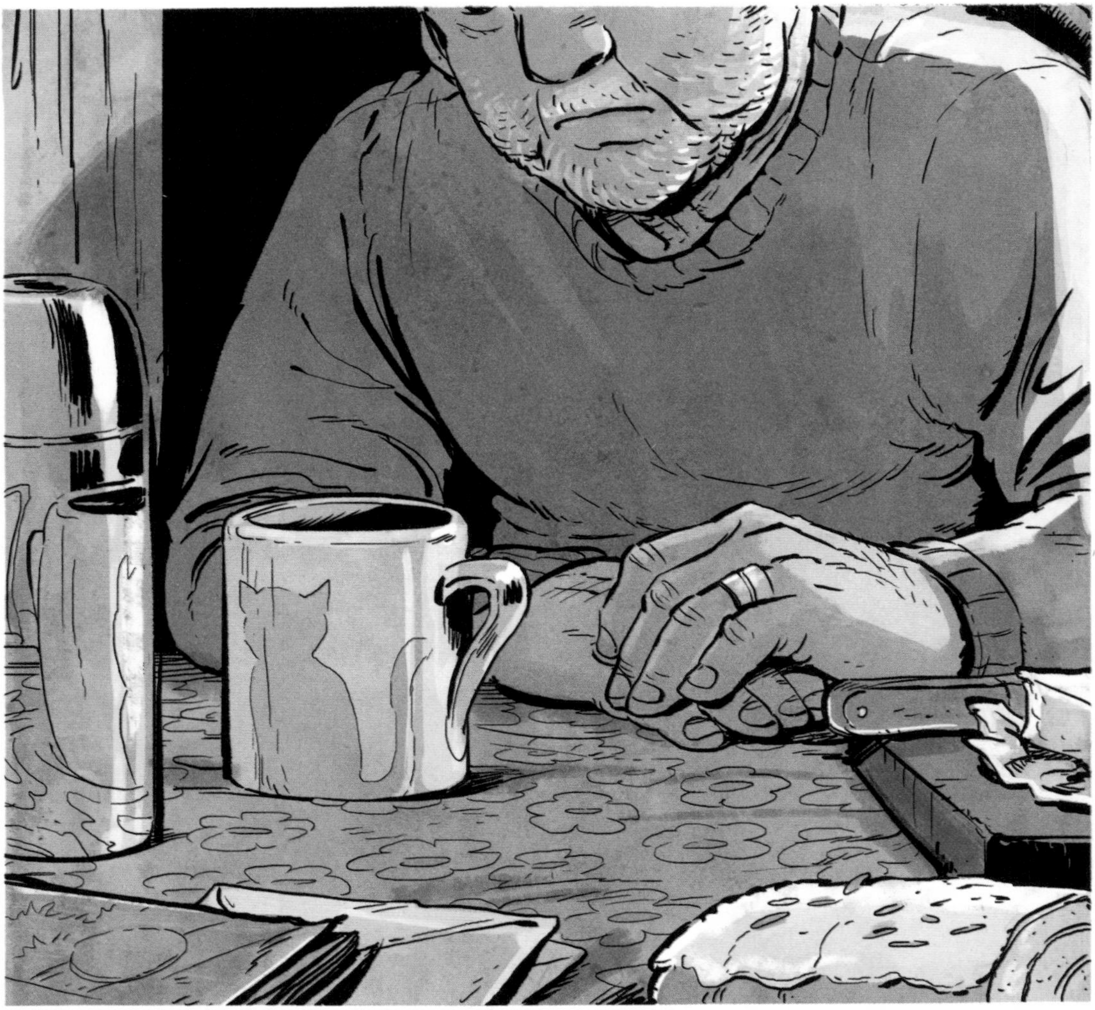

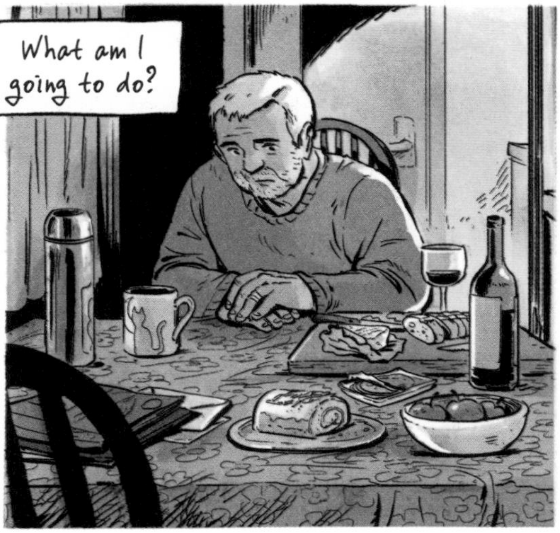
What am I going to do?

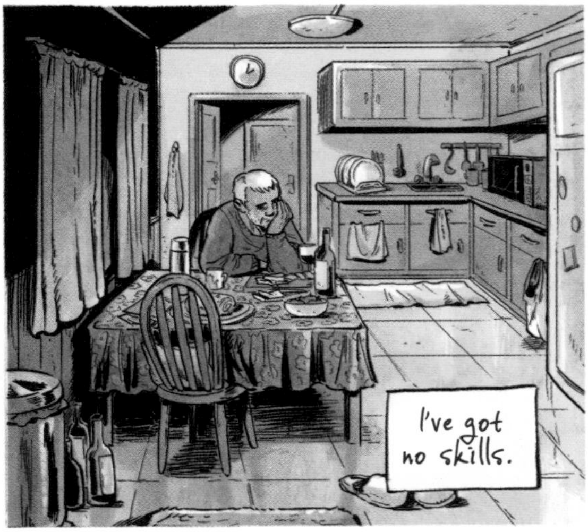
I've got no skills.

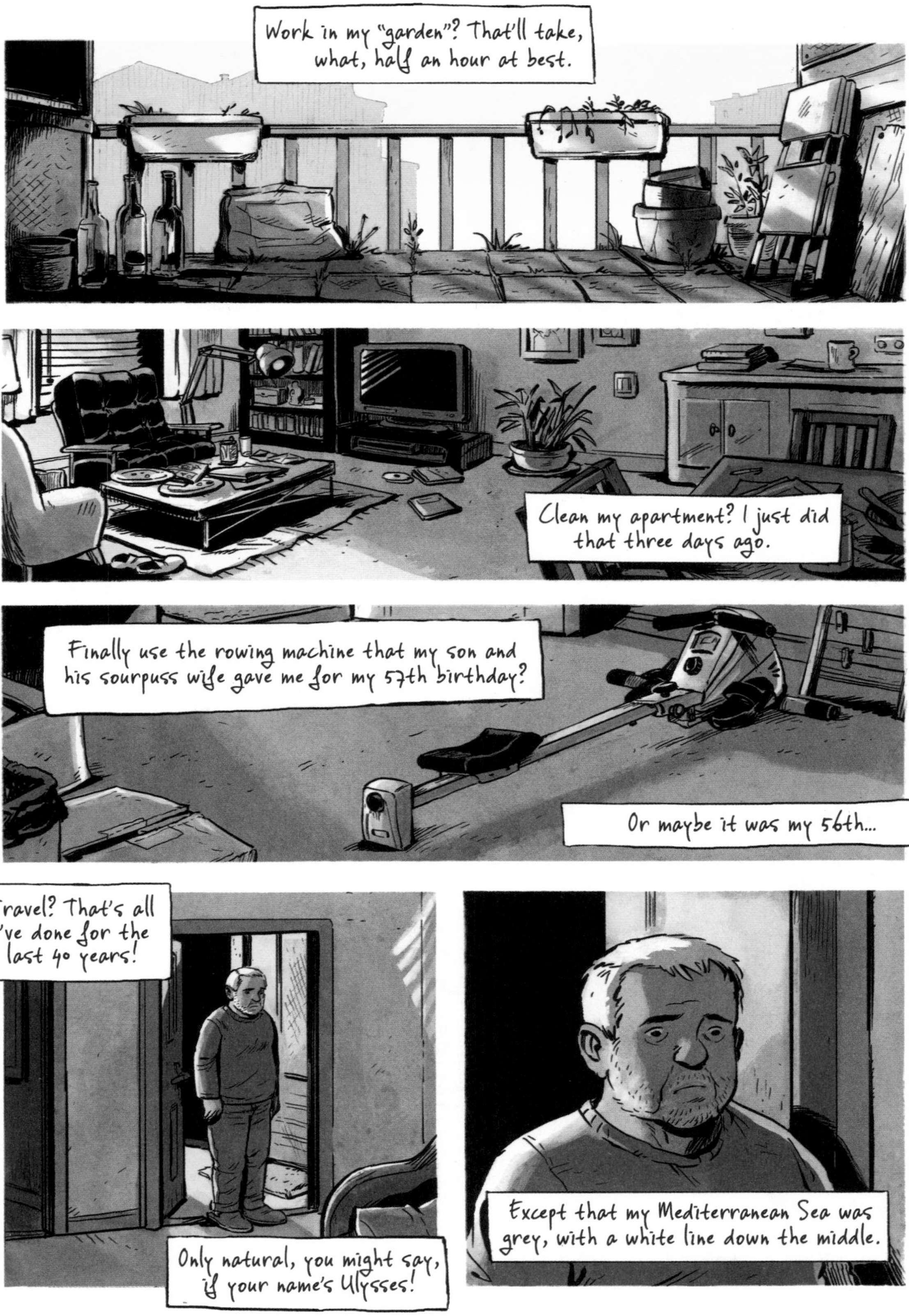
Work in my "garden"? That'll take, what, half an hour at best.
Clean my apartment? I just did that three days ago.
Finally use the rowing machine that my son and his sourpuss wife gave me for my 57th birthday?
Or maybe it was my 56th...
Travel? That's all I've done for the last 40 years!
Only natural, you might say, if your name's Ulysses!
Except that my Mediterranean Sea was grey, with a white line down the middle.

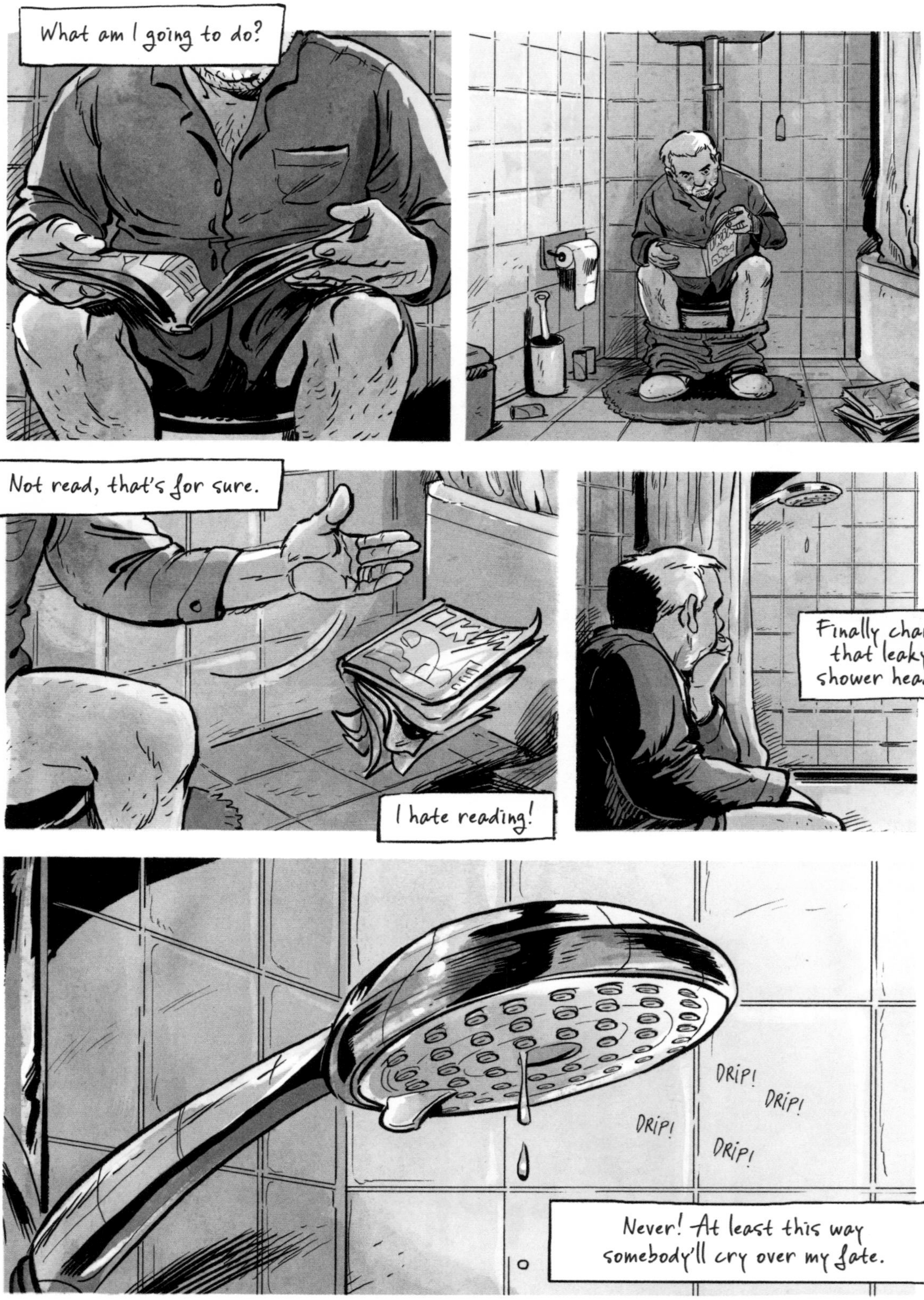
What am I going to do?
Not read, that's for sure.
I hate reading!
Finally change that leaky shower head?
DRIP!
DRIP!
DRIP!
DRIP!
Never! At least this way somebody'll cry over my fate.

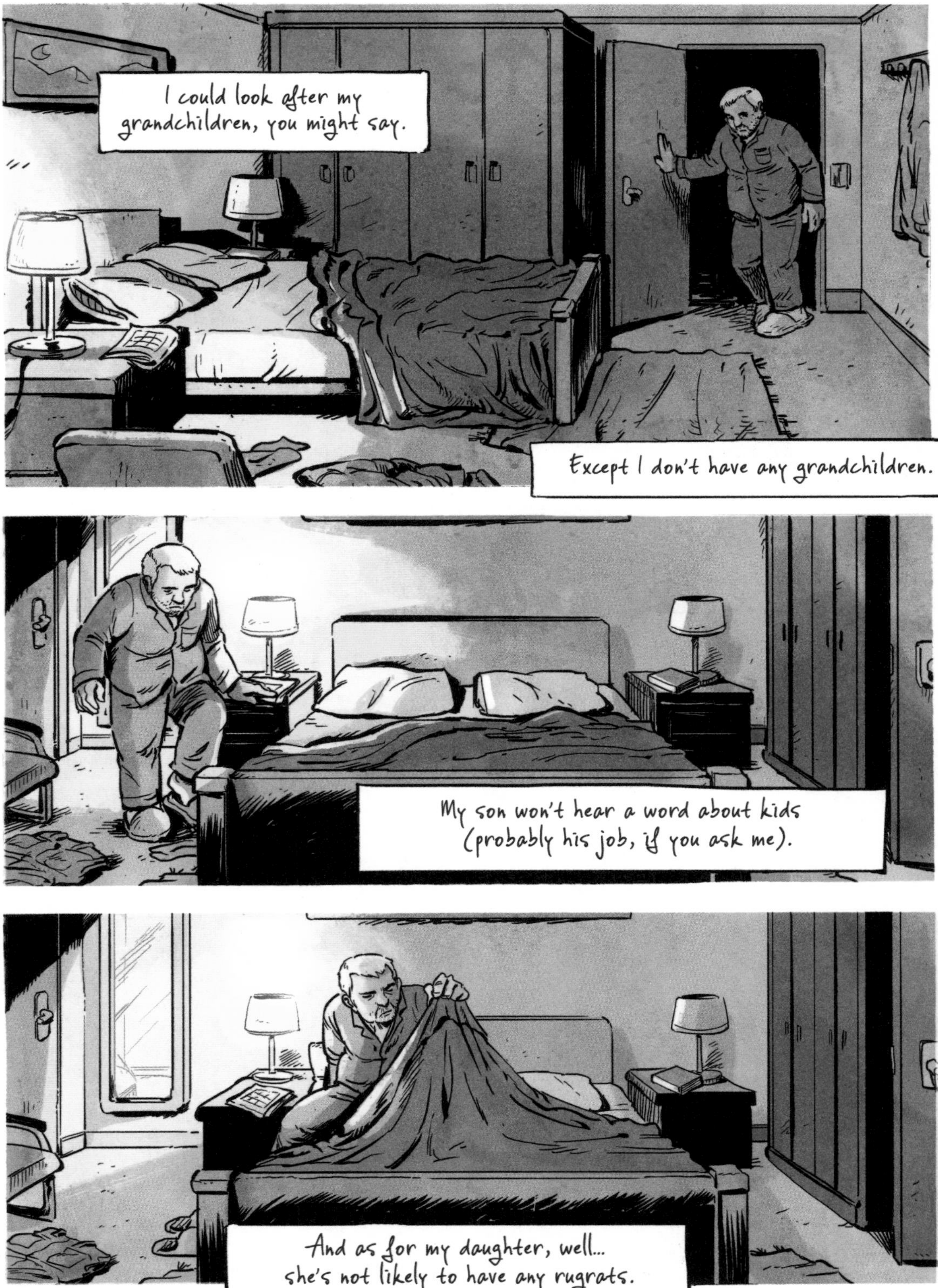
I could look after my grandchildren, you might say.
Except I don't have any grandchildren.
My son won't hear a word about kids (probably his job, if you ask me).
And as for my daughter, well... she's not likely to have any rugrats.

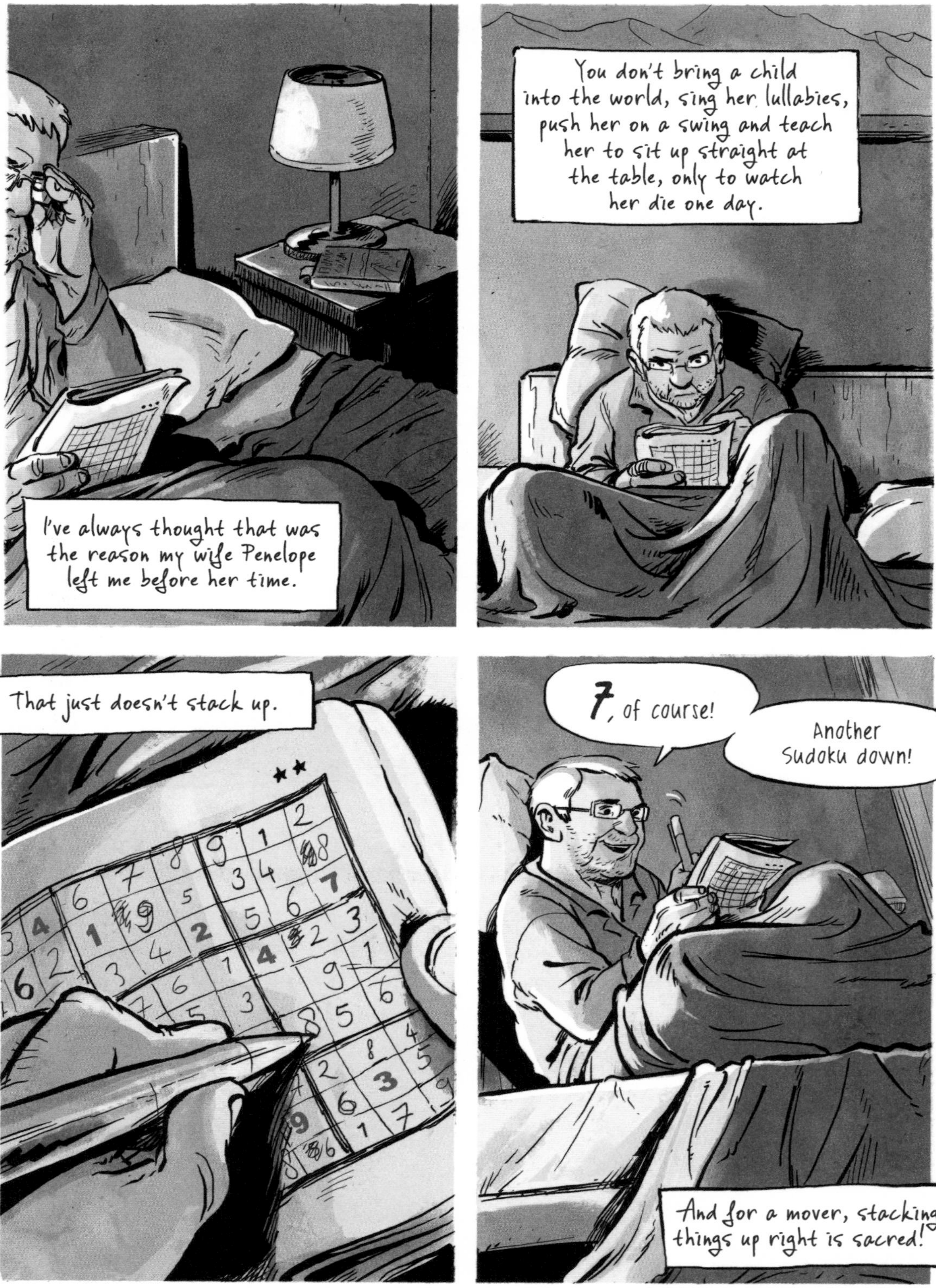
I've always thought that was the reason my wife Penelope left me before her time.
You don't bring a child into the world, sing her lullabies, push her on a swing and teach her to sit up straight at the table, only to watch her die one day.
That just doesn't stack up.
7, of course!
Another Sudoku down!
And for a mover, stacking things up right is sacred!

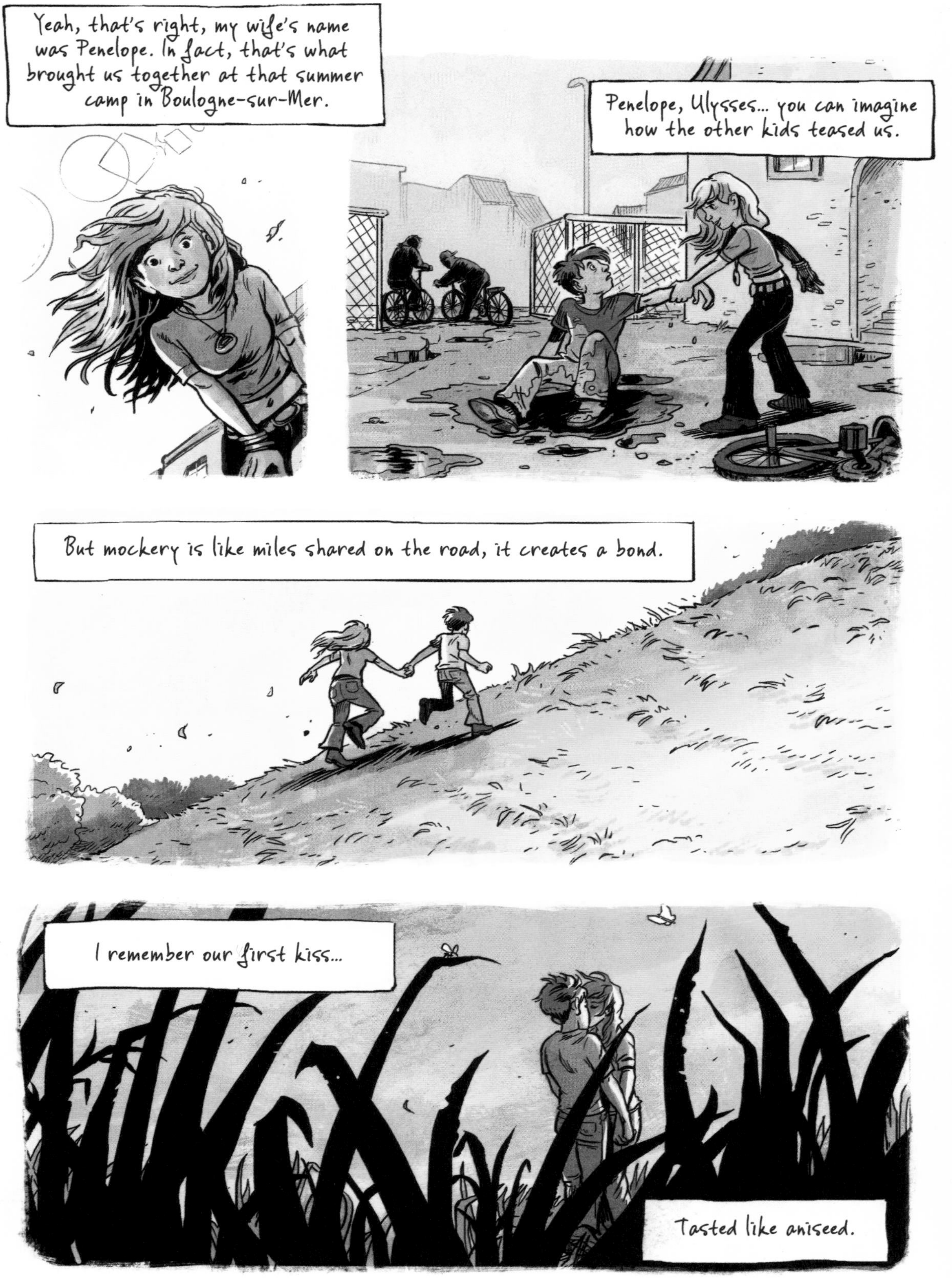
Yeah, that's right, my wife's name was Penelope. In fact, that's what brought us together at that summer camp in Boulogne-sur-Mer.
Penelope, Ulysses... you can imagine how the other kids teased us.
But mockery is like miles shared on the road, it creates a bond.
I remember our first kiss...
Tasted like aniseed.

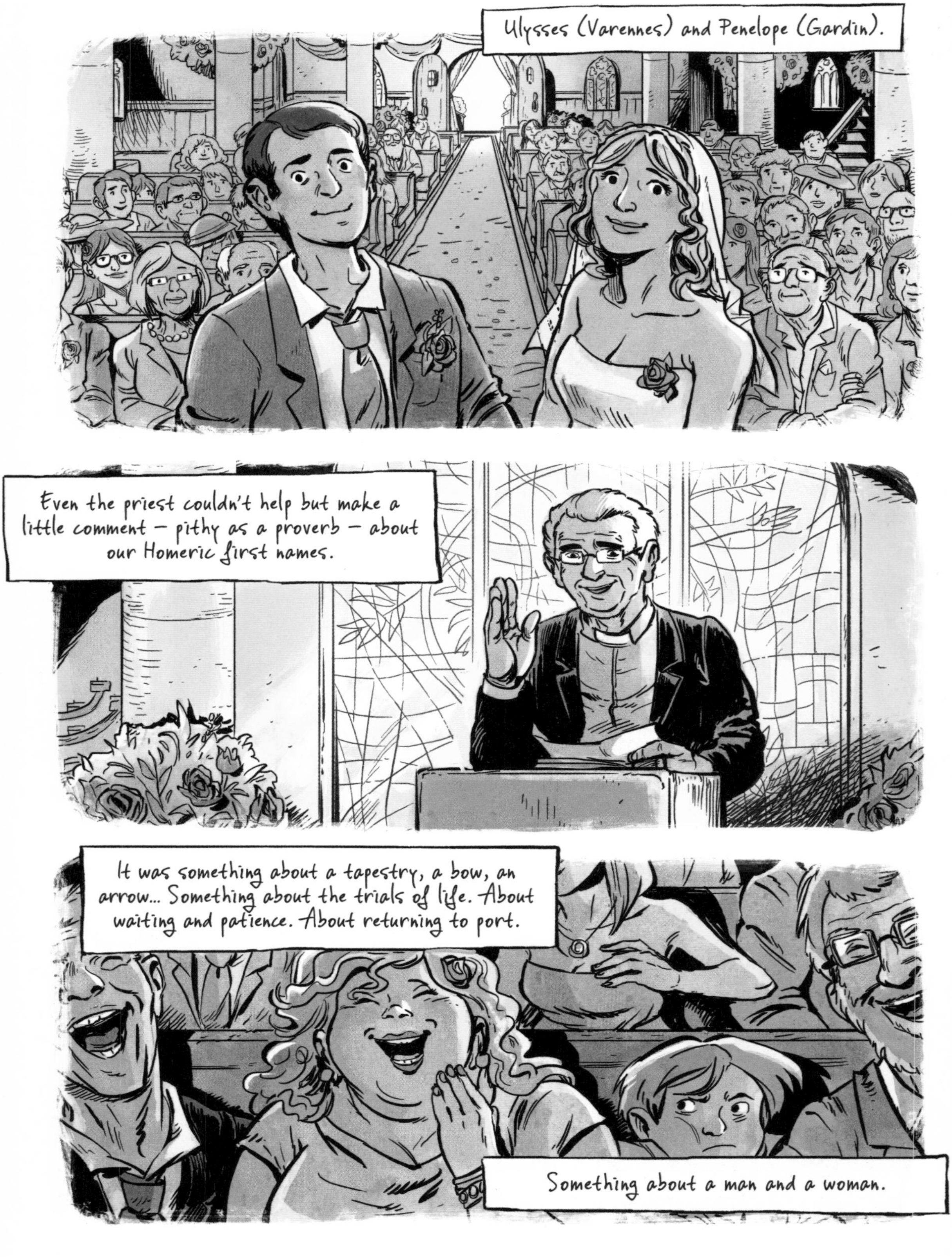
Ulysses (Varennes) and Penelope (Gardin).
Even the priest couldn't help but make a little comment – pithy as a proverb – about our Homeric first names.
It was something about a tapestry, a bow, an arrow... Something about the trials of life. About waiting and patience. About returning to port.
Something about a man and a woman.

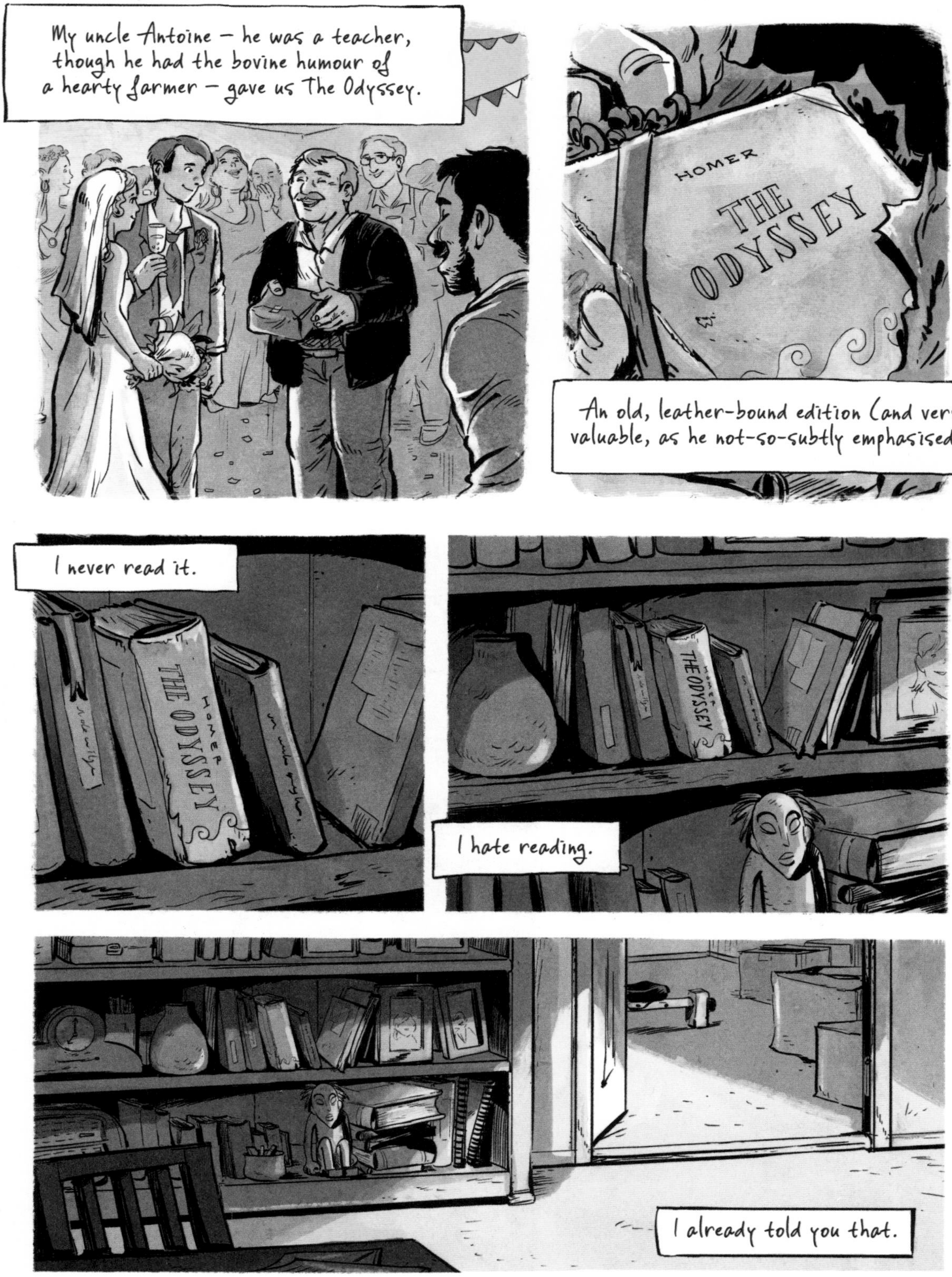
My uncle Antoine – he was a teacher, though he had the bovine humour of a hearty farmer – gave us The Odyssey.
HOMER
THE ODYSSEY
An old, leather-bound edition (and very valuable, as he not-so-subtly emphasised).
I never read it.
THE ODYSSEY
HOMER
HOMER
THE ODYSSEY
I hate reading.
I already told you that.

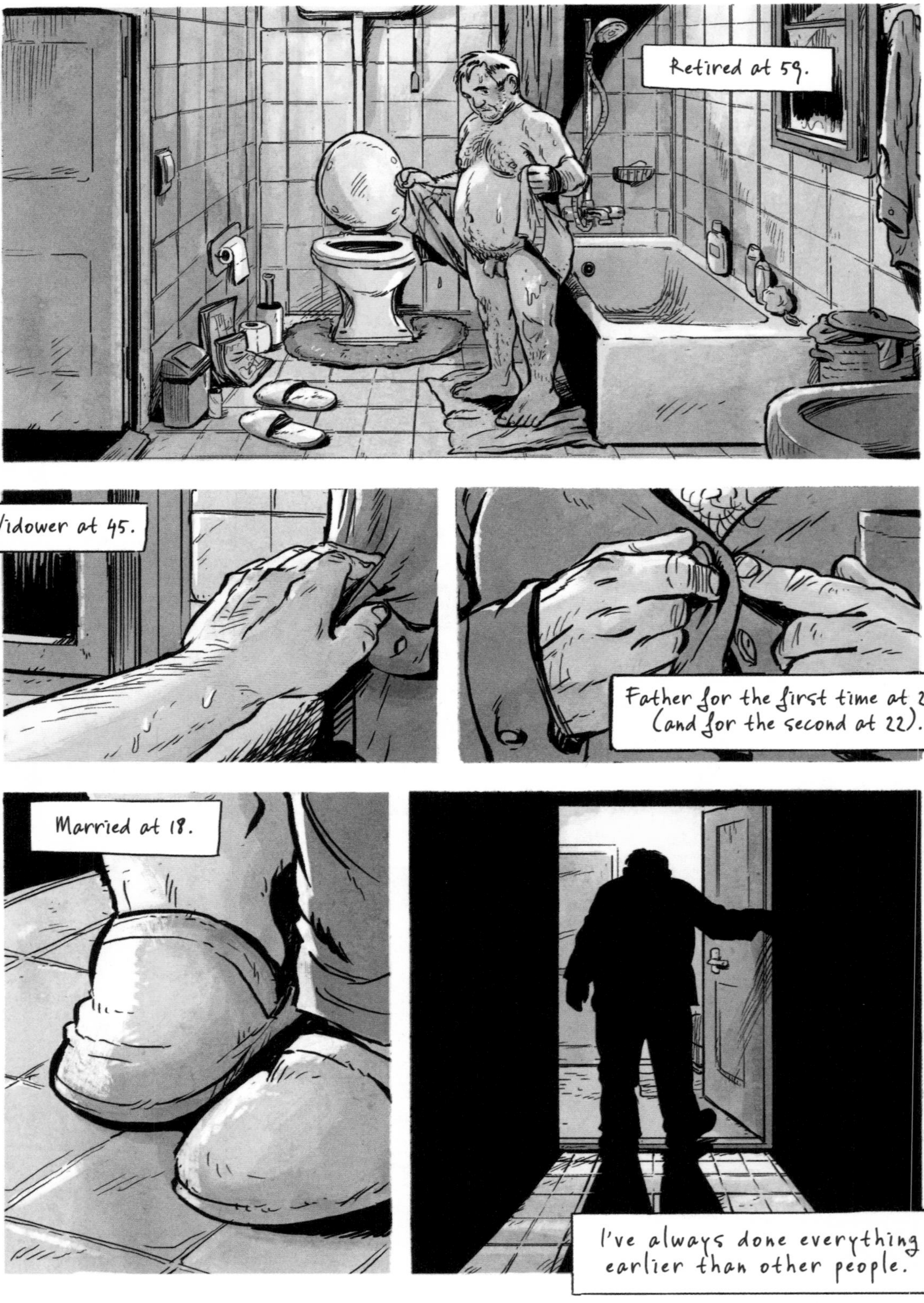
Retired at 59.
Widower at 45.
Father for the first time at 20 (and for the second at 22).
Married at 18.
I've always done everything earlier than other people.

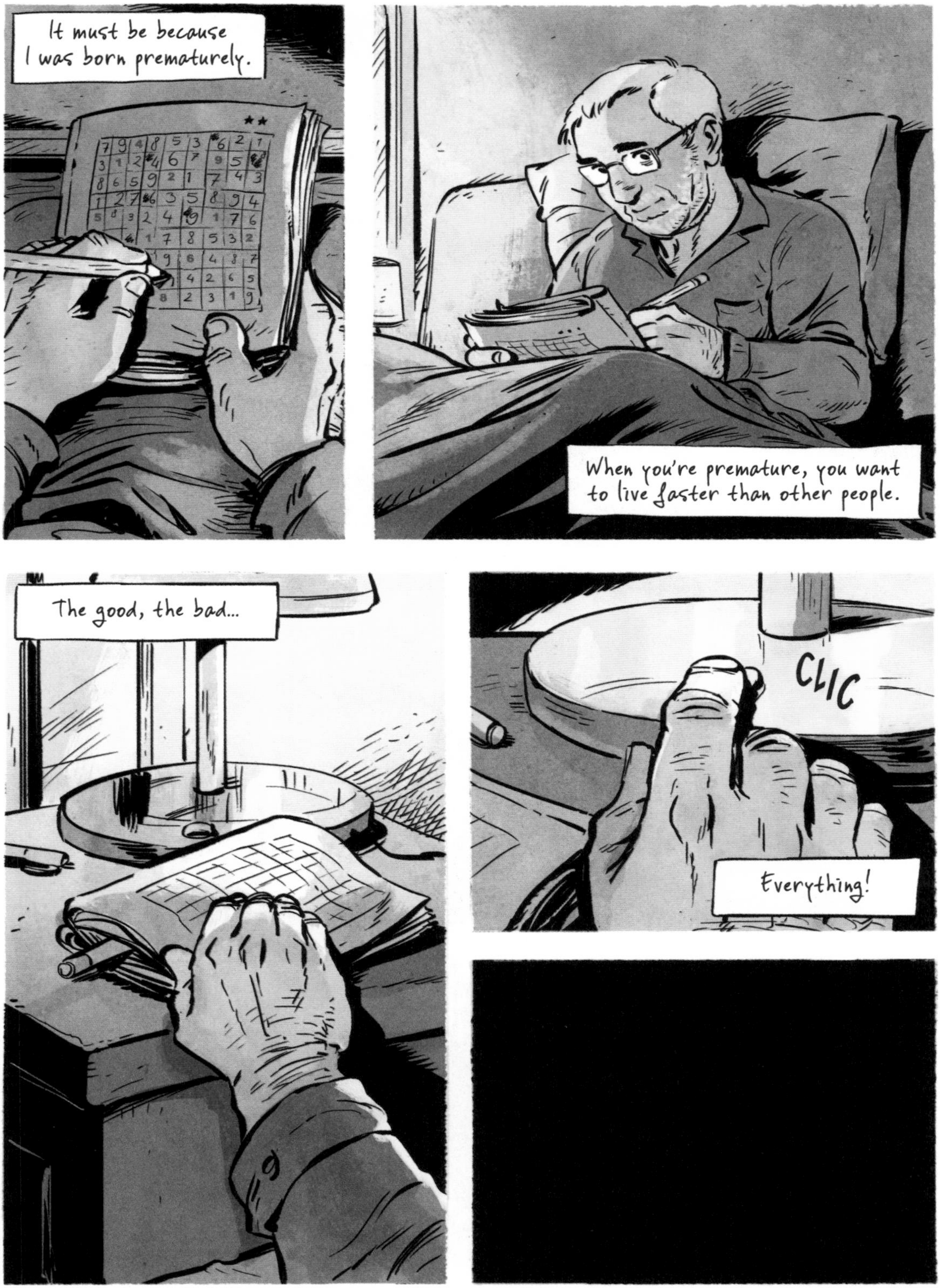
It must be because I was born prematurely.
When you're premature, you want to live faster than other people.
The good, the bad...
CLIC
Everything!

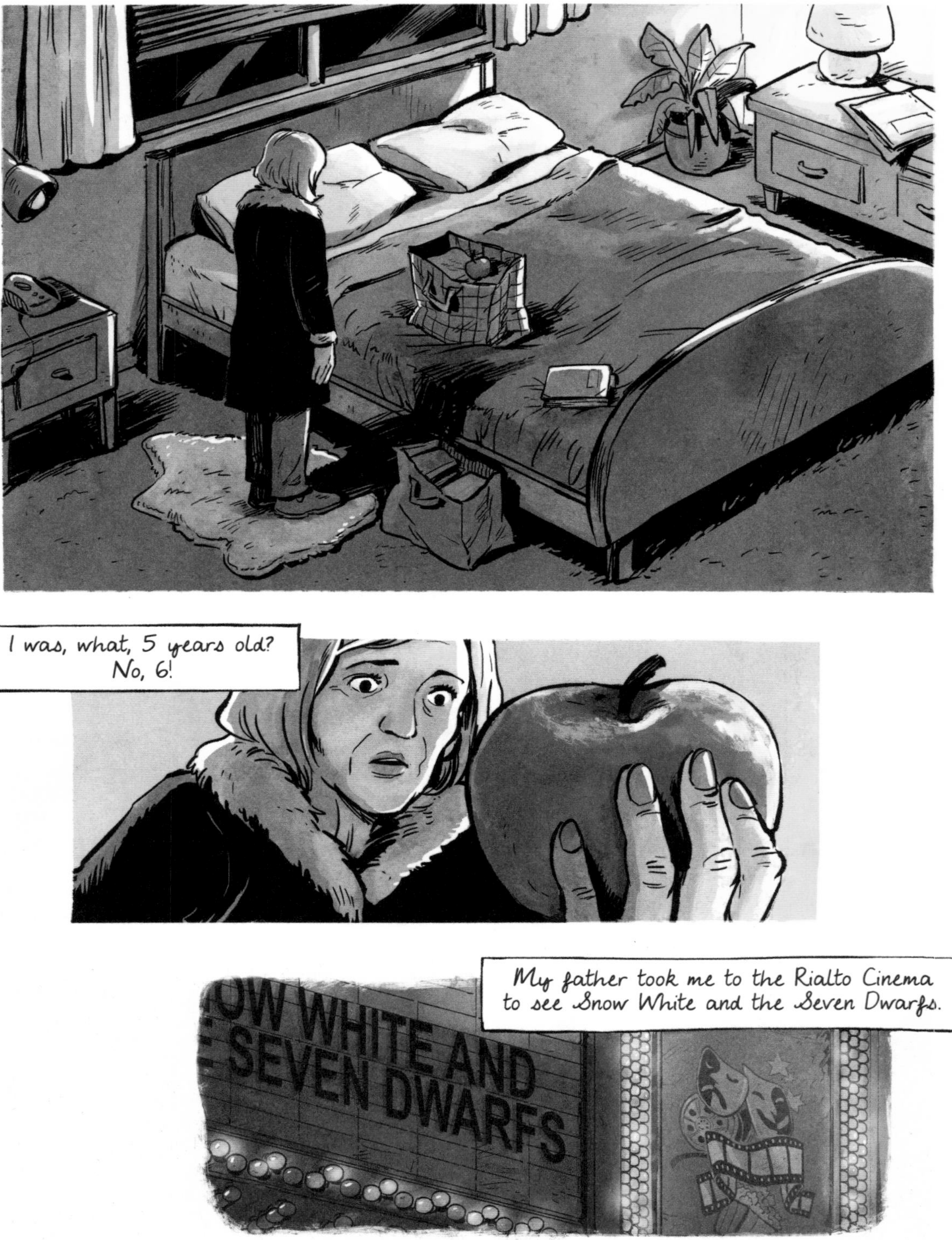
I was, what, 5 years old? No, 6!
My father took me to the Rialto Cinema to see Snow White and the Seven Dwarfs.
OW WHITE AND
SEVEN DWARFS

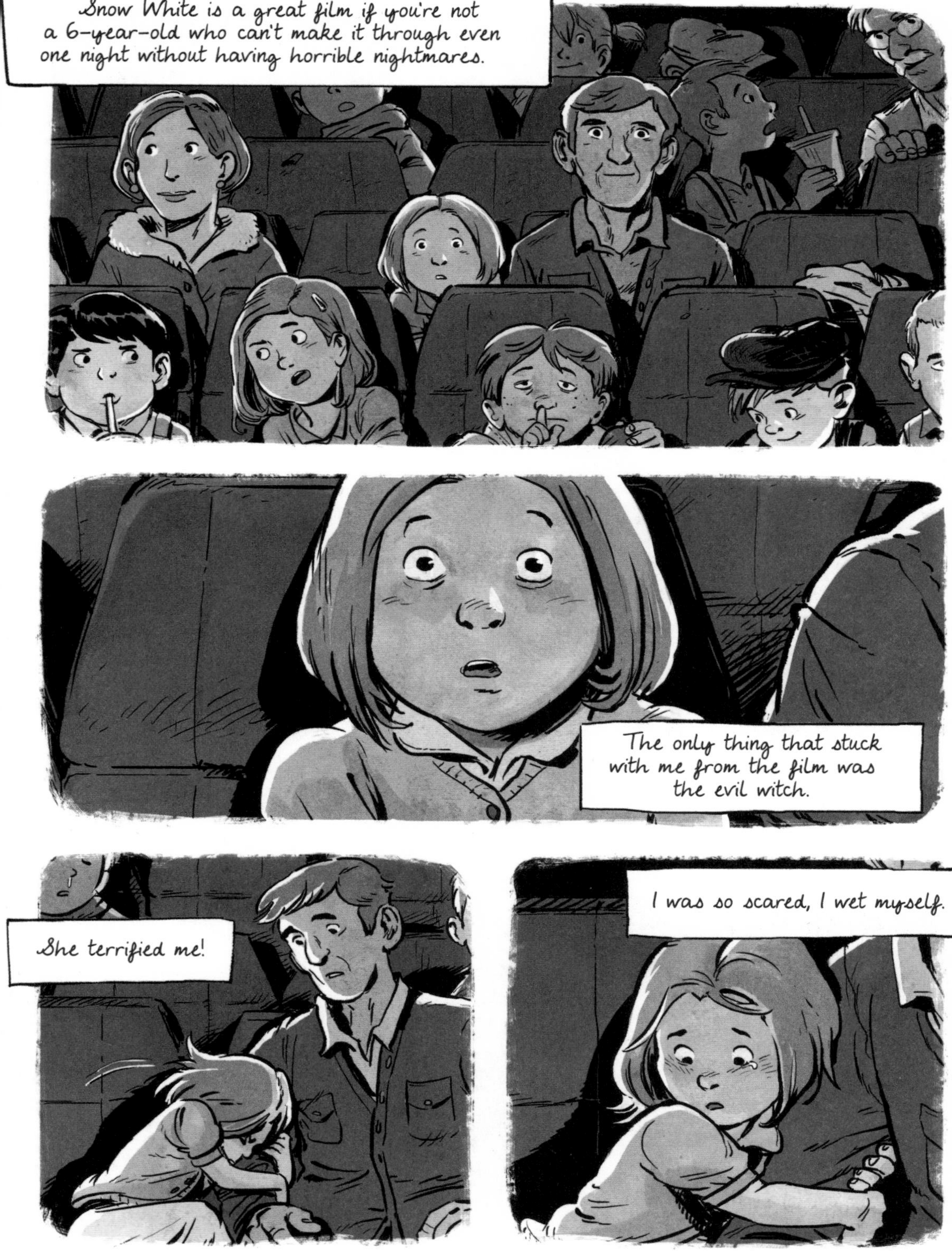
Snow White is a great film if you're not a 6-year-old who can't make it through even one night without having horrible nightmares.
The only thing that stuck with me from the film was the evil witch.
She terrified me!
I was so scared, I wet myself.

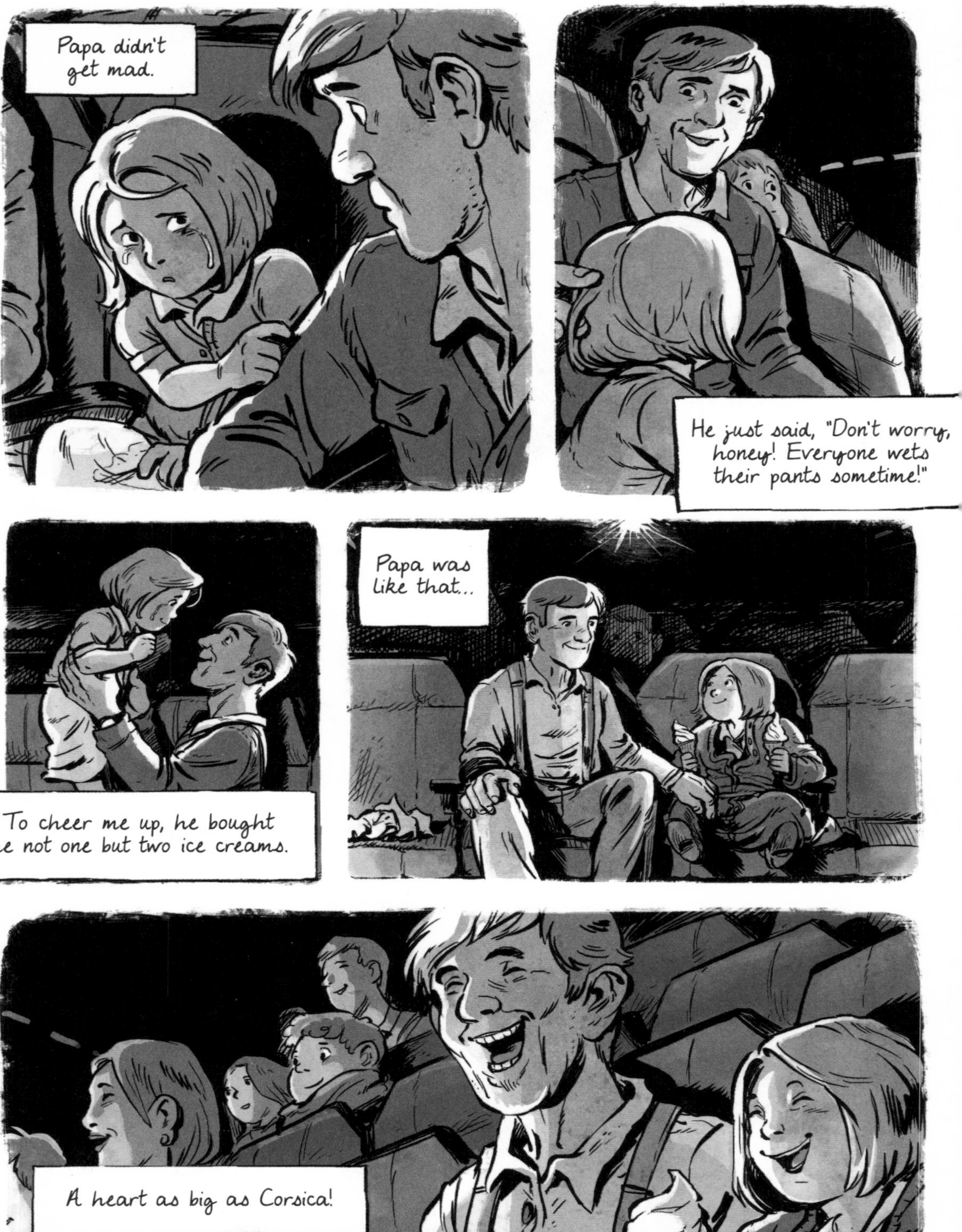

Papa didn't get mad.
He just said, "Don't worry, honey! Everyone wets their pants sometime!"
To cheer me up, he bought me not one but two ice creams.
Papa was like that...
A heart as big as Corsica!

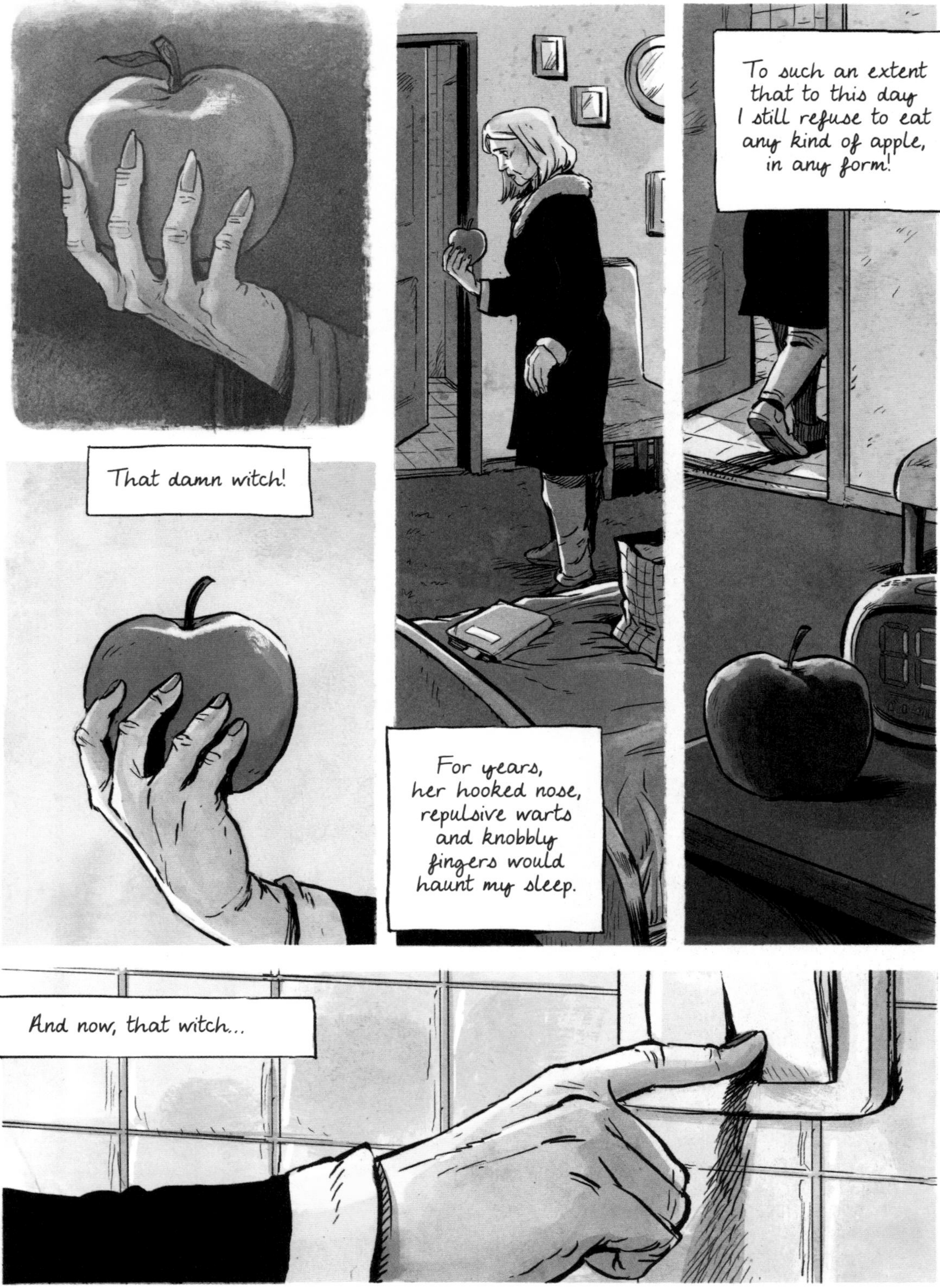
That damn witch!
For years, her hooked nose, repulsive warts and knobbly fingers would haunt my sleep.
To such an extent that to this day I still refuse to eat any kind of apple, in any form!
And now, that witch...

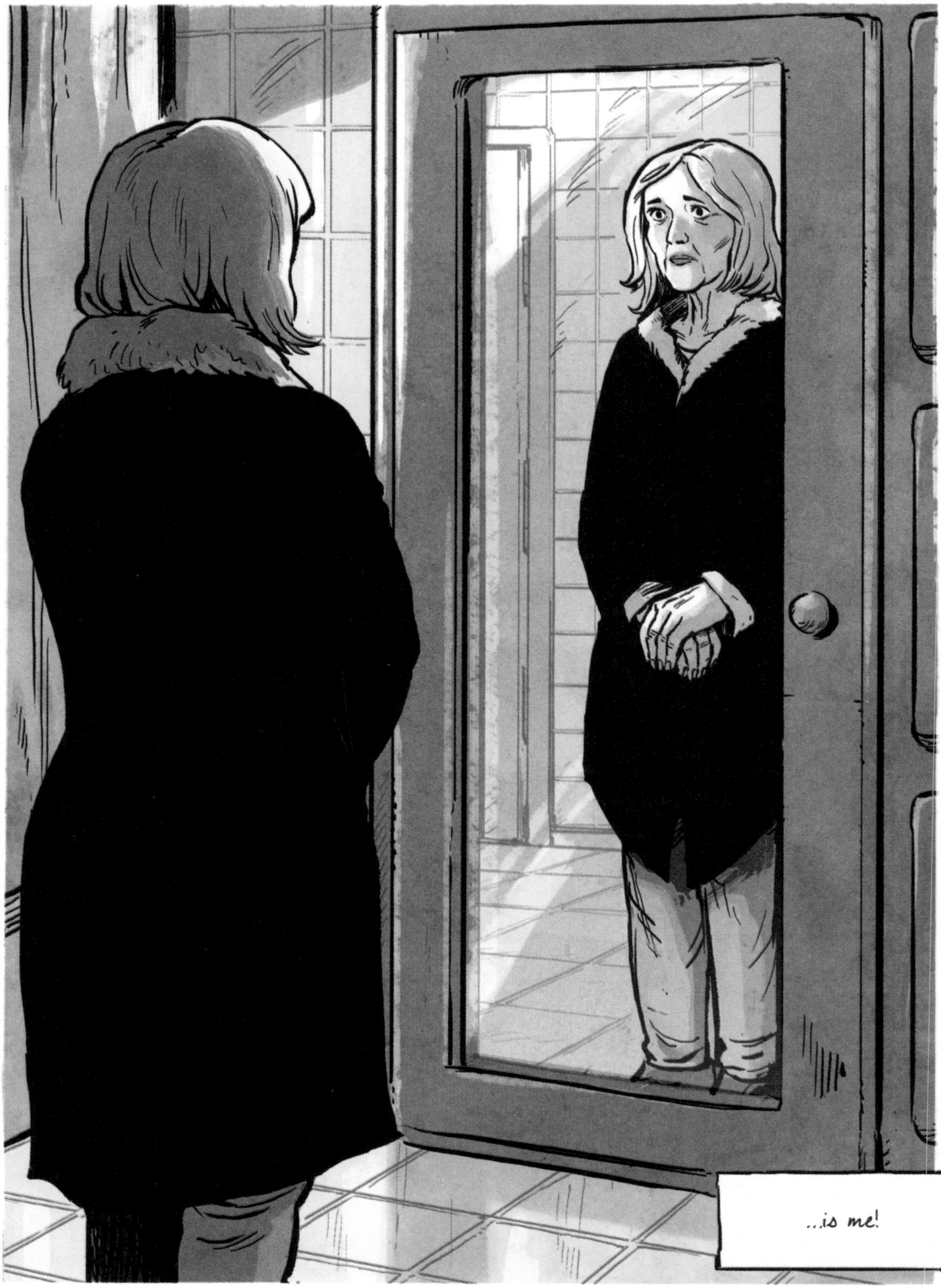
...is me!

2.

The rest of what's left

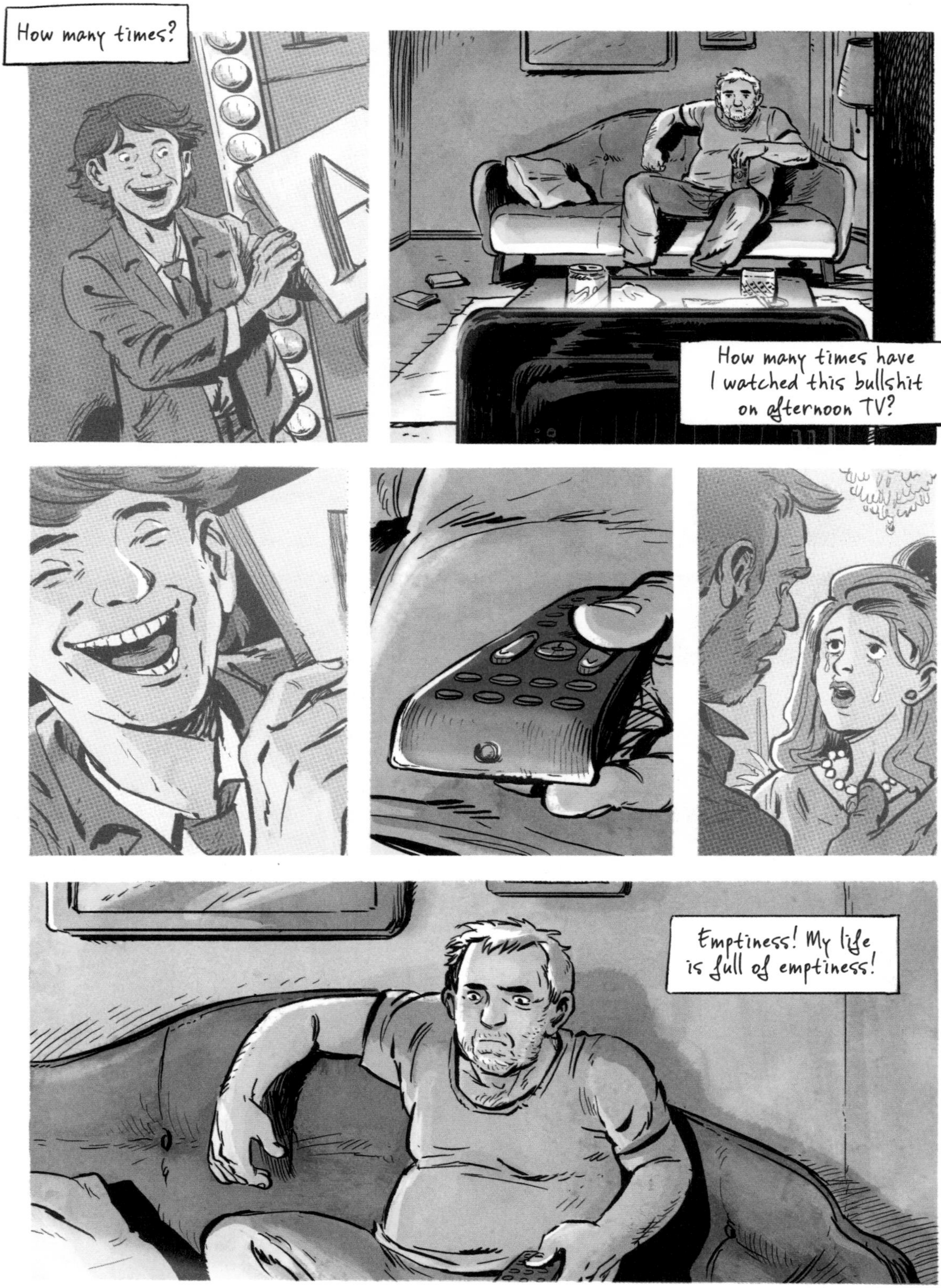
How many times?
How many times have I watched this bullshit on afternoon TV?
Emptiness! My life is full of emptiness!

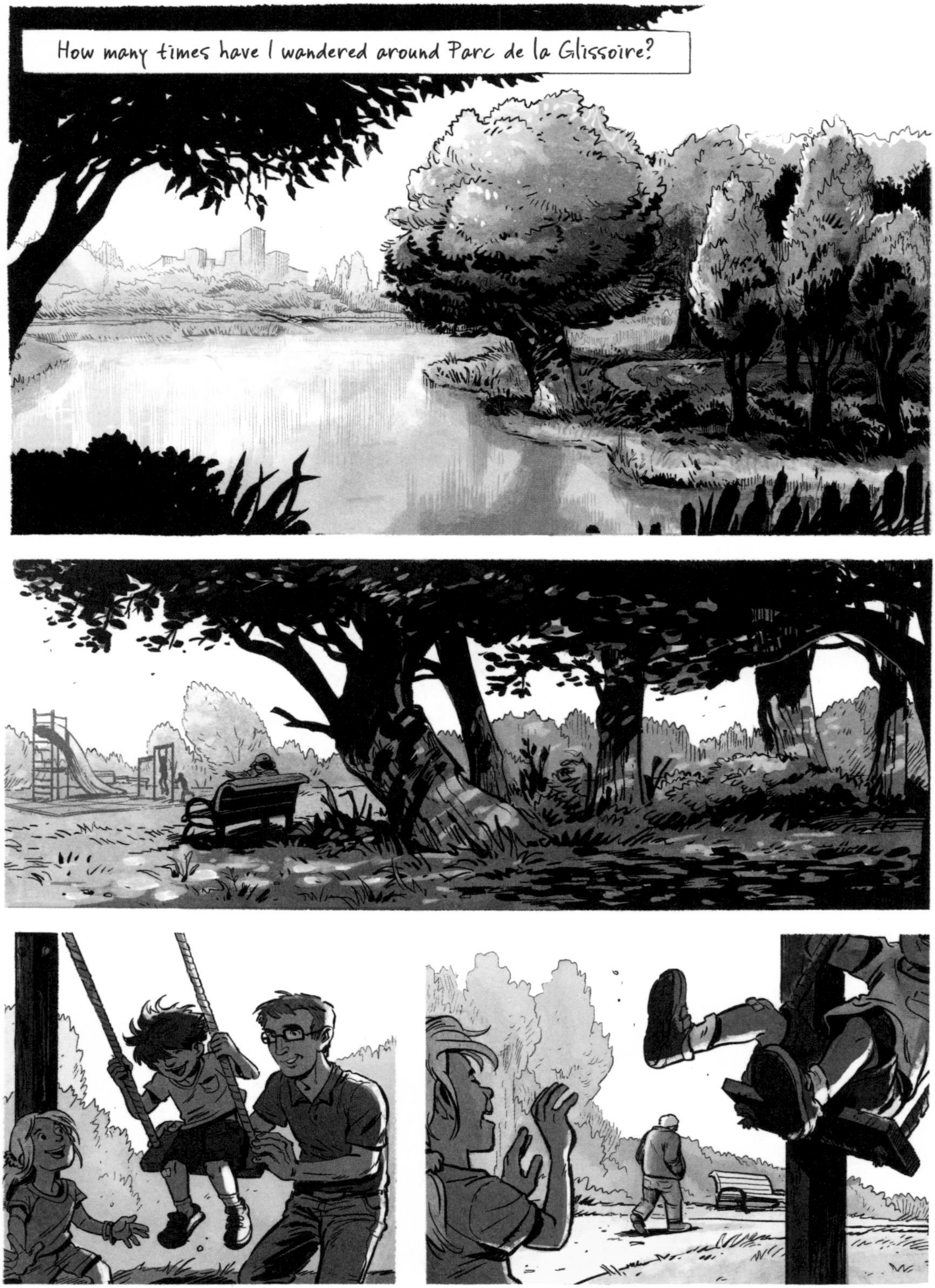
How many times have I wandered around Parc de la Glissoire?

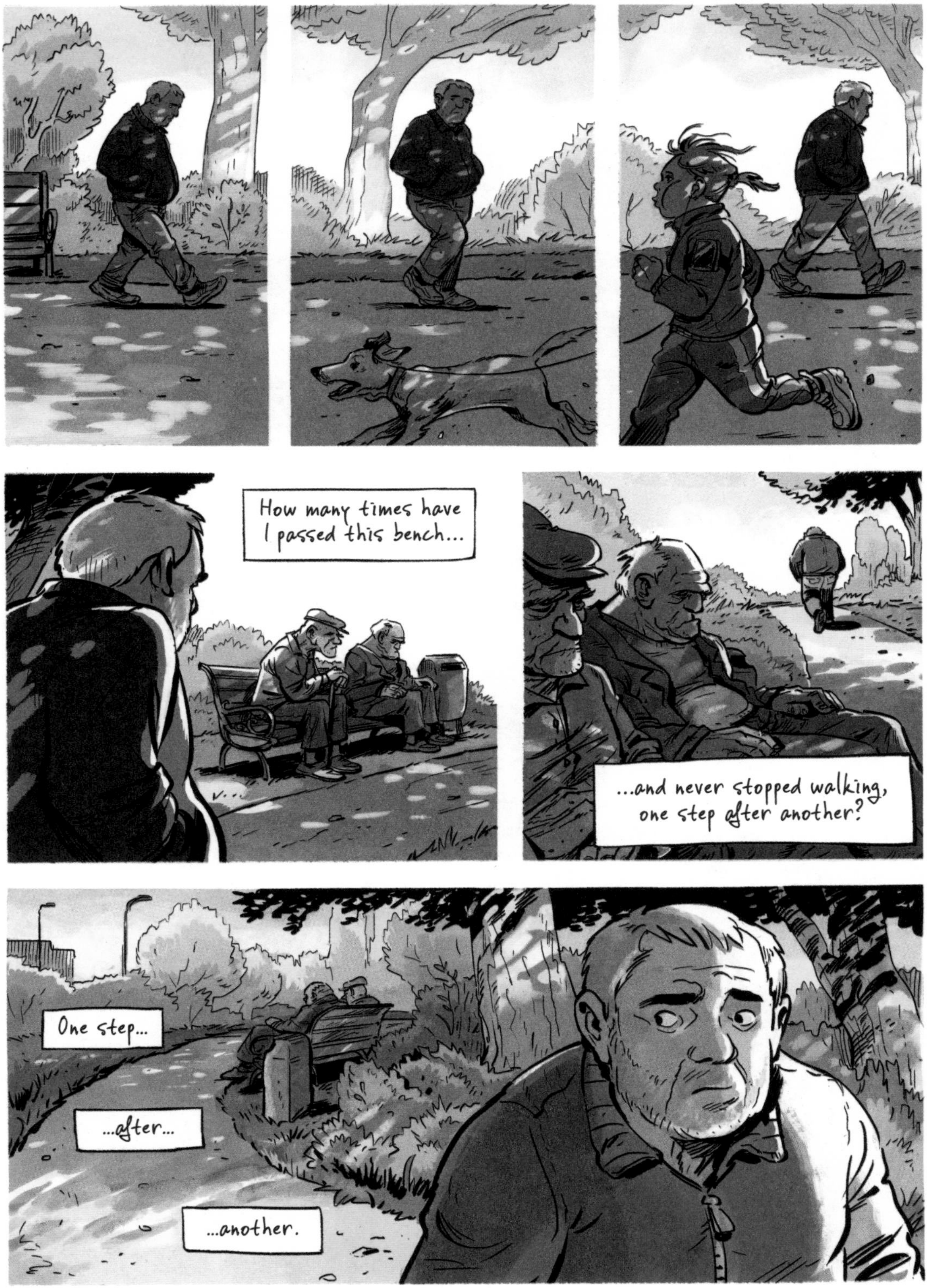
How many times have I passed this bench...
...and never stopped walking, one step after another?
One step...
...after...
...another.

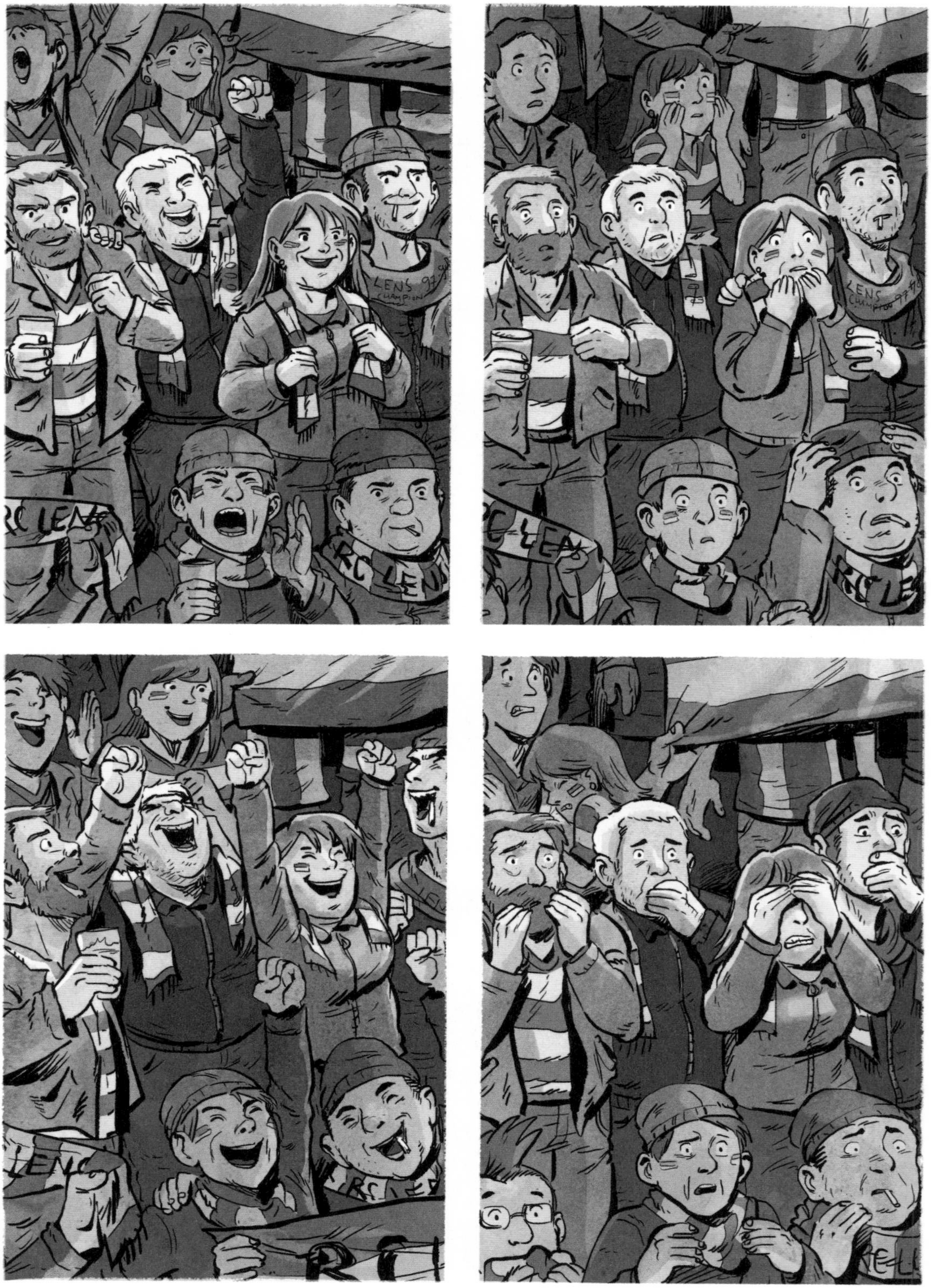
LENS 97
CHAMPION

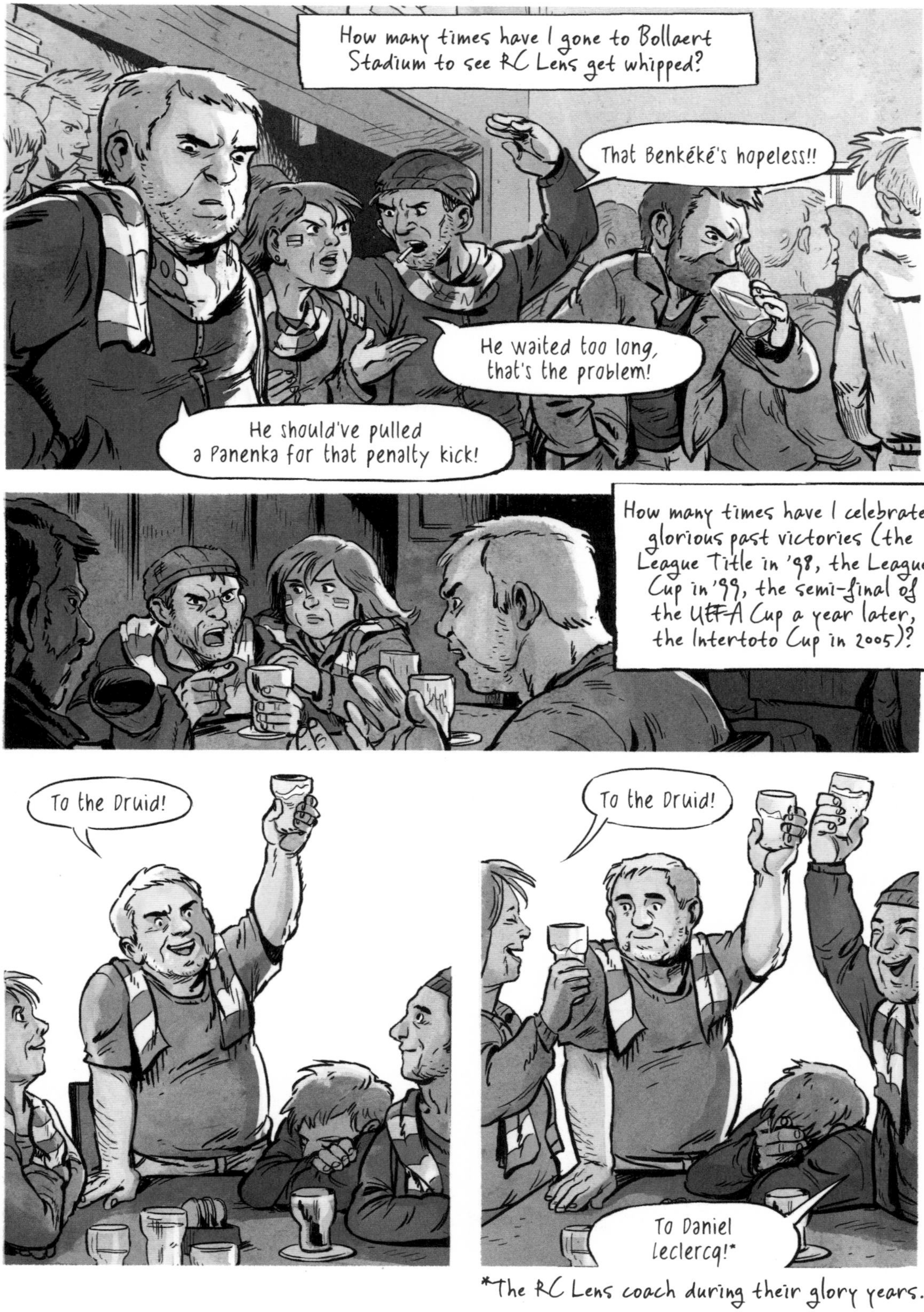
How many times have I gone to Bollaert Stadium to see RC Lens get whipped?
That Benkéké's hopeless!!
He waited too long, that's the problem!
He should've pulled a Panenka for that penalty kick!
How many times have I celebrated glorious past victories (the League Title in '98, the League Cup in '99, the semi-final of the UEFA Cup a year later, the Intertoto Cup in 2005)?
To the Druid!
To the Druid!
To Daniel Leclercq!*

*The RC Lens coach during their glory years.

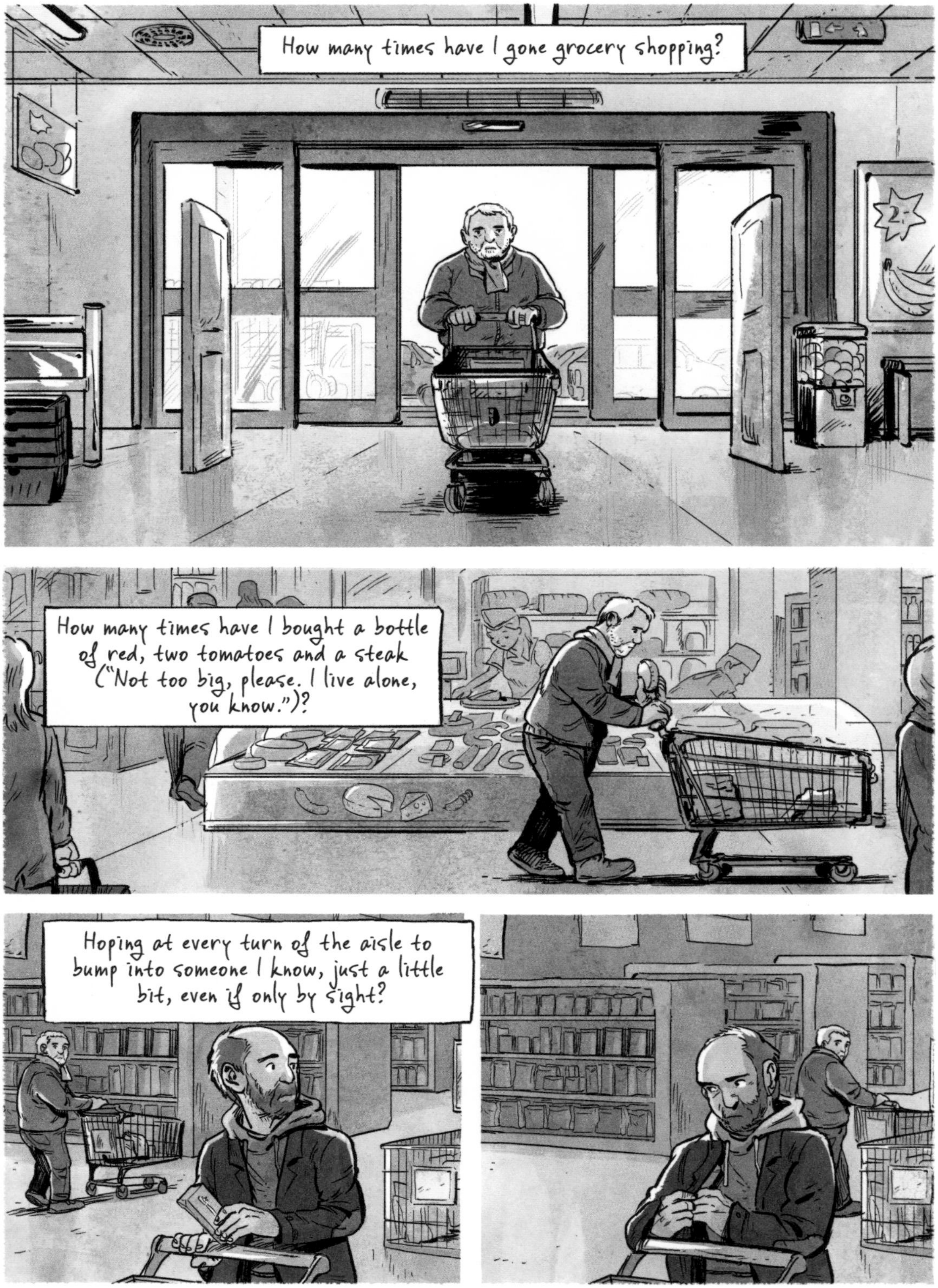
How many times have I gone grocery shopping?
How many times have I bought a bottle of red, two tomatoes and a steak ("Not too big, please. I live alone, you know.")?
Hoping at every turn of the aisle to bump into someone I know, just a little bit, even if only by sight?

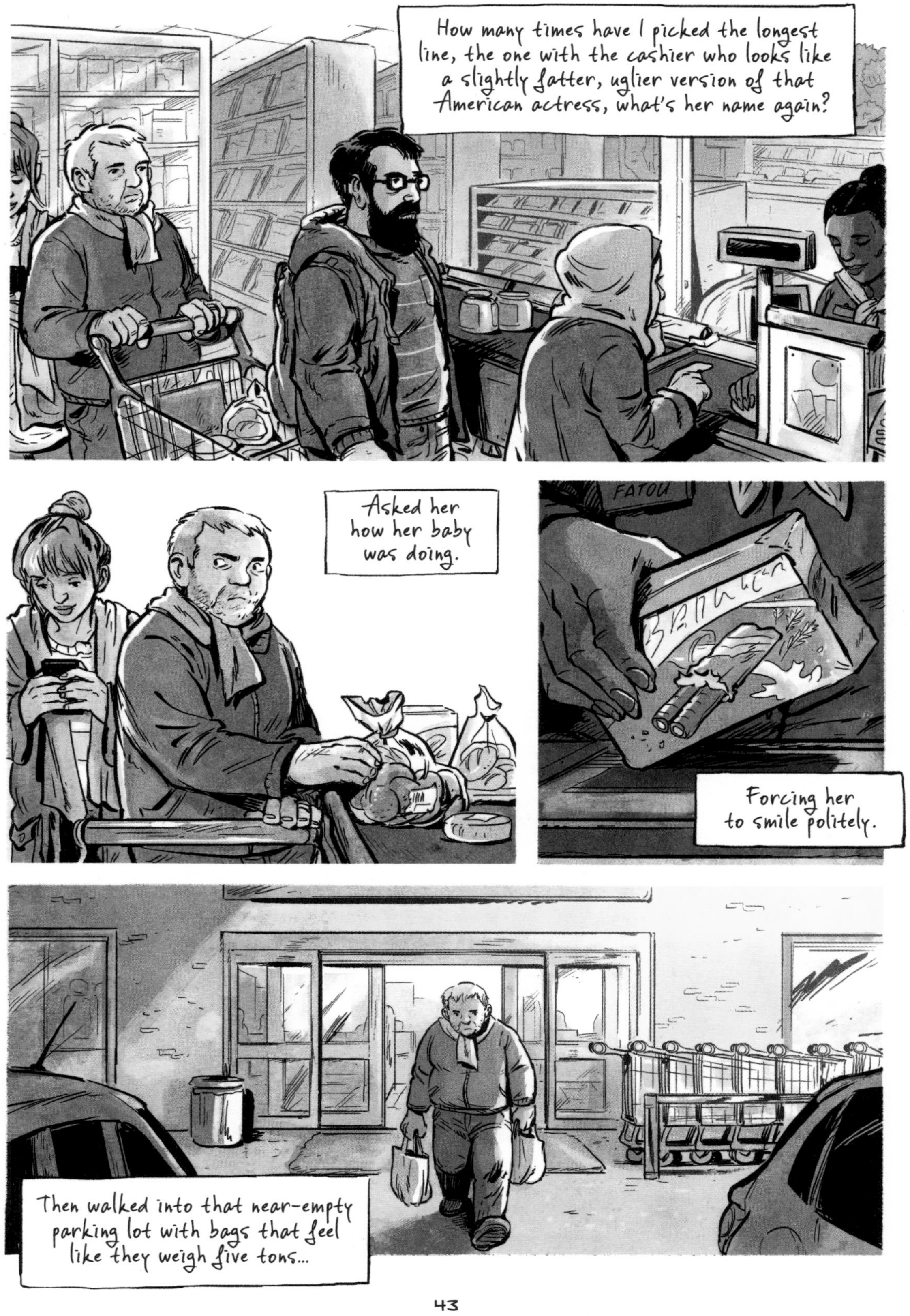
How many times have I picked the longest line, the one with the cashier who looks like a slightly fatter, uglier version of that American actress, what's her name again?
Asked her how her baby was doing.
FATOU
Forcing her to smile politely.
Then walked into that near-empty parking lot with bags that feel like they weigh five tons...

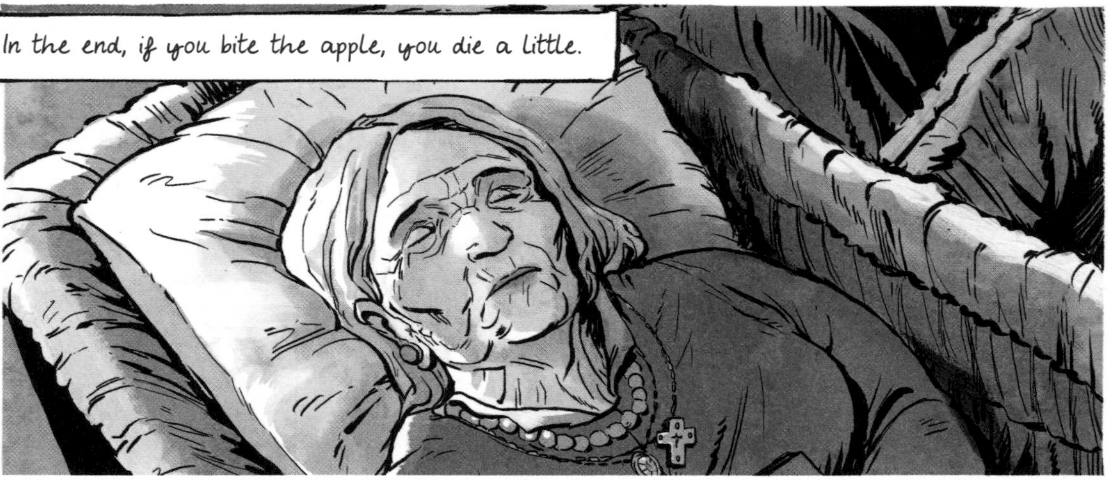
In the end, if you bite the apple, you die a little.

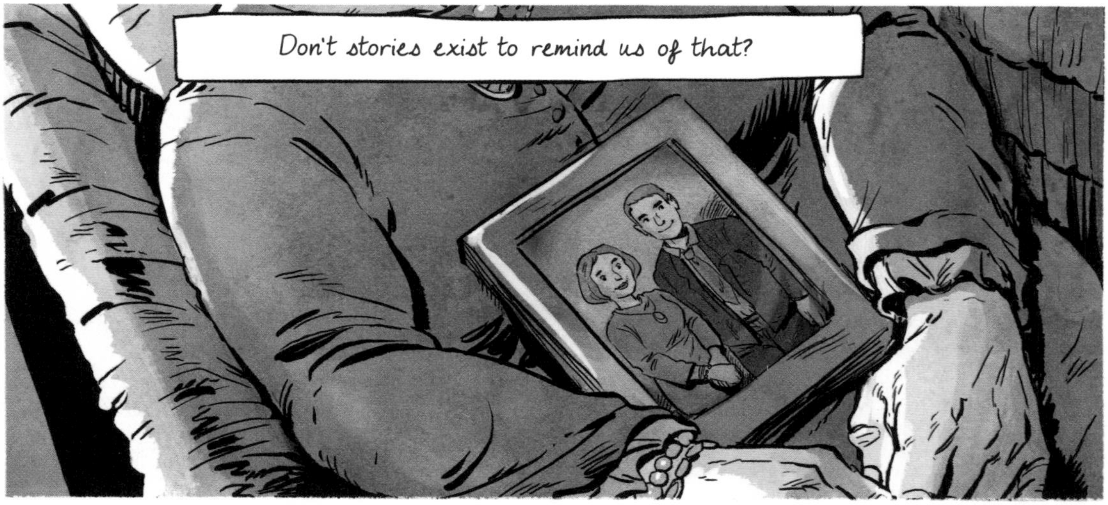
Don't stories exist to remind us of that?

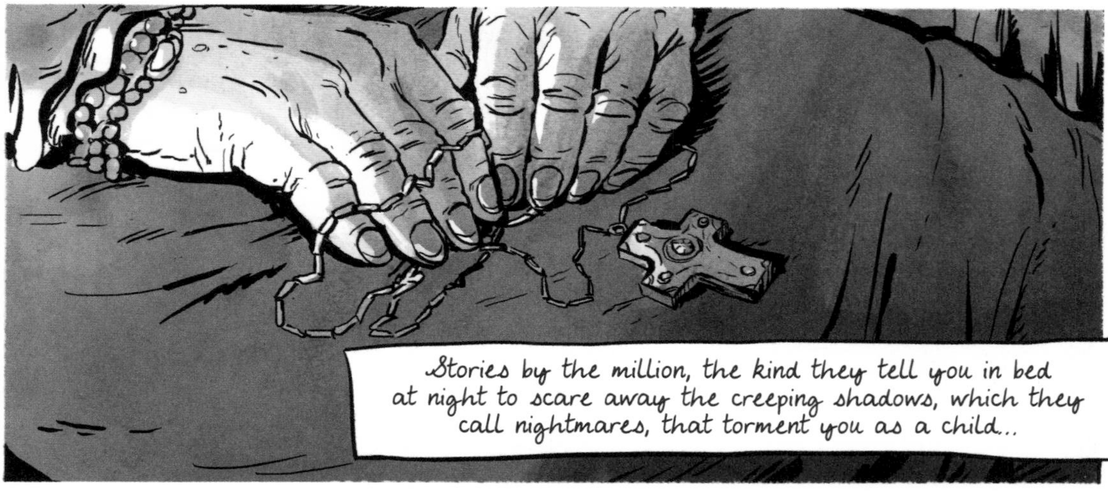
Stories by the million, the kind they tell you in bed at night to scare away the creeping shadows, which they call nightmares, that torment you as a child...

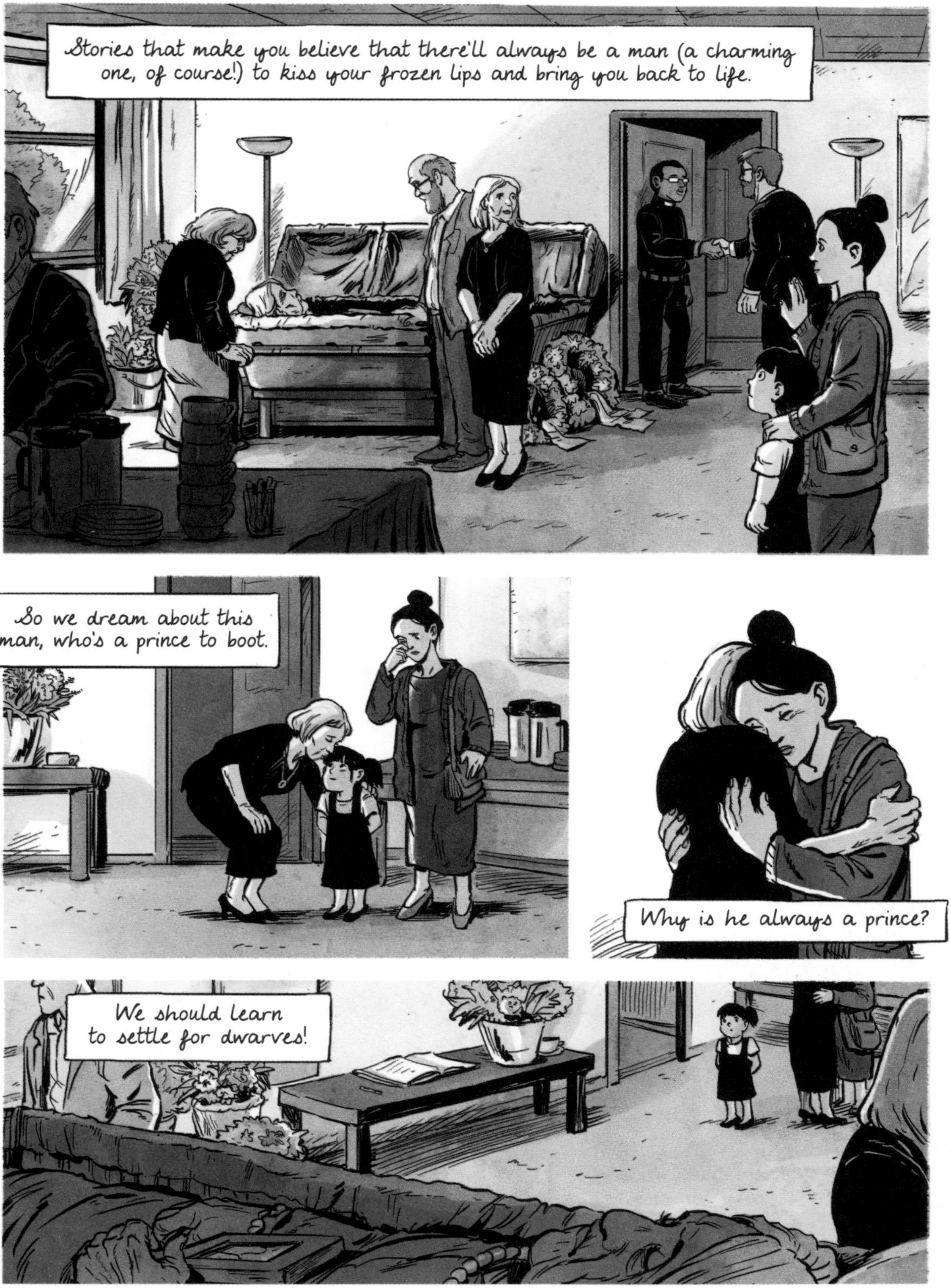
Stories that make you believe that there'll always be a man (a charming one, of course!) to kiss your frozen lips and bring you back to life.
So we dream about this man, who's a prince to boot.
Why is he always a prince?
We should learn to settle for dwarves!

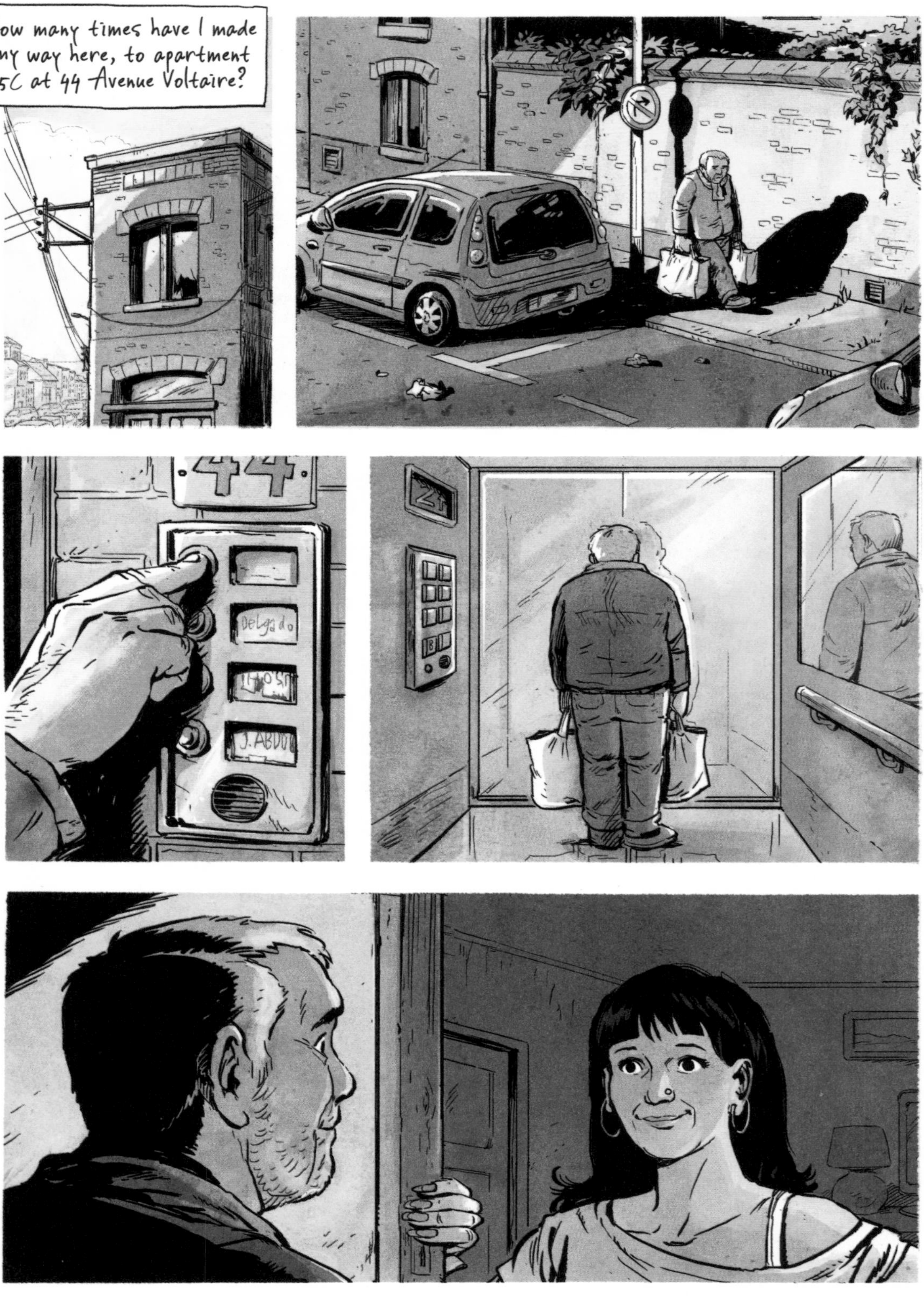
How many times have I made my way here, to apartment 5C at 44 Avenue Voltaire?
44
Delgado

How many times have I pitifully pulled 100 euros from my wallet, more ashamed than a kid who has to strip down for the nurse on the day of his medical check-up?

How many times have I seen that sweet, kind smile on the face of this woman who could be my daughter...

...but who treats me as if she were my mother?

  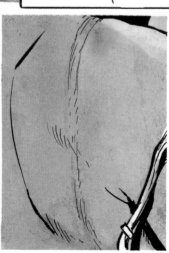

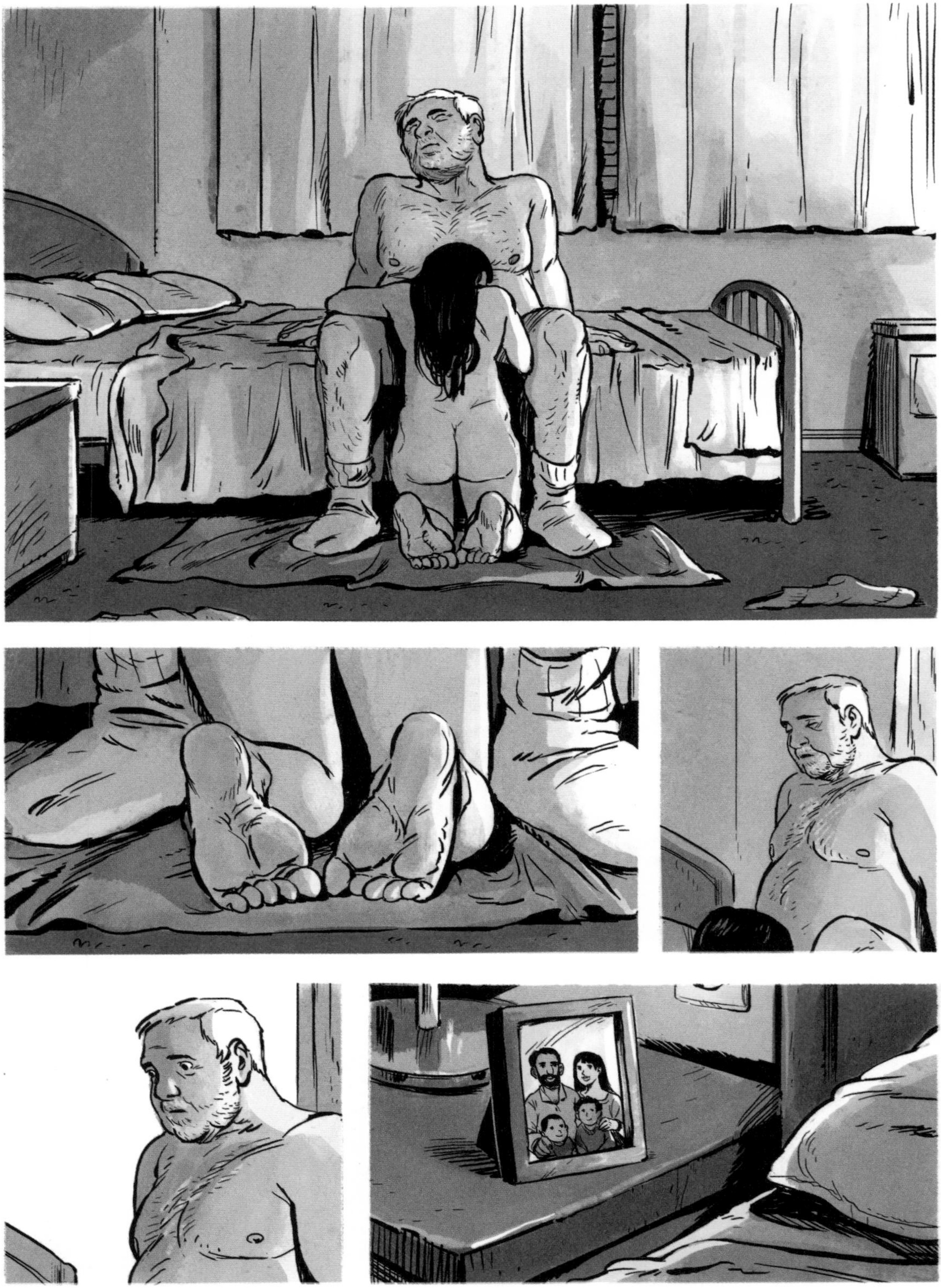

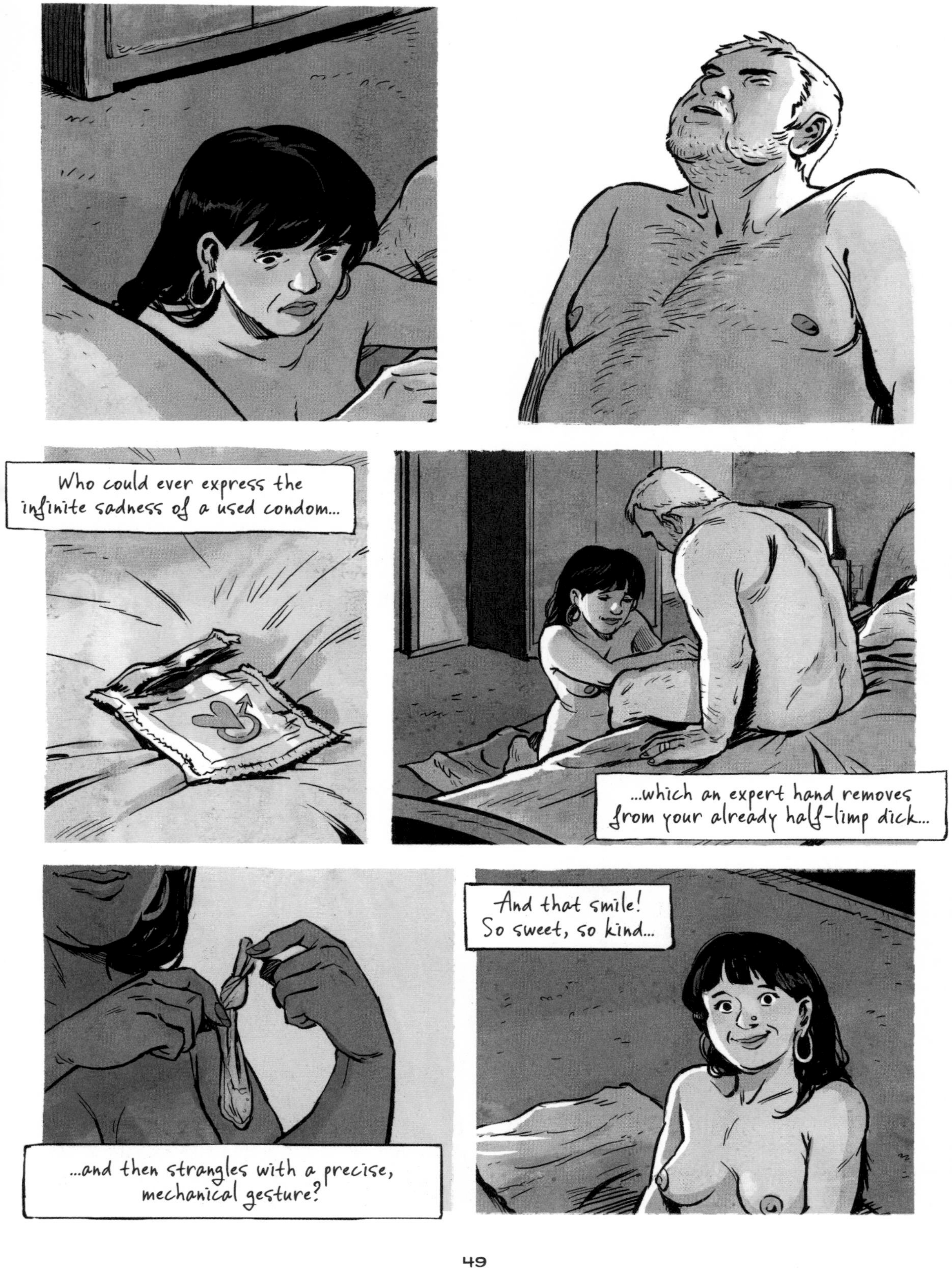
Who could ever express the infinite sadness of a used condom...
...which an expert hand removes from your already half-limp dick...
...and then strangles with a precise, mechanical gesture?
And that smile! So sweet, so kind...

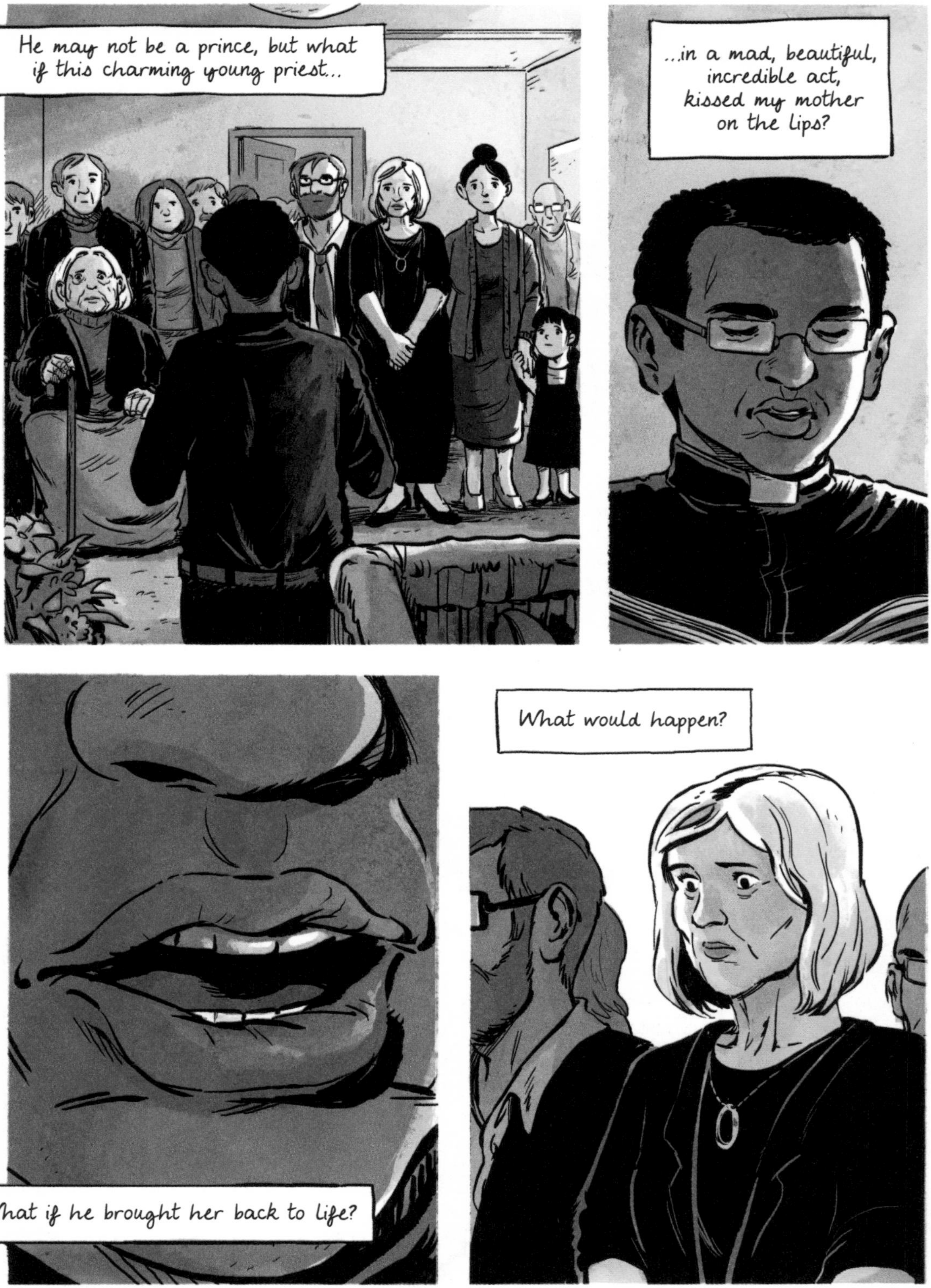
He may not be a prince, but what if this charming young priest...
...in a mad, beautiful, incredible act, kissed my mother on the lips?
What if he brought her back to life?
What would happen?

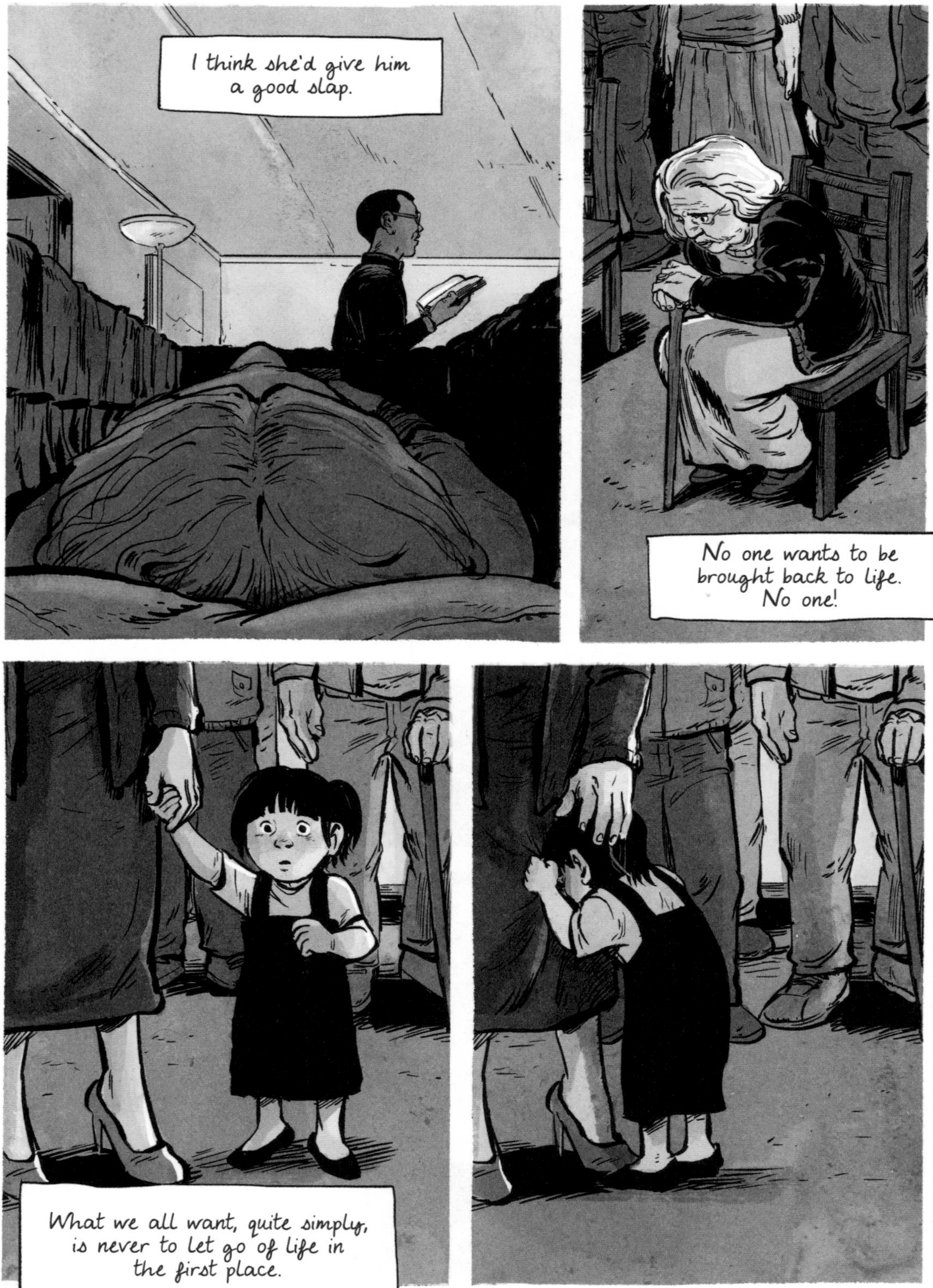
I think she'd give him a good slap.
No one wants to be brought back to life. No one!
What we all want, quite simply, is never to let go of life in the first place.

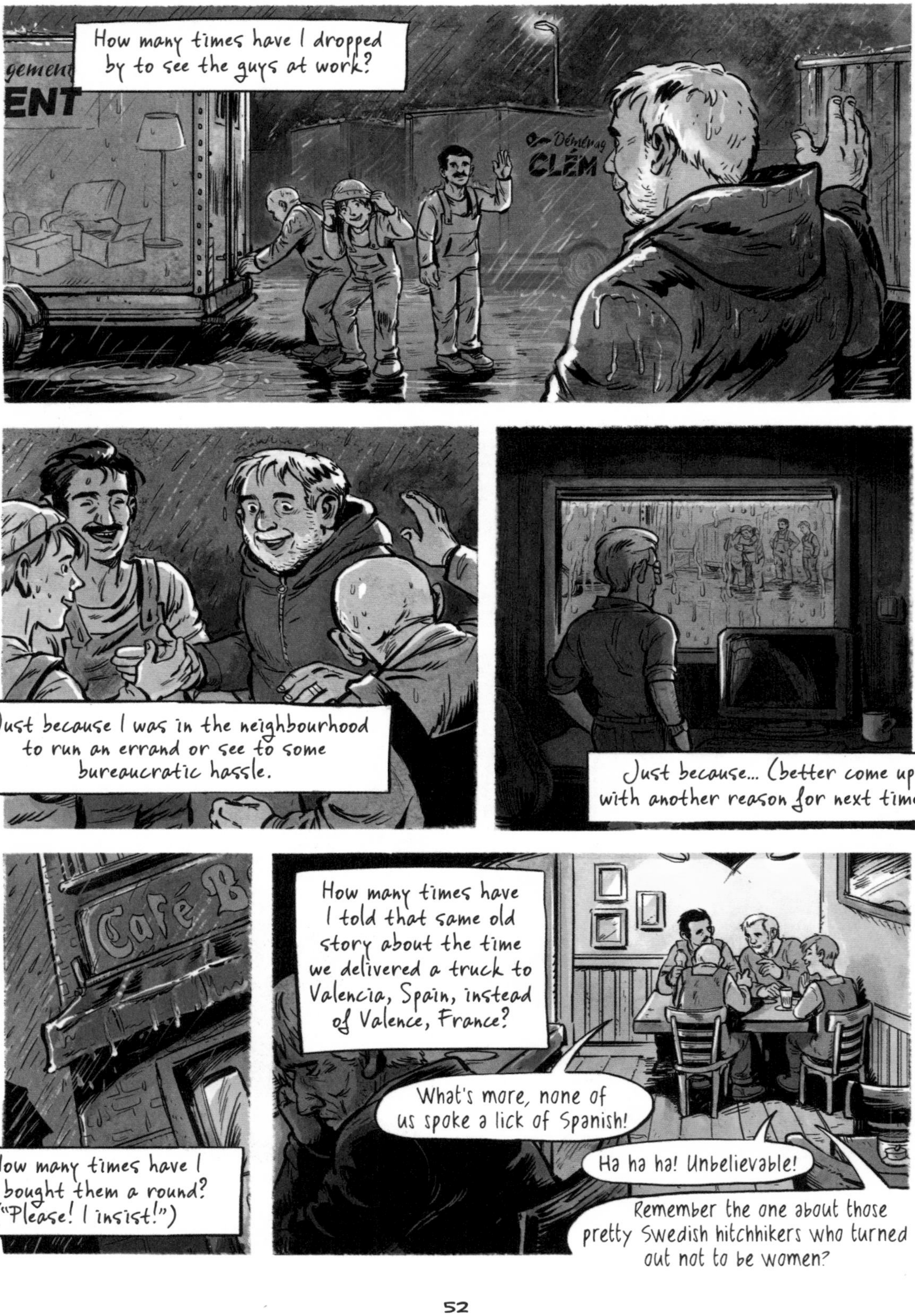
How many times have I dropped by to see the guys at work?
CLÉM
Just because I was in the neighbourhood to run an errand or see to some bureaucratic hassle.
Just because... (better come up with another reason for next time!)
Café
How many times have I bought them a round? ("Please! I insist!")
How many times have I told that same old story about the time we delivered a truck to Valencia, Spain, instead of Valence, France?
What's more, none of us spoke a lick of Spanish!
Ha ha ha! Unbelievable!
Remember the one about those pretty Swedish hitchhikers who turned out not to be women?

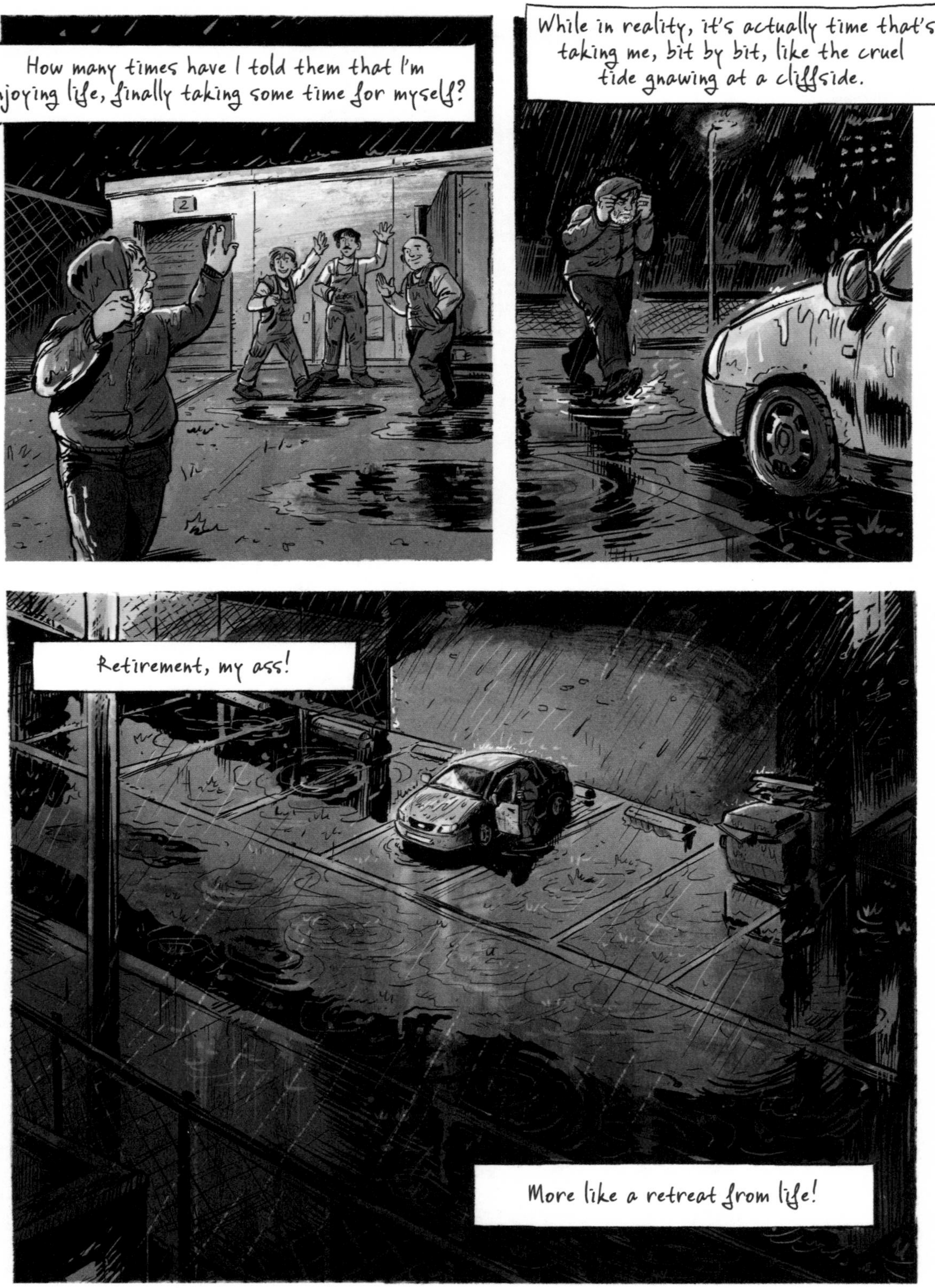
How many times have I told them that I'm enjoying life, finally taking some time for myself?
While in reality, it's actually time that's taking me, bit by bit, like the cruel tide gnawing at a cliffside.
Retirement, my ass!
More like a retreat from life!

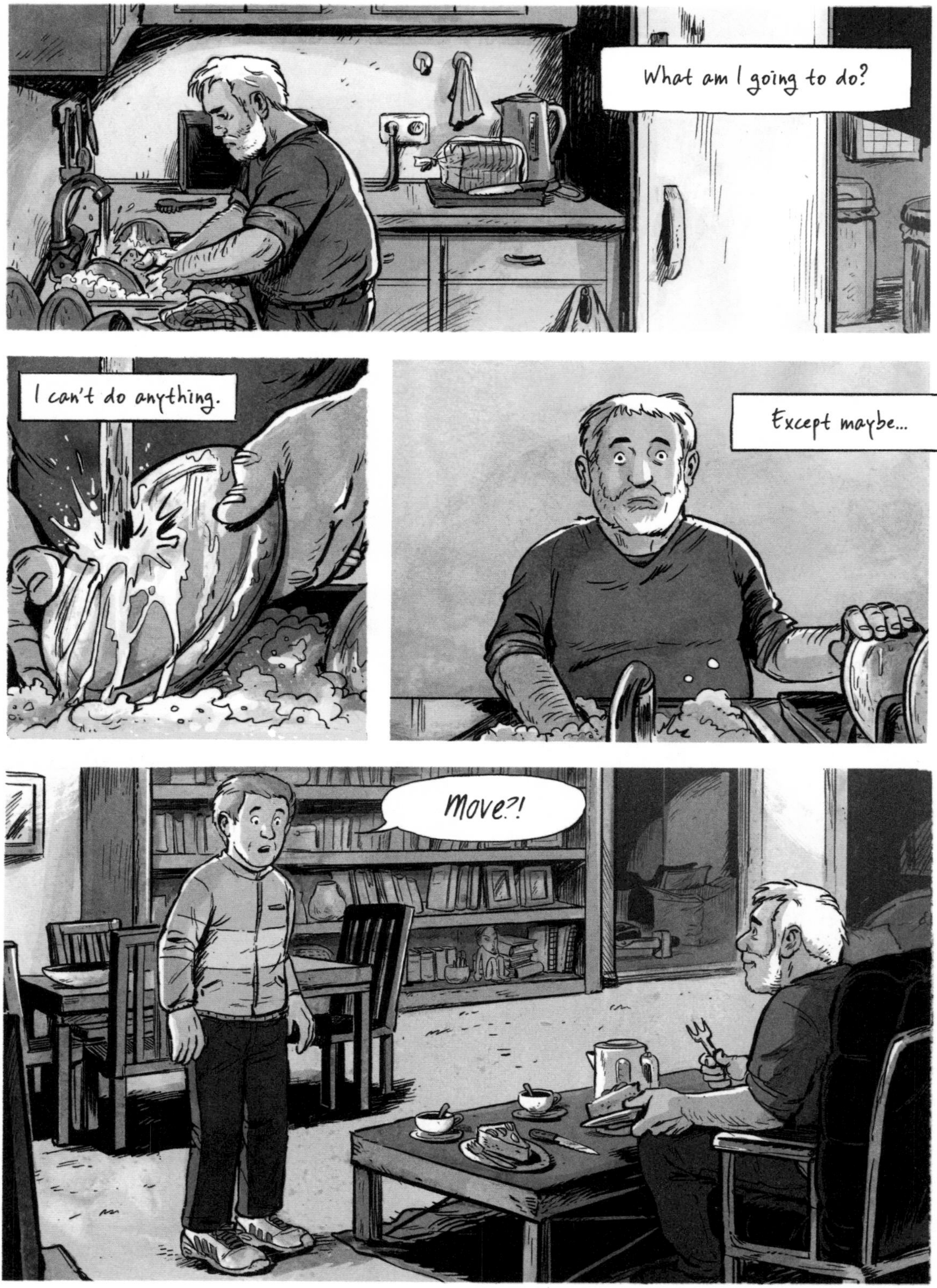
What am I going to do?
I can't do anything.
Except maybe...
Move?!

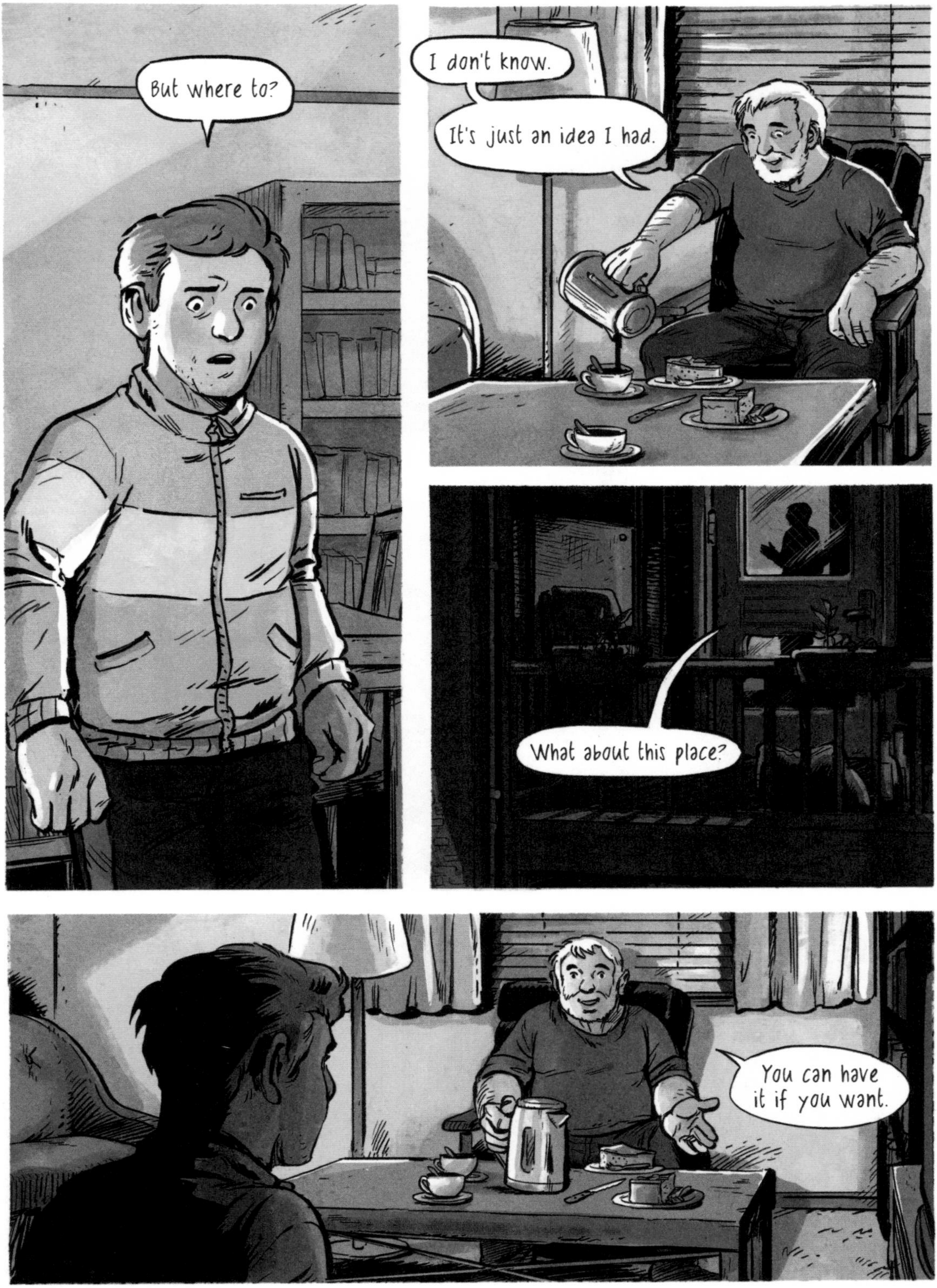
But where to?
I don't know.
It's just an idea I had.
What about this place?
You can have it if you want.

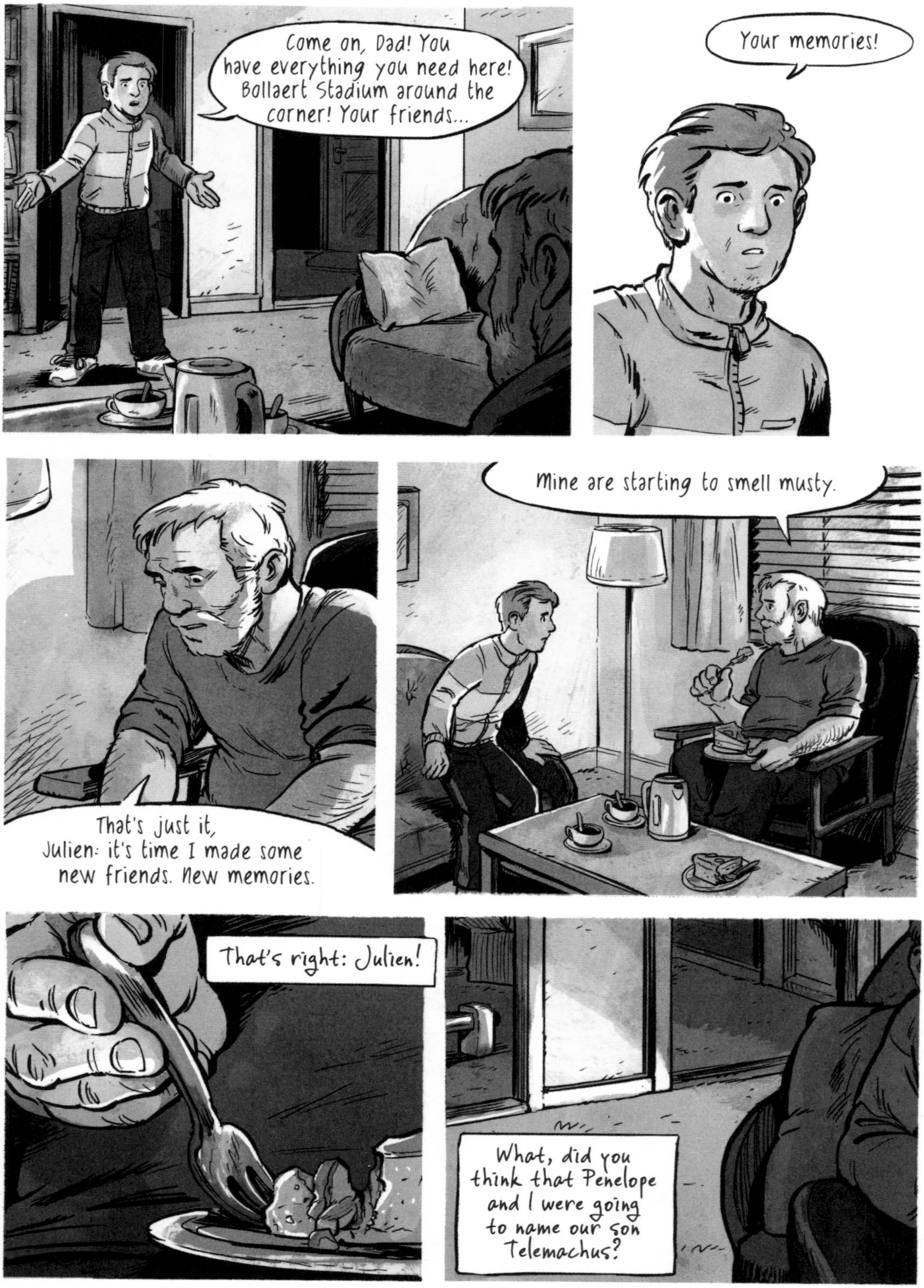
Come on, Dad! You have everything you need here! Bollaert Stadium around the corner! Your friends...
Your memories!
That's just it, Julien: it's time I made some new friends. New memories.
Mine are starting to smell musty.
That's right: Julien!
What, did you think that Penelope and I were going to name our son Telemachus?

3.

Cover girl

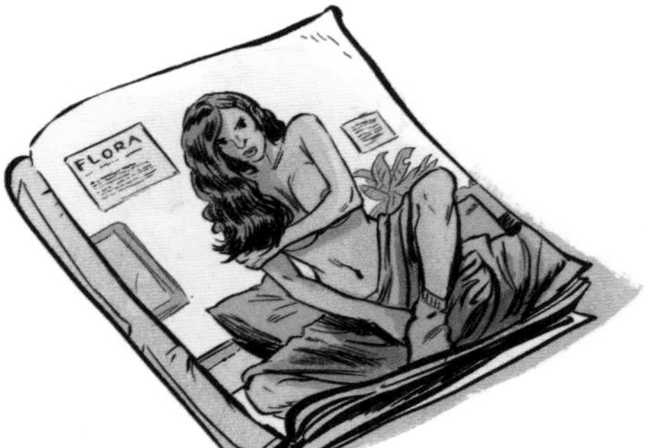
FLORA

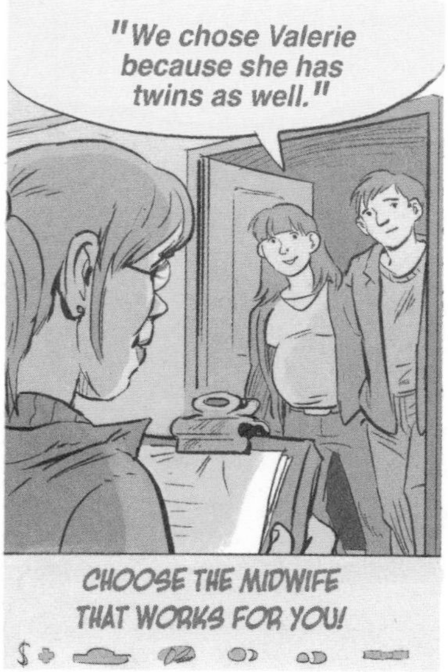
"We chose Valerie because she has twins as well."
CHOOSE THE MIDWIFE THAT WORKS FOR YOU!
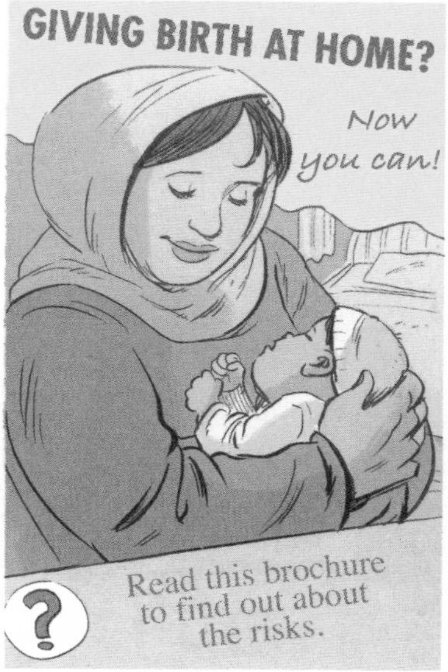
GIVING BIRTH AT HOME?
Now you can!
Read this brochure to find out about the risks.
?
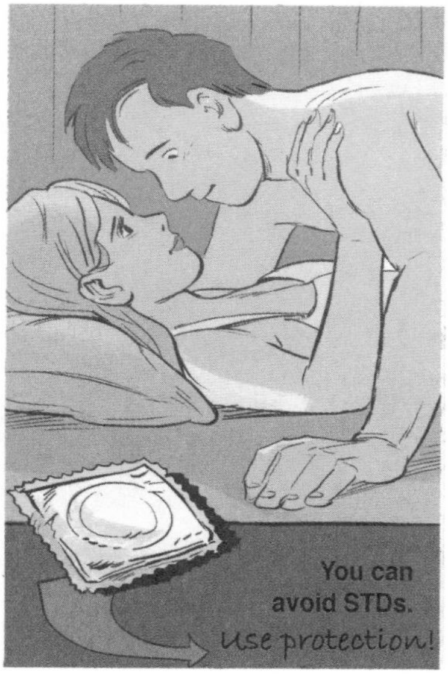
You can avoid STDs.
Use protection!
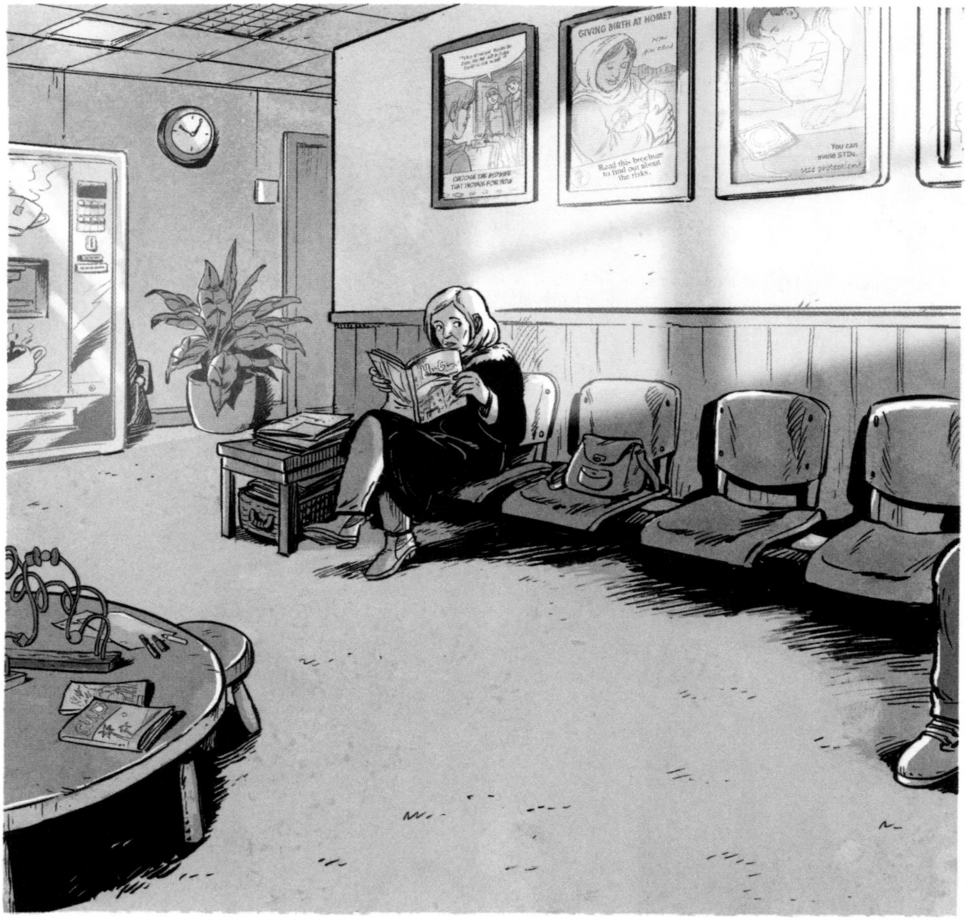
GIVING BIRTH AT HOME?
CHOOSE THE MIDWIFE THAT WORKS FOR YOU!
Read this brochure to find out about the risks.
You can avoid STDs.

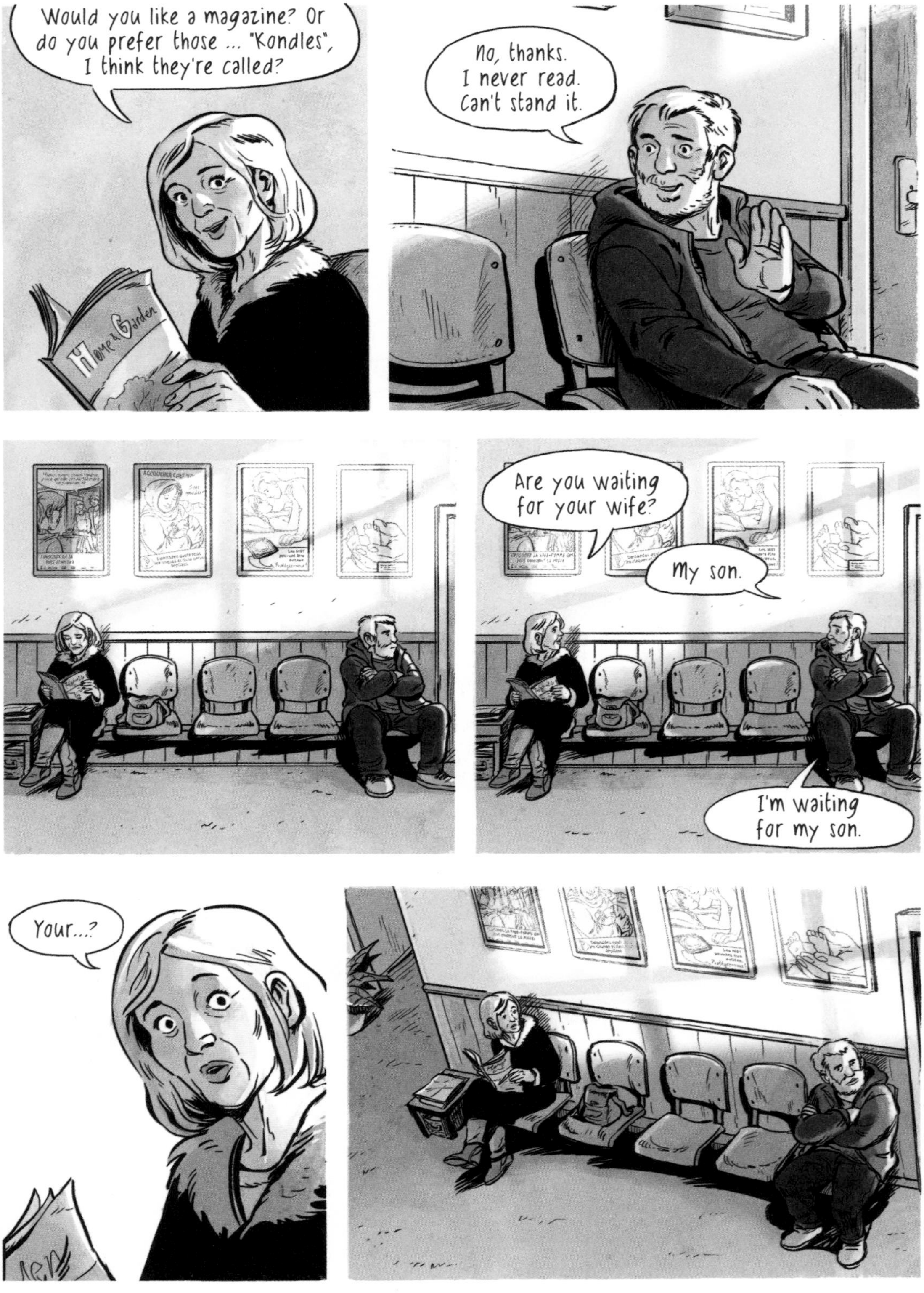
Would you like a magazine? Or do you prefer those ... "Kondles", I think they're called?
Home&Garden
No, thanks. I never read. Can't stand it.
Are you waiting for your wife?
My son.
I'm waiting for my son.
Your...?

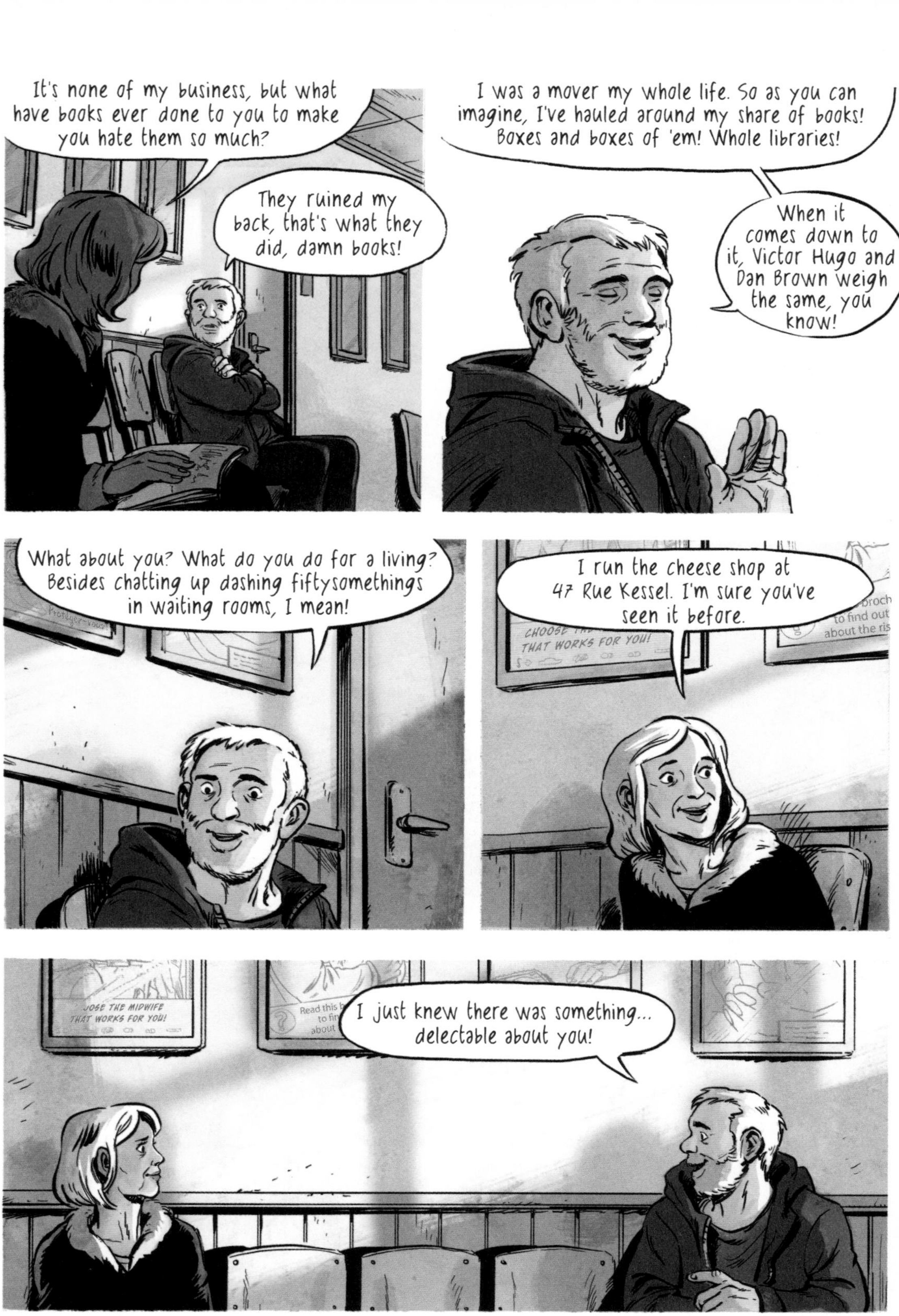
It's none of my business, but what have books ever done to you to make you hate them so much?
They ruined my back, that's what they did, damn books!
I was a mover my whole life. So as you can imagine, I've hauled around my share of books! Boxes and boxes of 'em! Whole libraries!
When it comes down to it, Victor Hugo and Dan Brown weigh the same, you know!
What about you? What do you do for a living? Besides chatting up dashing fiftysomethings in waiting rooms, I mean!
I run the cheese shop at 47 Rue Kessel. I'm sure you've seen it before.
THAT WORKS FOR YOU!
I just knew there was something... delectable about you!
JOSE THE MIDWIFE
THAT WORKS FOR YOU!

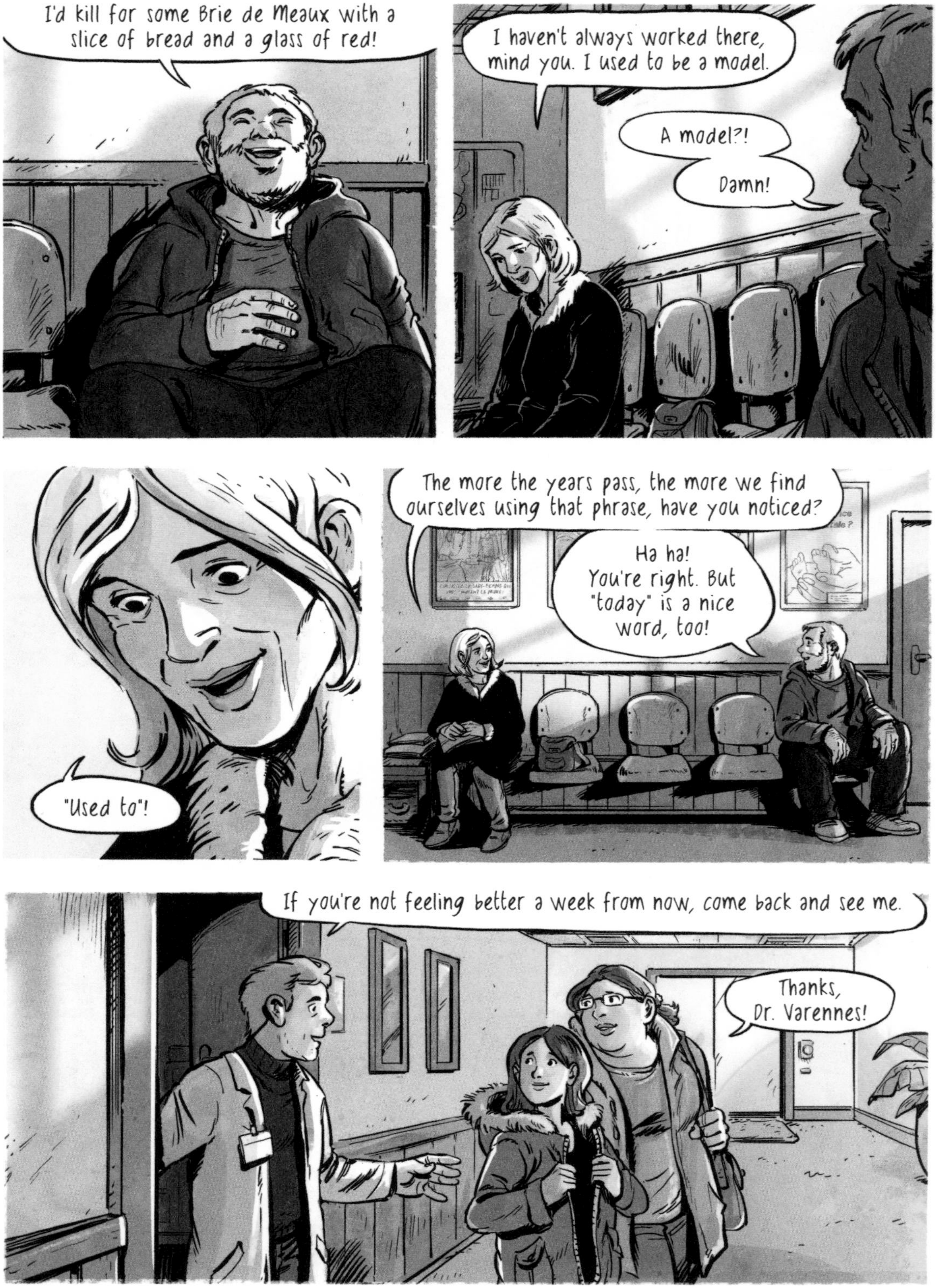
I'd kill for some Brie de Meaux with a slice of bread and a glass of red!
I haven't always worked there, mind you. I used to be a model.
A model?!
Damn!
"Used to"!
The more the years pass, the more we find ourselves using that phrase, have you noticed?
Ha ha! You're right. But "today" is a nice word, too!
If you're not feeling better a week from now, come back and see me.
Thanks, Dr. Varennes!

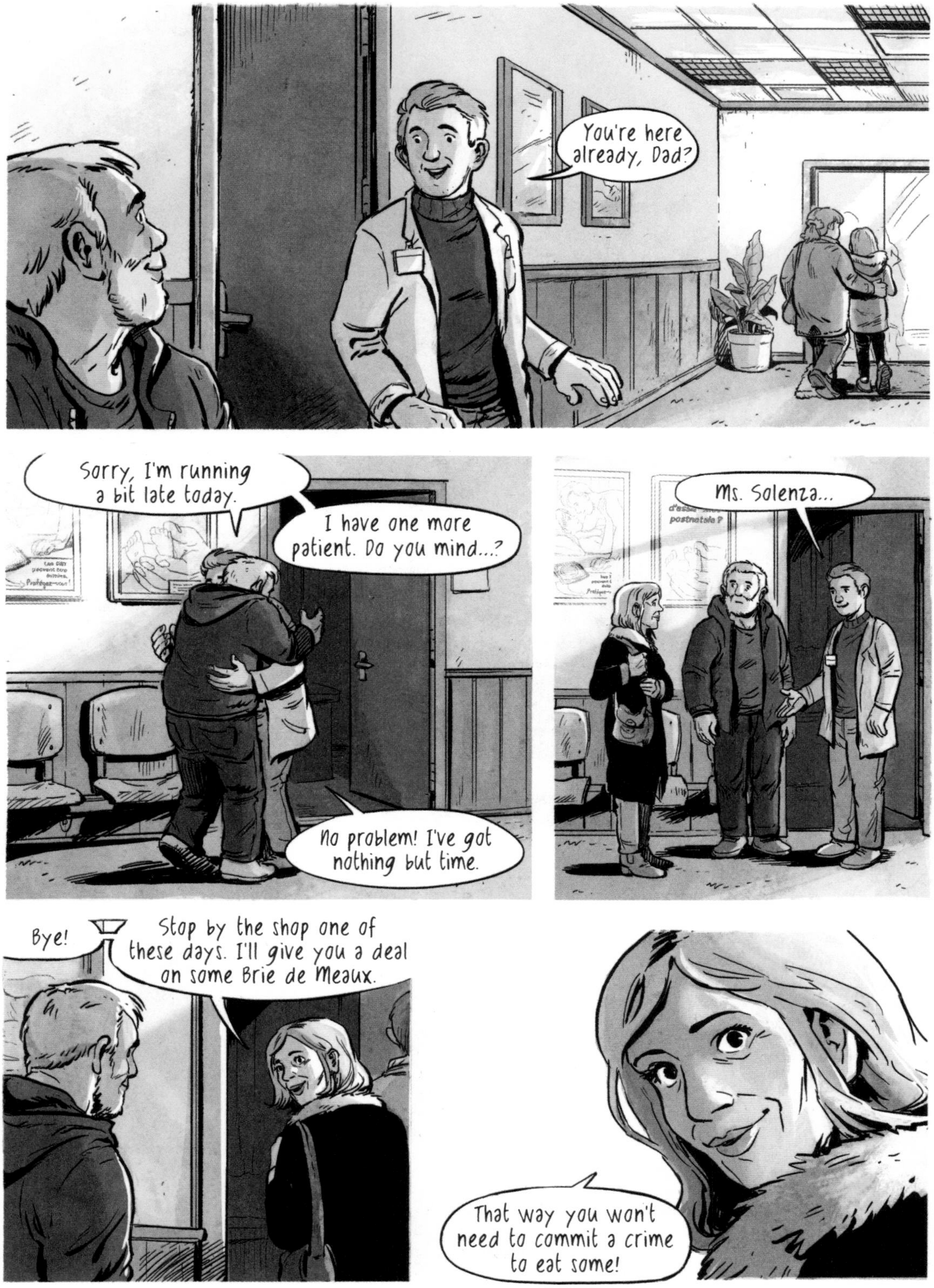

You're here already, Dad?
Sorry, I'm running a bit late today.
I have one more patient. Do you mind...?
No problem! I've got nothing but time.
Ms. Solenza...
Bye!
Stop by the shop one of these days. I'll give you a deal on some Brie de Meaux.
That way you won't need to commit a crime to eat some!

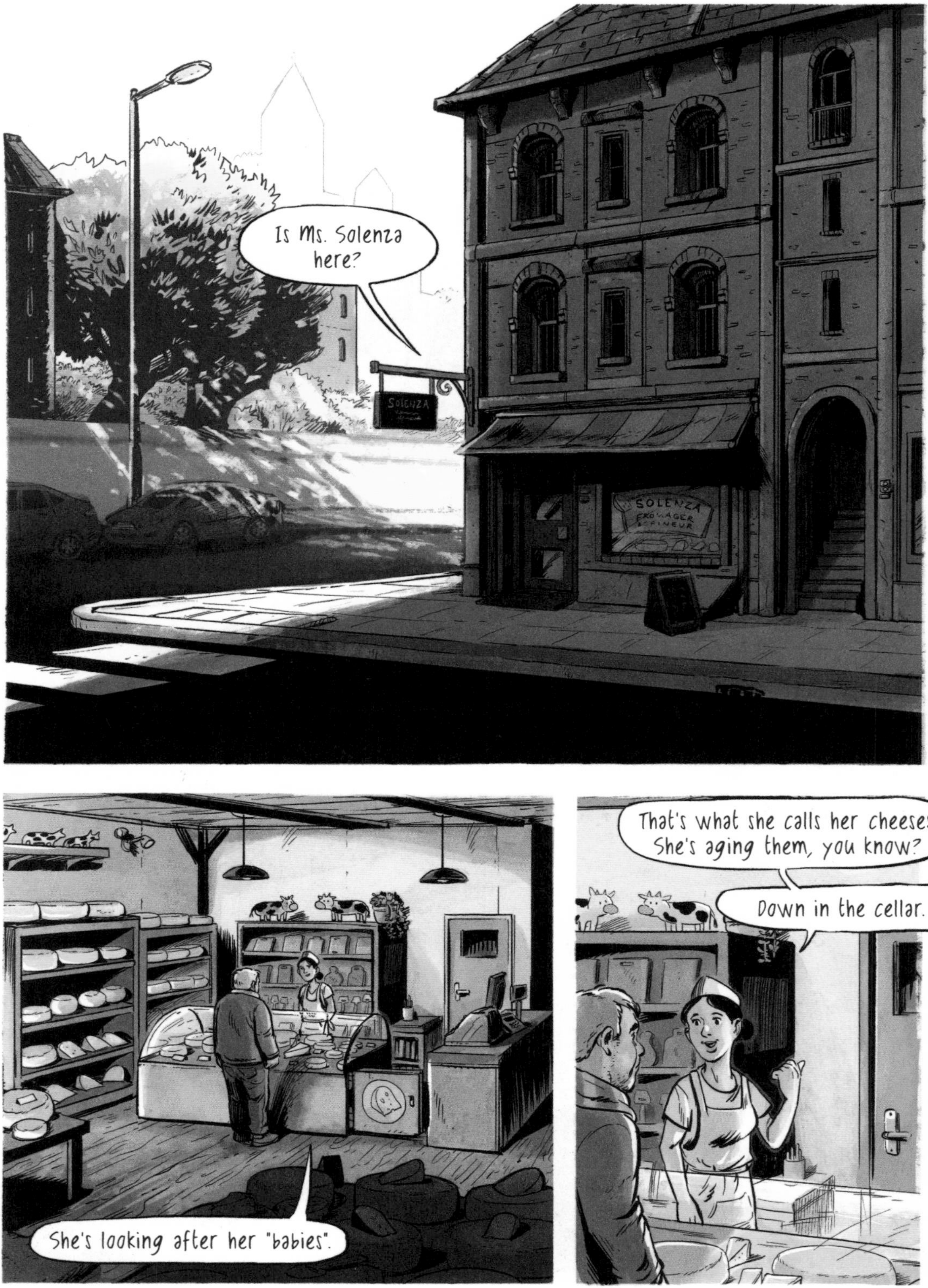
Is Ms. Solenza here?
SOLENZA
She's looking after her "babies".
That's what she calls her cheeses. She's aging them, you know?
Down in the cellar.

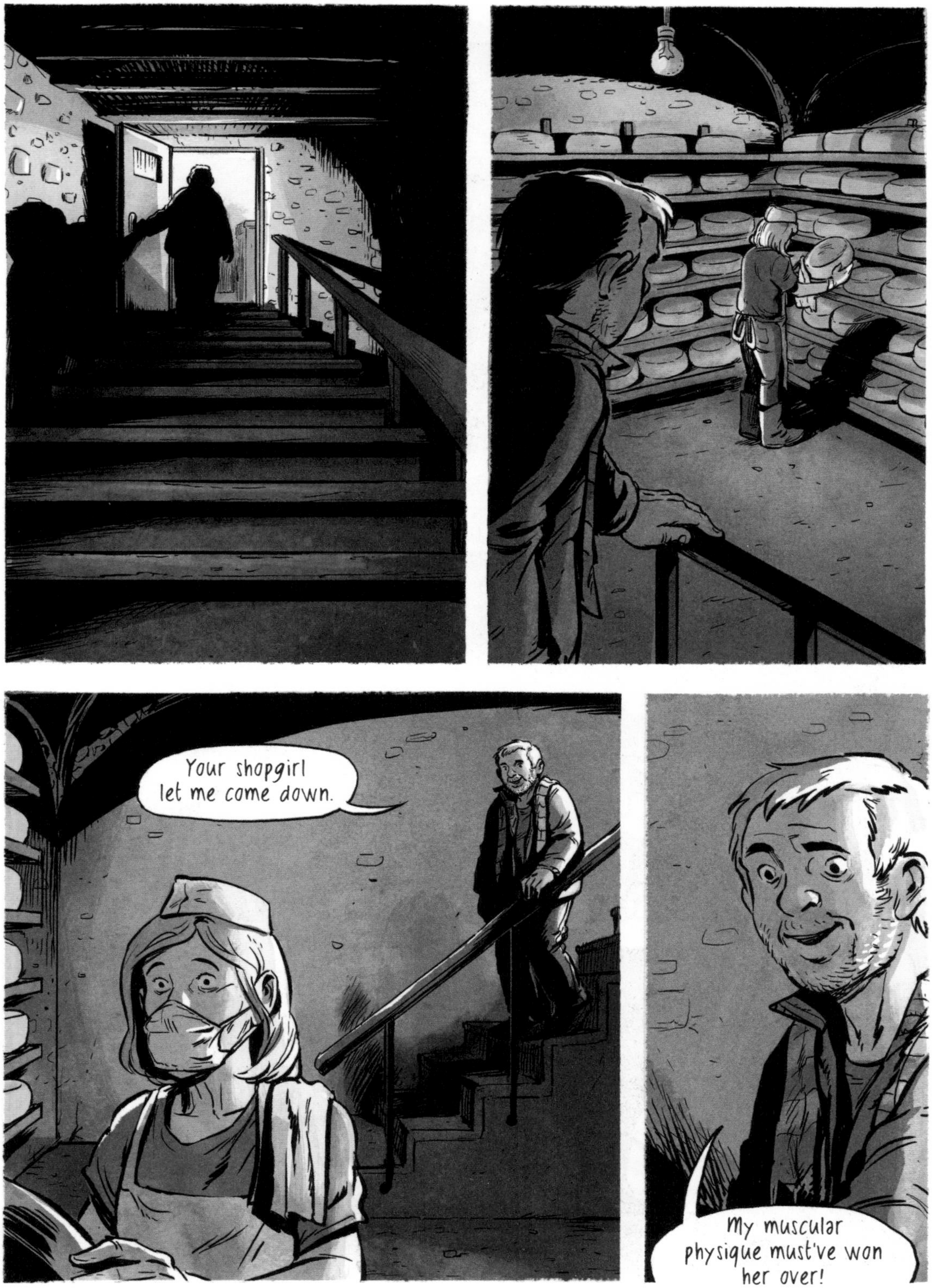
Your shopgirl let me come down.
My muscular physique must've won her over!

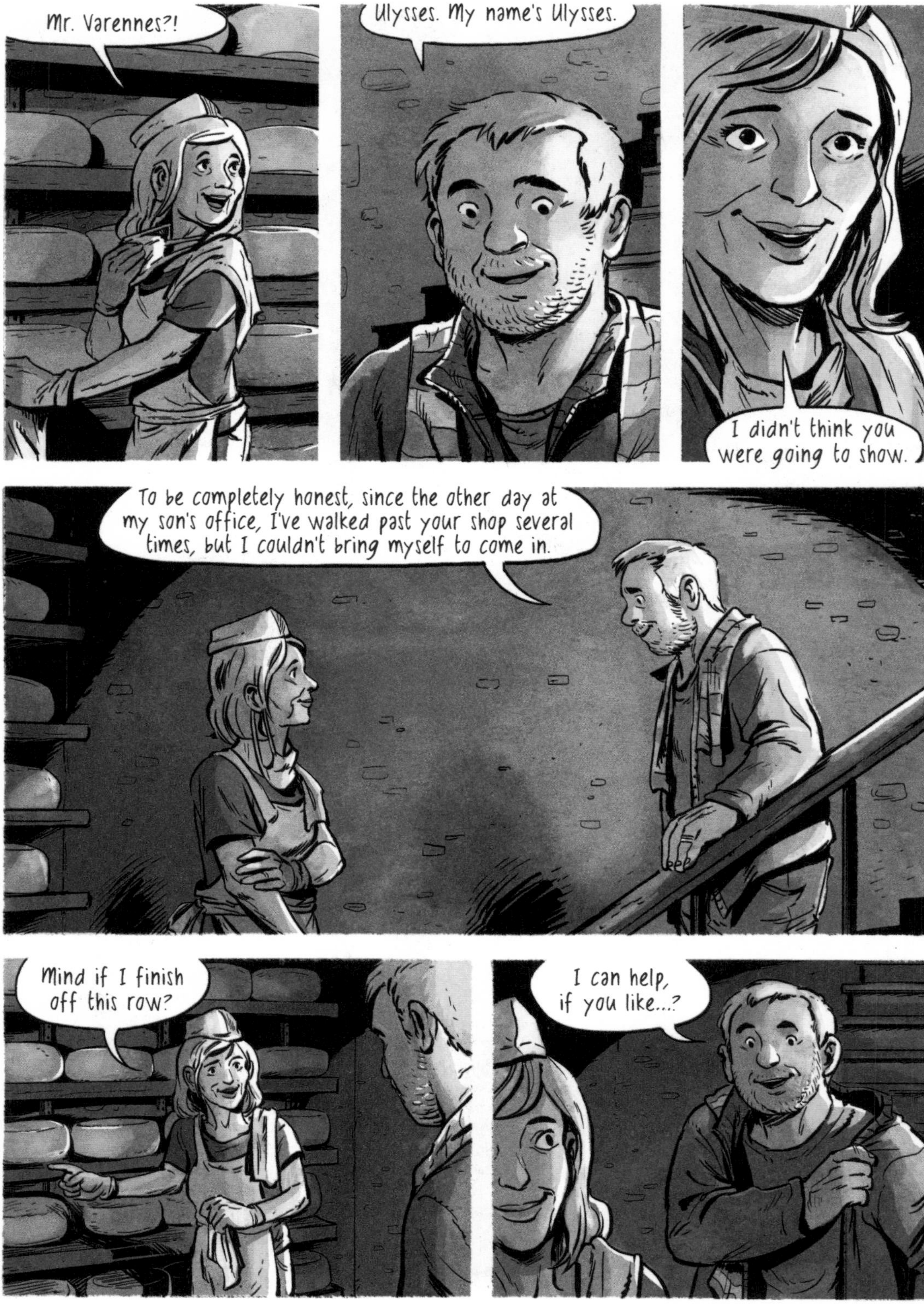
Mr. Varennes?!
Ulysses. My name's Ulysses.
I didn't think you were going to show.
To be completely honest, since the other day at my son's office, I've walked past your shop several times, but I couldn't bring myself to come in.
Mind if I finish off this row?
I can help, if you like...?

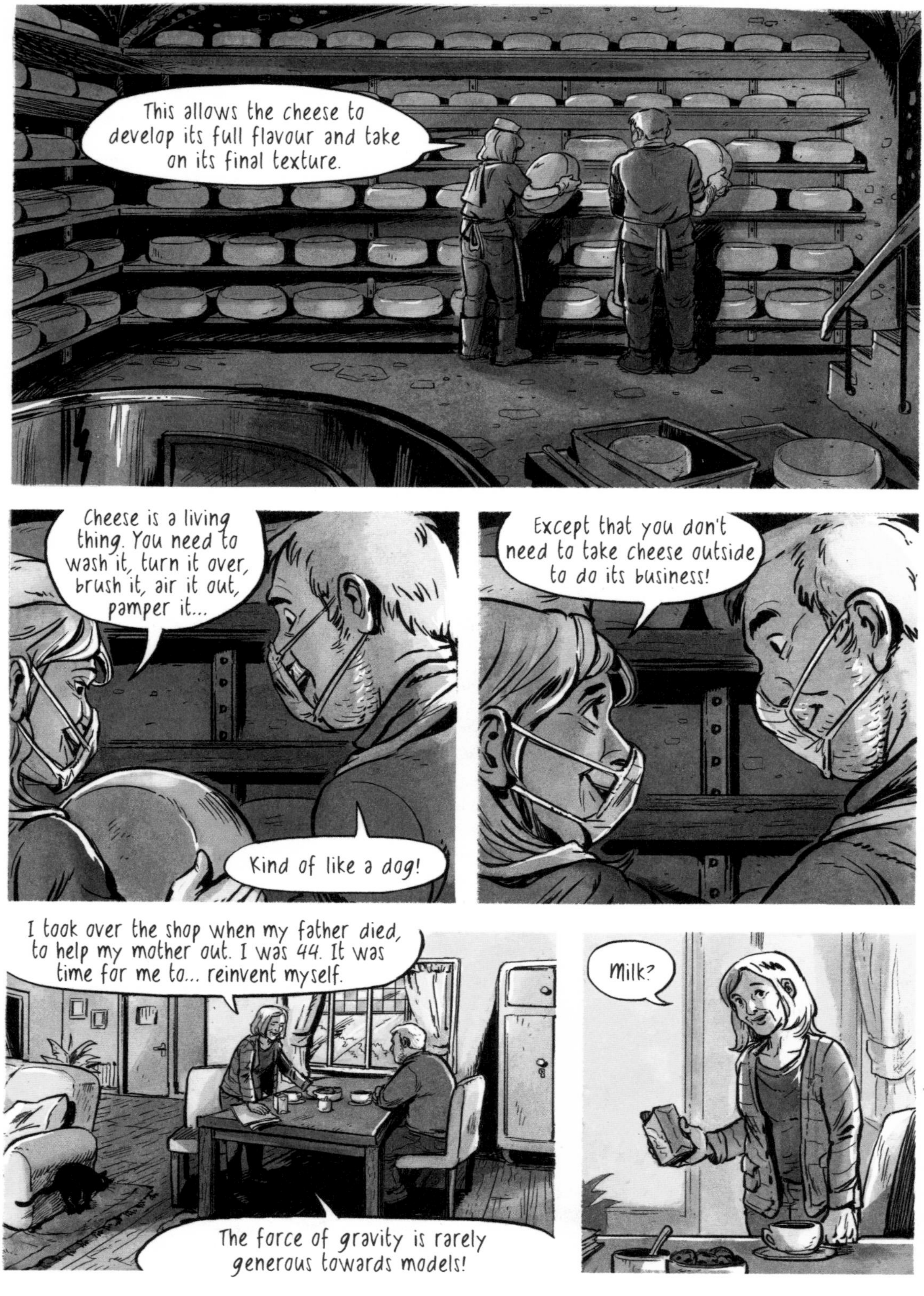

This allows the cheese to develop its full flavour and take on its final texture.
Cheese is a living thing. You need to wash it, turn it over, brush it, air it out, pamper it...
Kind of like a dog!
Except that you don't need to take cheese outside to do its business!
I took over the shop when my father died, to help my mother out. I was 44. It was time for me to... reinvent myself.
The force of gravity is rarely generous towards models!
Milk?

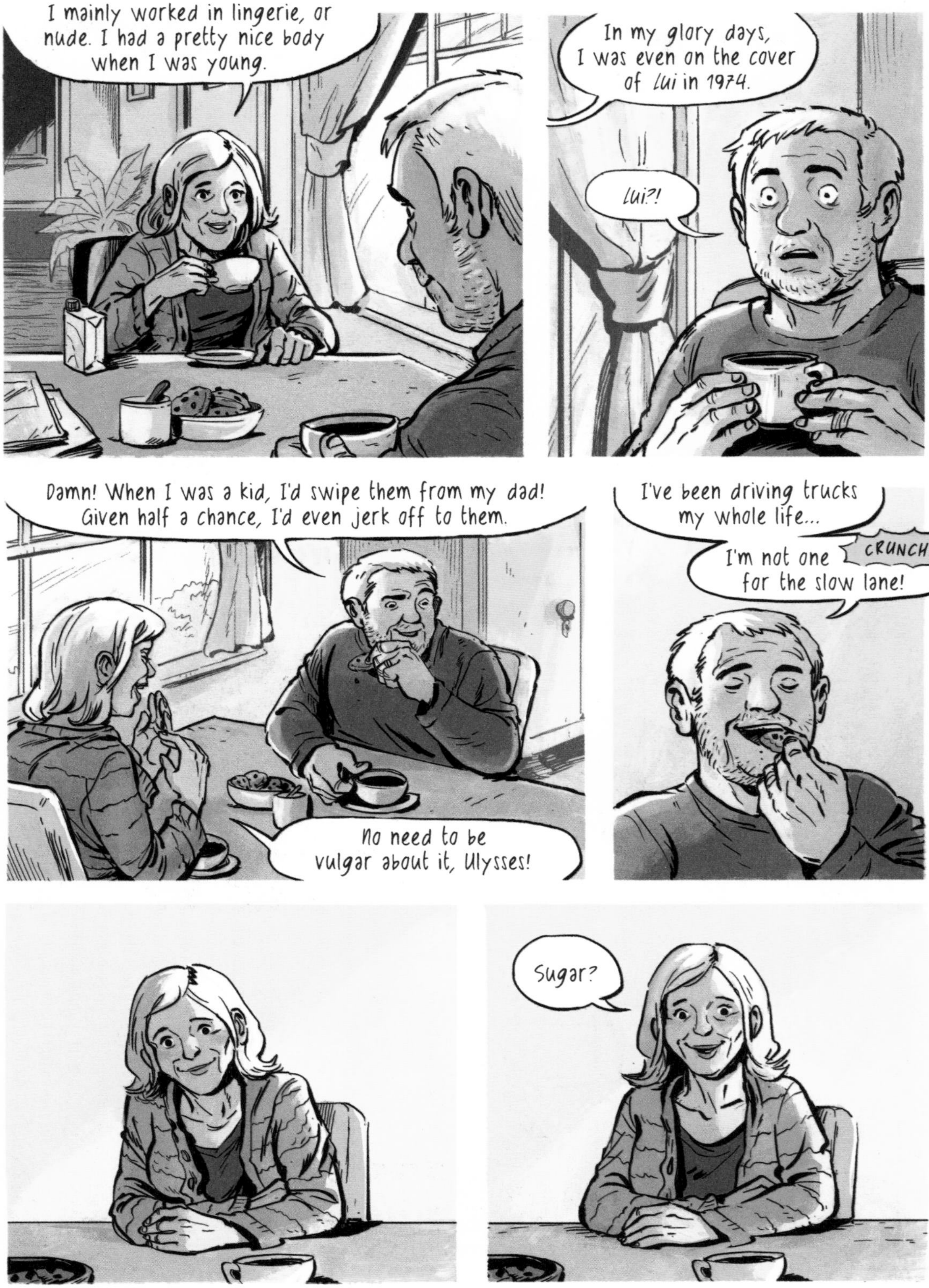
I mainly worked in lingerie, or nude. I had a pretty nice body when I was young.
In my glory days, I was even on the cover of *Lui* in 1974.
Lui?!
Damn! When I was a kid, I'd swipe them from my dad! Given half a chance, I'd even jerk off to them.
No need to be vulgar about it, Ulysses!
I've been driving trucks my whole life...
I'm not one for the slow lane!
CRUNCH!
Sugar?

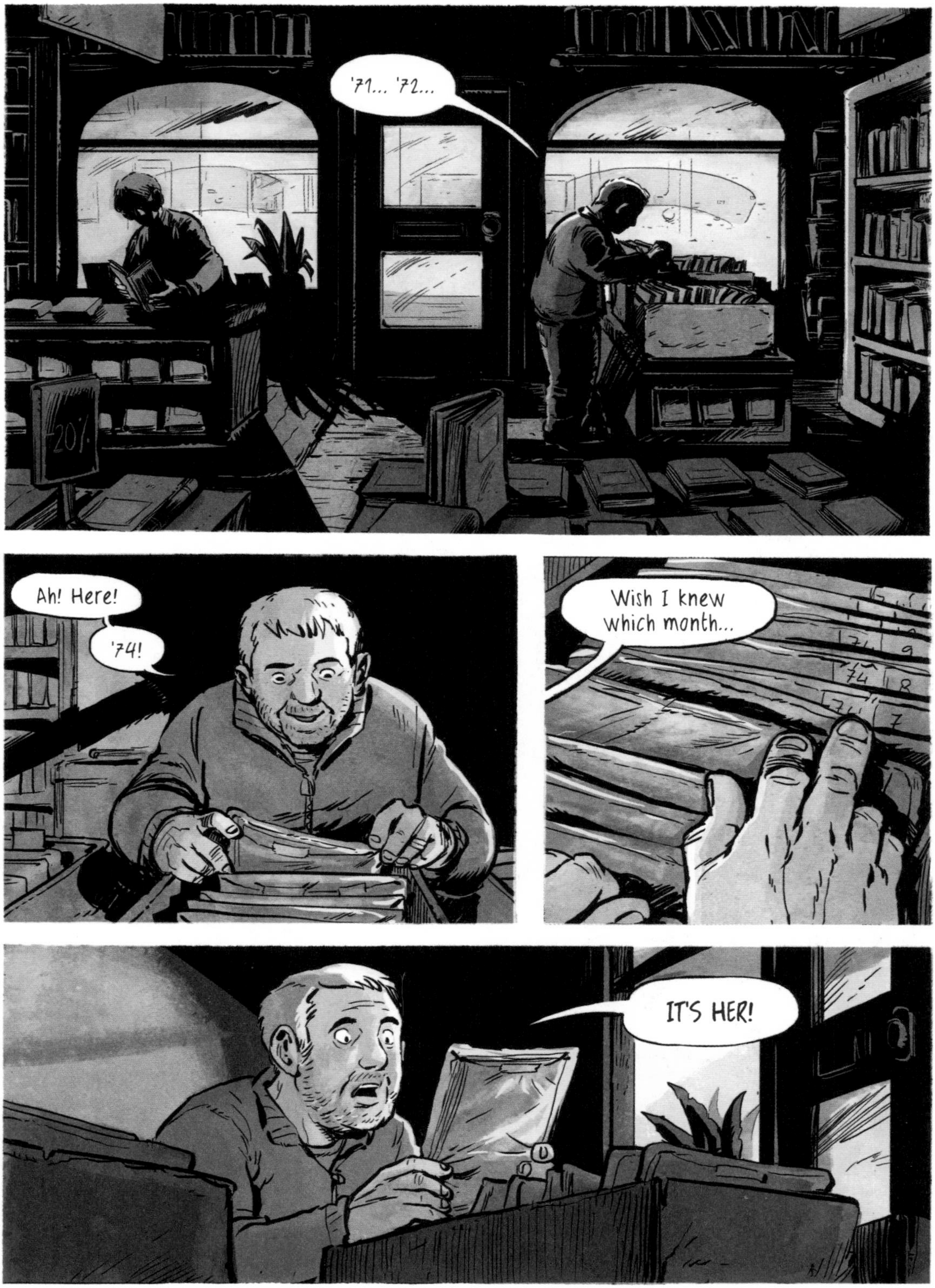
'71... '72...
20%
Ah! Here!
'74!
Wish I knew which month...
IT'S HER!

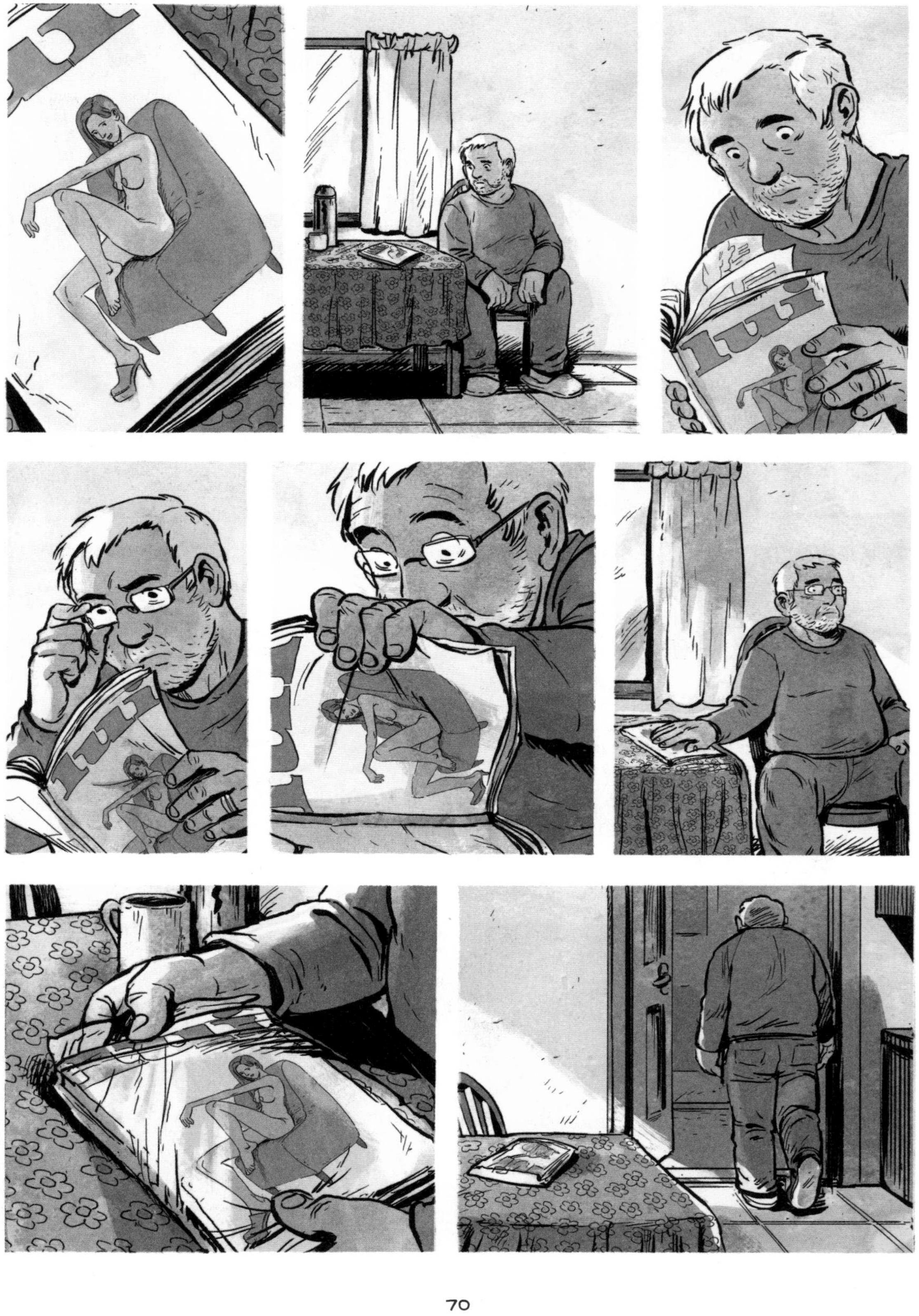
lui

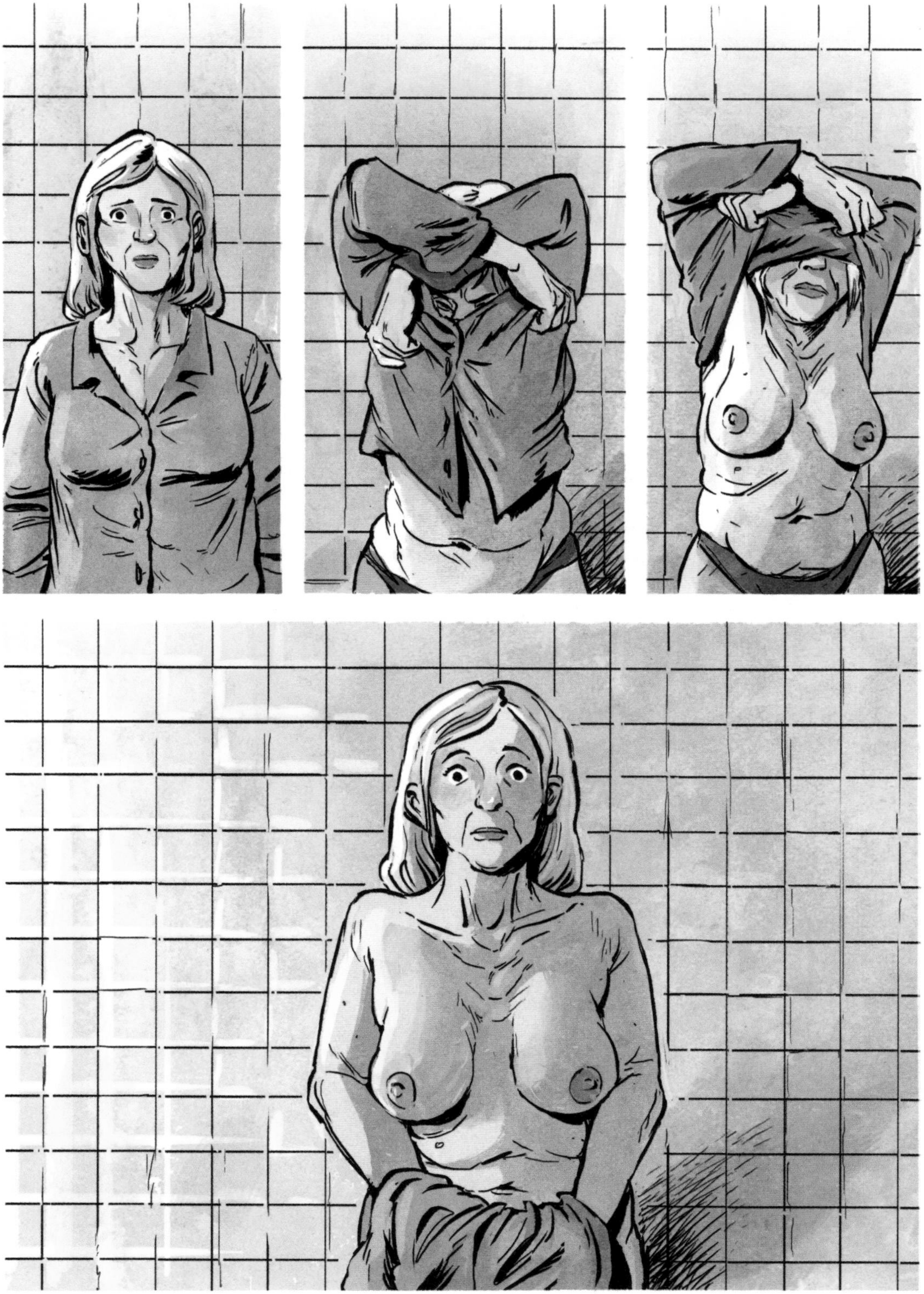

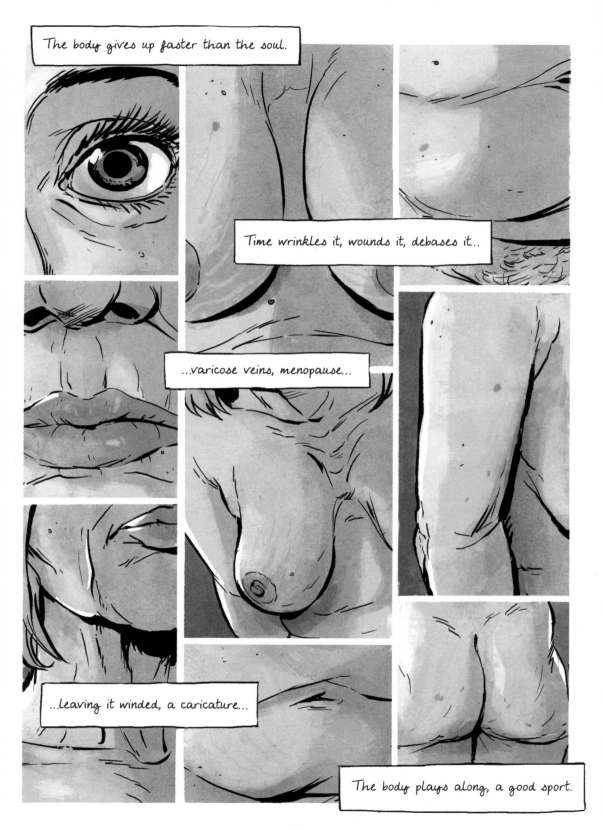

The body gives up faster than the soul.

Time wrinkles it, wounds it, debases it...

...varicose veins, menopause...

...leaving it winded, a caricature...

The body plays along, a good sport.

72

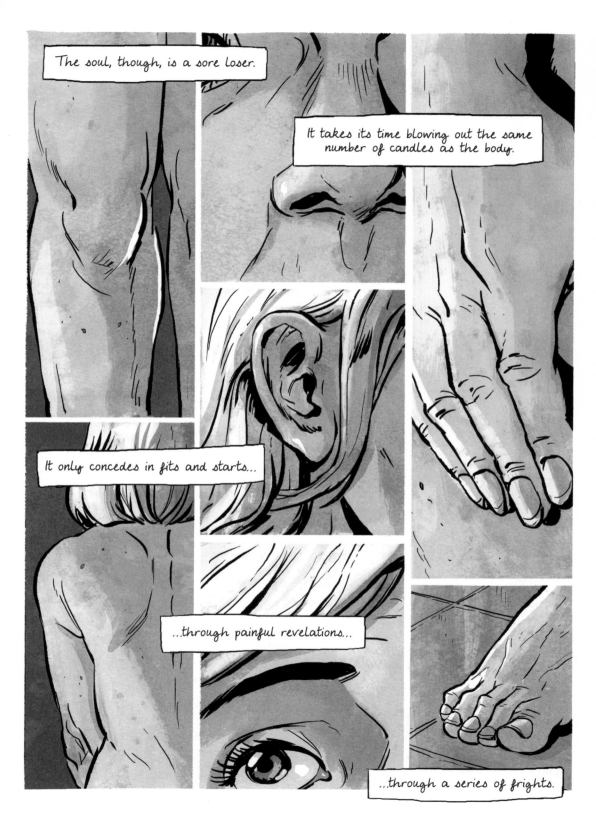

The soul, though, is a sore loser.

It takes its time blowing out the same number of candles as the body.

It only concedes in fits and starts...

...through painful revelations...

...through a series of frights.

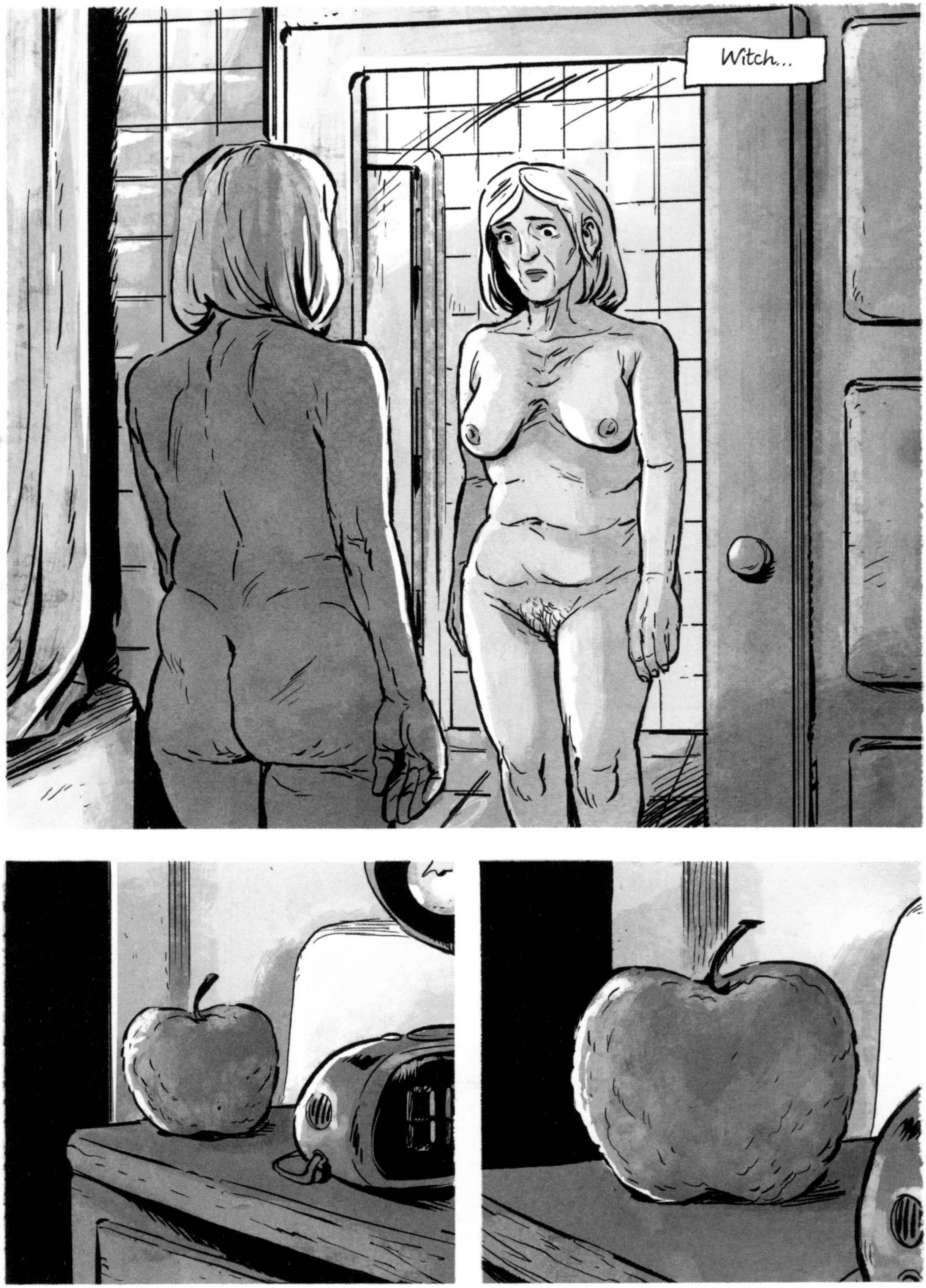
Witch...

4.

The little girl laughing in the photo

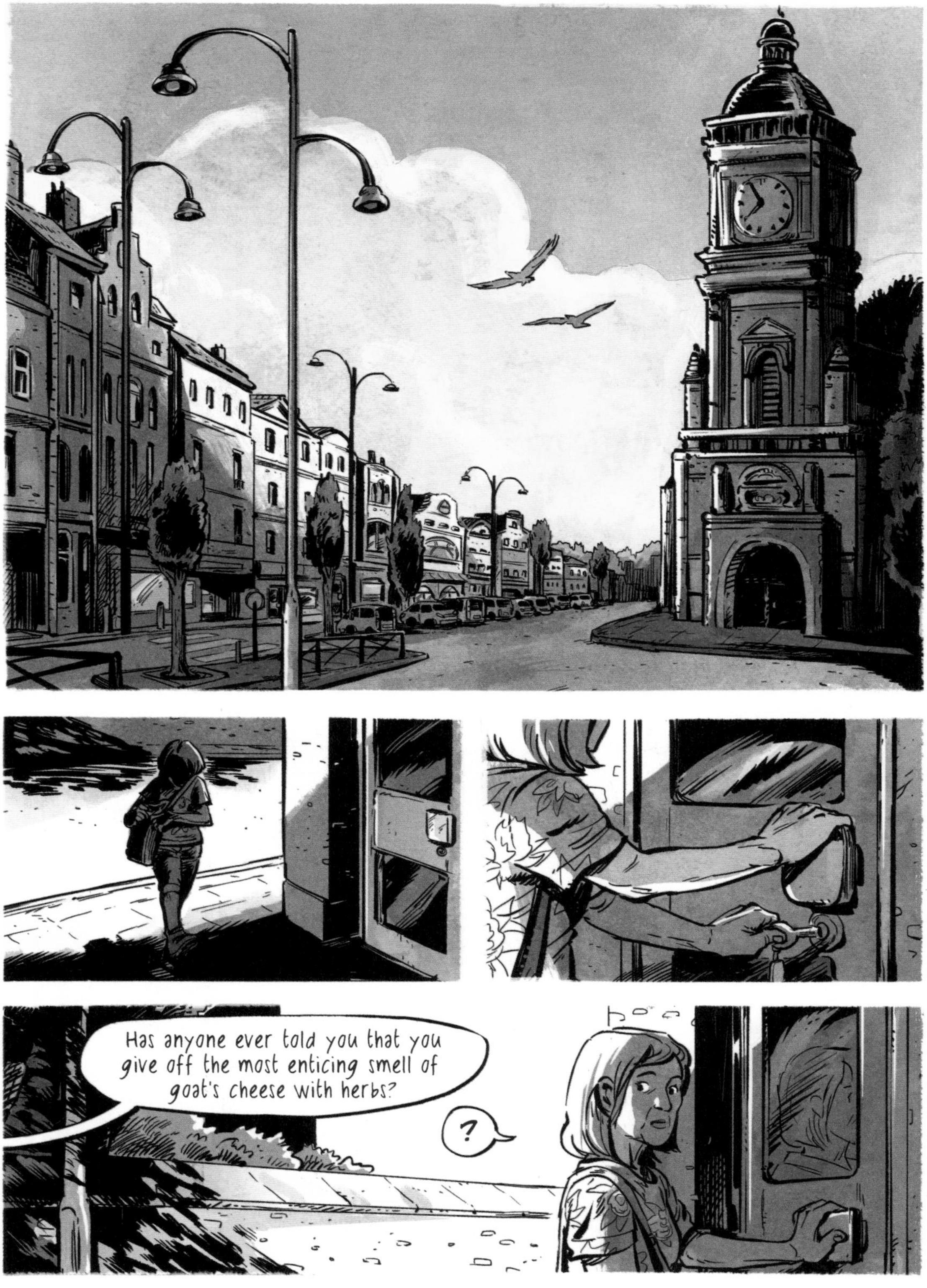
Has anyone ever told you that you give off the most enticing smell of goat's cheese with herbs?
?

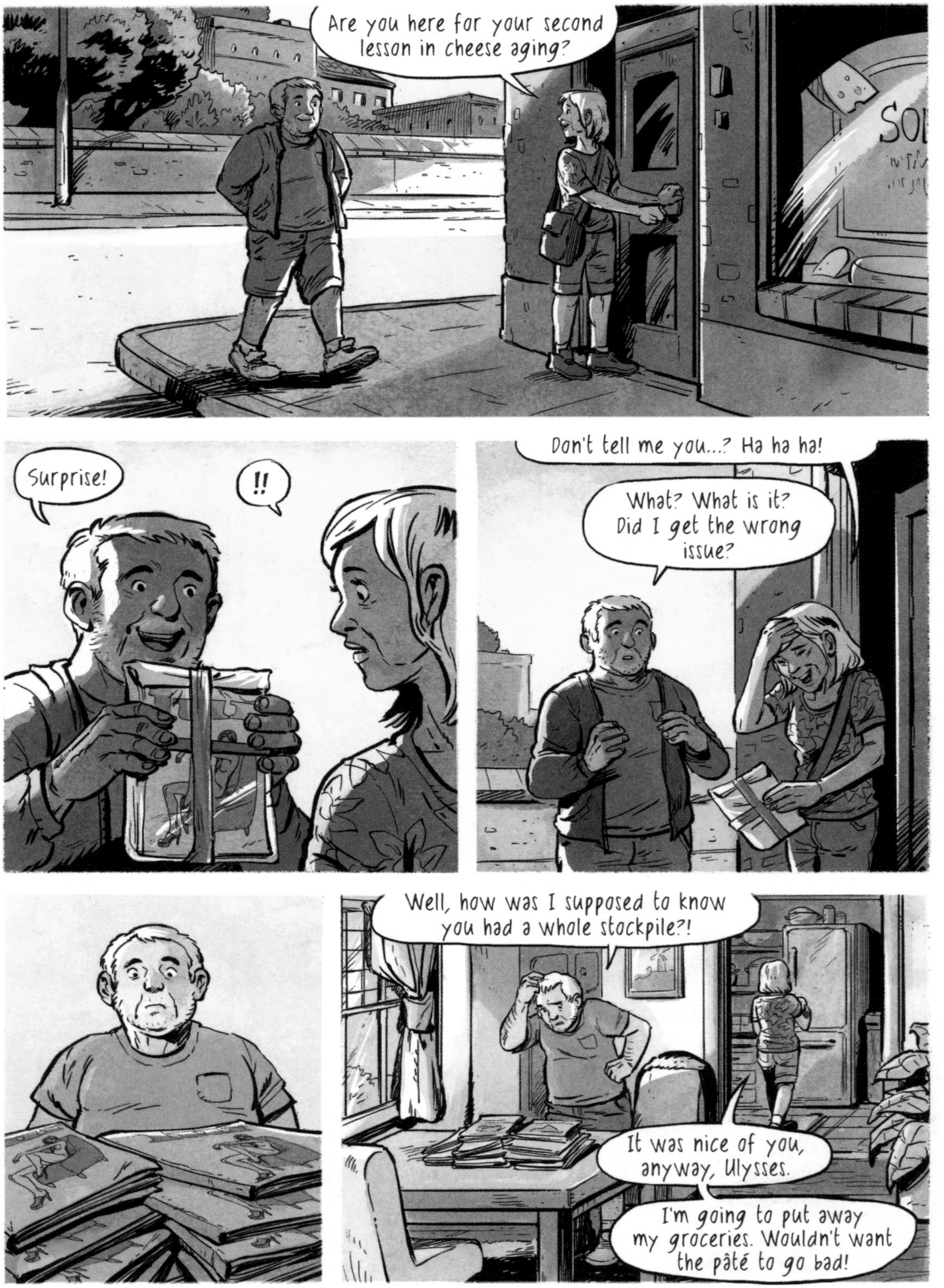
Are you here for your second lesson in cheese aging?
Surprise!
!!
Don't tell me you...? Ha ha ha!
What? What is it? Did I get the wrong issue?
Well, how was I supposed to know you had a whole stockpile?!
It was nice of you, anyway, Ulysses.
I'm going to put away my groceries. Wouldn't want the pâté to go bad!

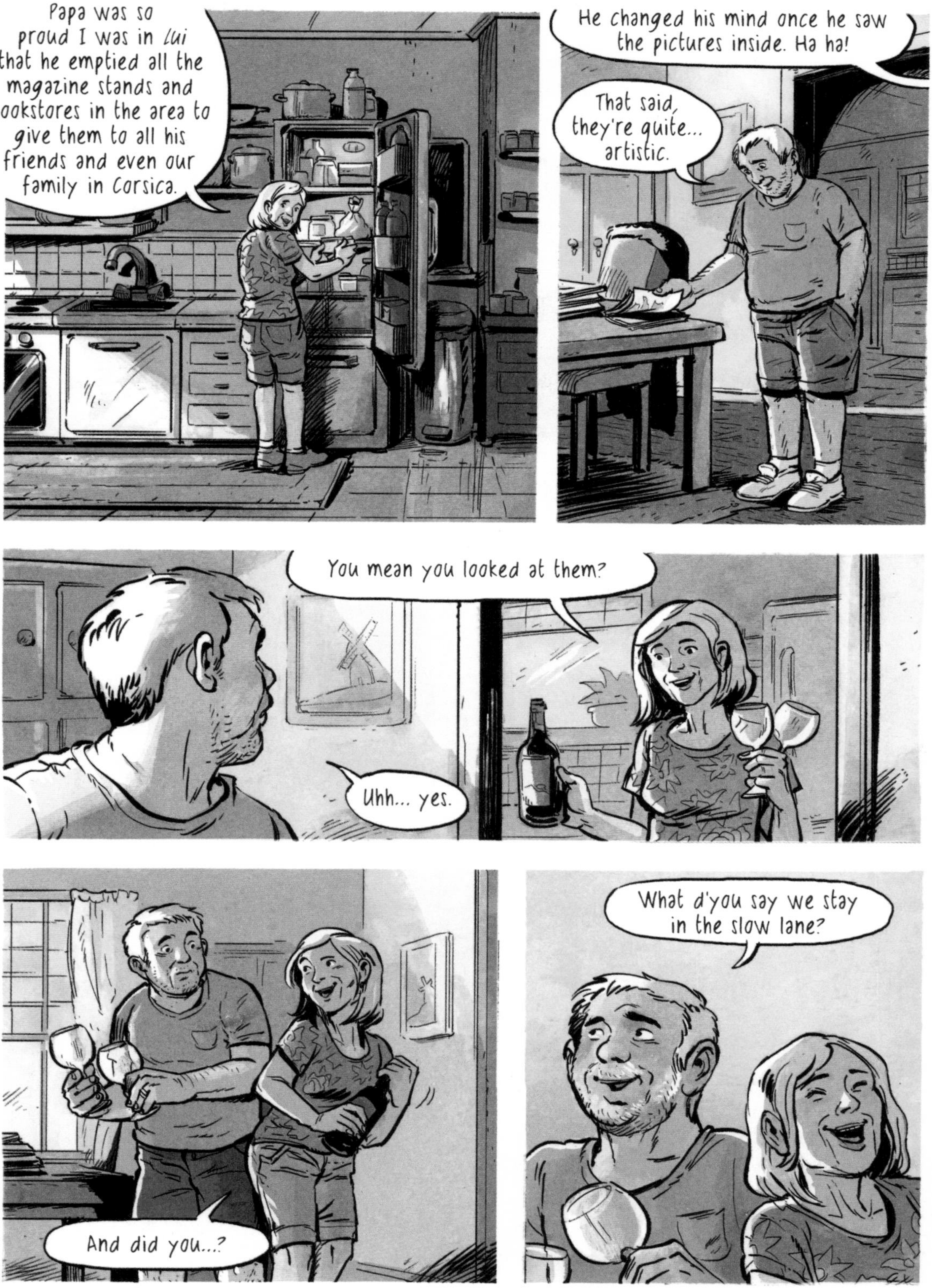
Papa was so proud I was in *Lui* that he emptied all the magazine stands and bookstores in the area to give them to all his friends and even our family in Corsica.
He changed his mind once he saw the pictures inside. Ha ha!
That said, they're quite... artistic.
You mean you looked at them?
Uhh... yes.
And did you...?
What d'you say we stay in the slow lane?

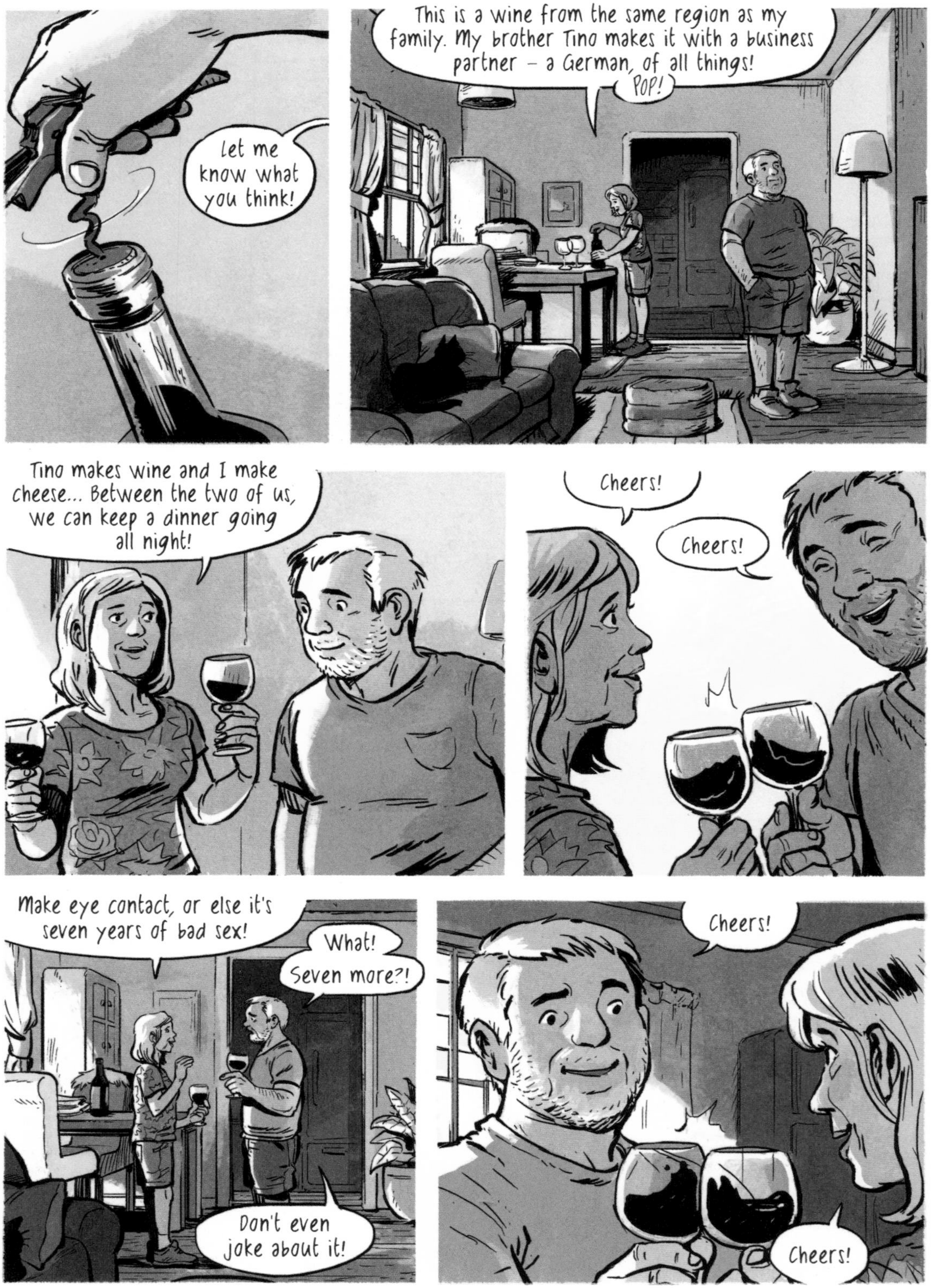
Let me know what you think!
This is a wine from the same region as my family. My brother Tino makes it with a business partner – a German, of all things!
POP!
Tino makes wine and I make cheese... Between the two of us, we can keep a dinner going all night!
Cheers!
Cheers!
Make eye contact, or else it's seven years of bad sex!
What! Seven more?!
Don't even joke about it!
Cheers!
Cheers!

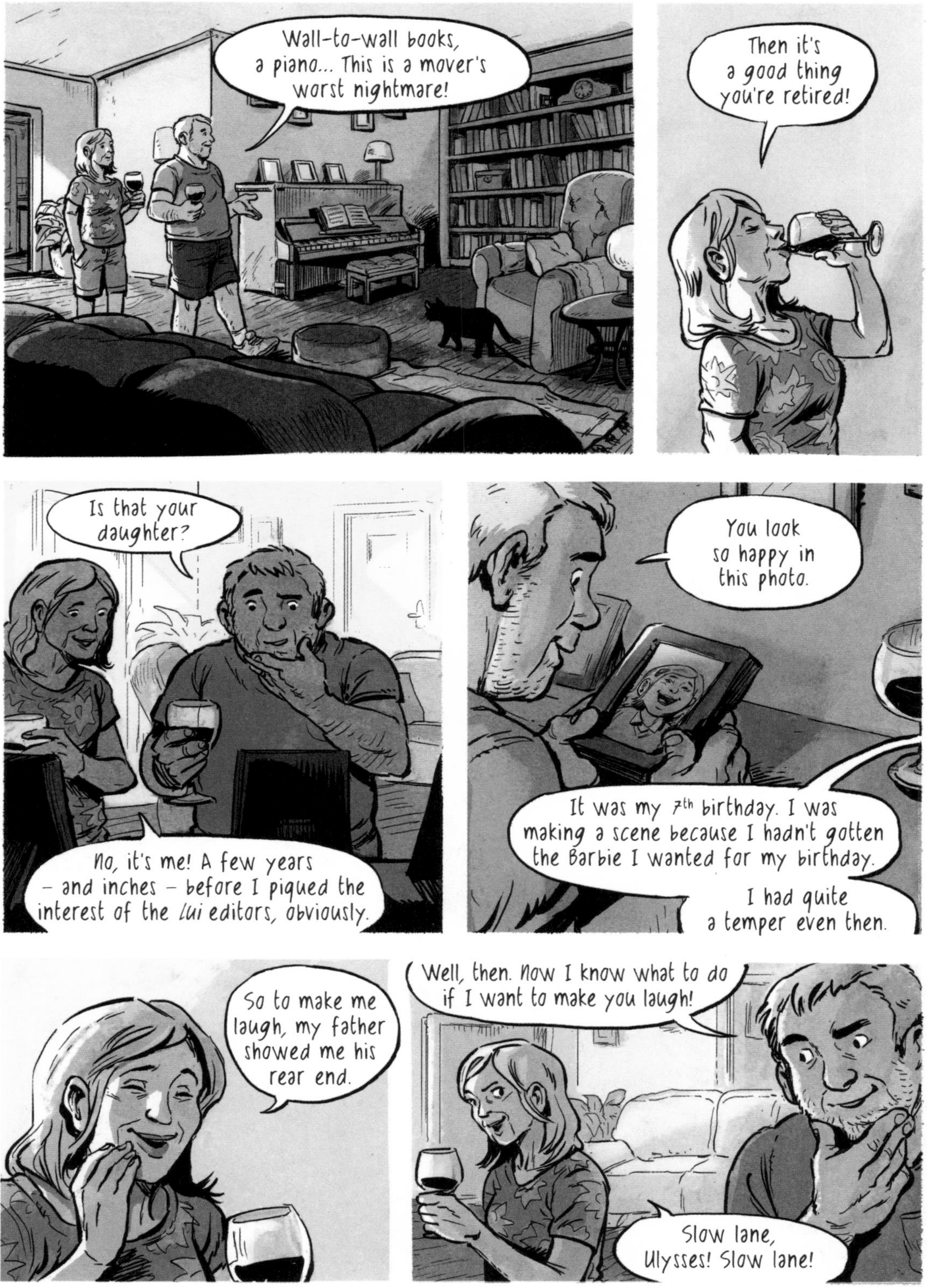
Wall-to-wall books, a piano... This is a mover's worst nightmare!
Then it's a good thing you're retired!
Is that your daughter?
No, it's me! A few years – and inches – before I piqued the interest of the Lui editors, obviously.
You look so happy in this photo.
It was my 7th birthday. I was making a scene because I hadn't gotten the Barbie I wanted for my birthday.
I had quite a temper even then.
So to make me laugh, my father showed me his rear end.
Well, then. Now I know what to do if I want to make you laugh!
Slow lane, Ulysses! Slow lane!

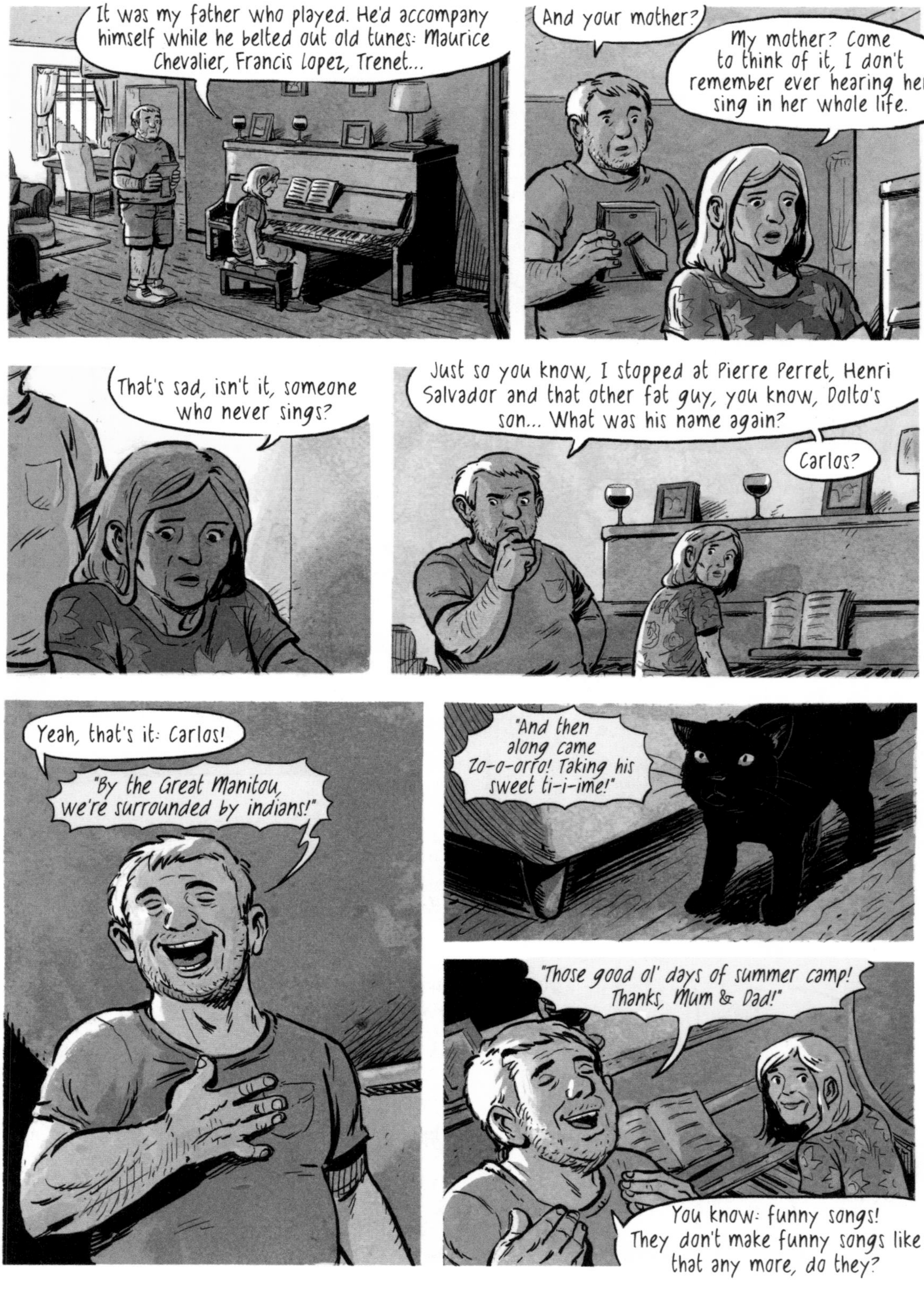
It was my father who played. He'd accompany himself while he belted out old tunes: Maurice Chevalier, Francis Lopez, Trenet...
And your mother?
My mother? Come to think of it, I don't remember ever hearing her sing in her whole life.
That's sad, isn't it, someone who never sings?
Just so you know, I stopped at Pierre Perret, Henri Salvador and that other fat guy, you know, Dolto's son... What was his name again?
Carlos?
Yeah, that's it: Carlos!
"By the Great Manitou, we're surrounded by indians!"
"And then along came Zo-o-orro! Taking his sweet ti-i-ime!"
"Those good ol' days of summer camp! Thanks, Mum & Dad!"
You know: funny songs! They don't make funny songs like that any more, do they?

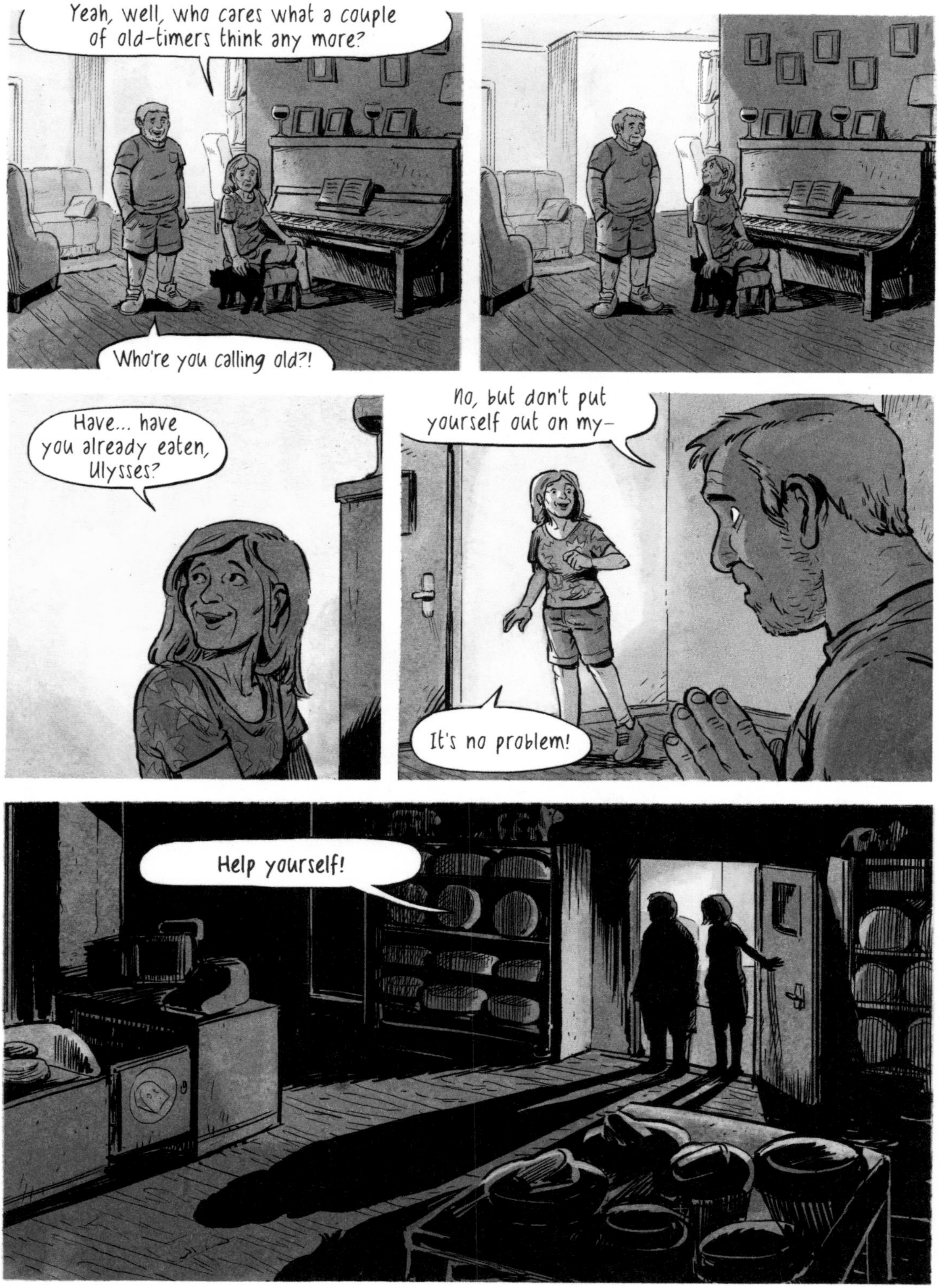
Yeah, well, who cares what a couple of old-timers think any more?
Who're you calling old?!
Have... have you already eaten, Ulysses?
No, but don't put yourself out on my-
It's no problem!
Help yourself!

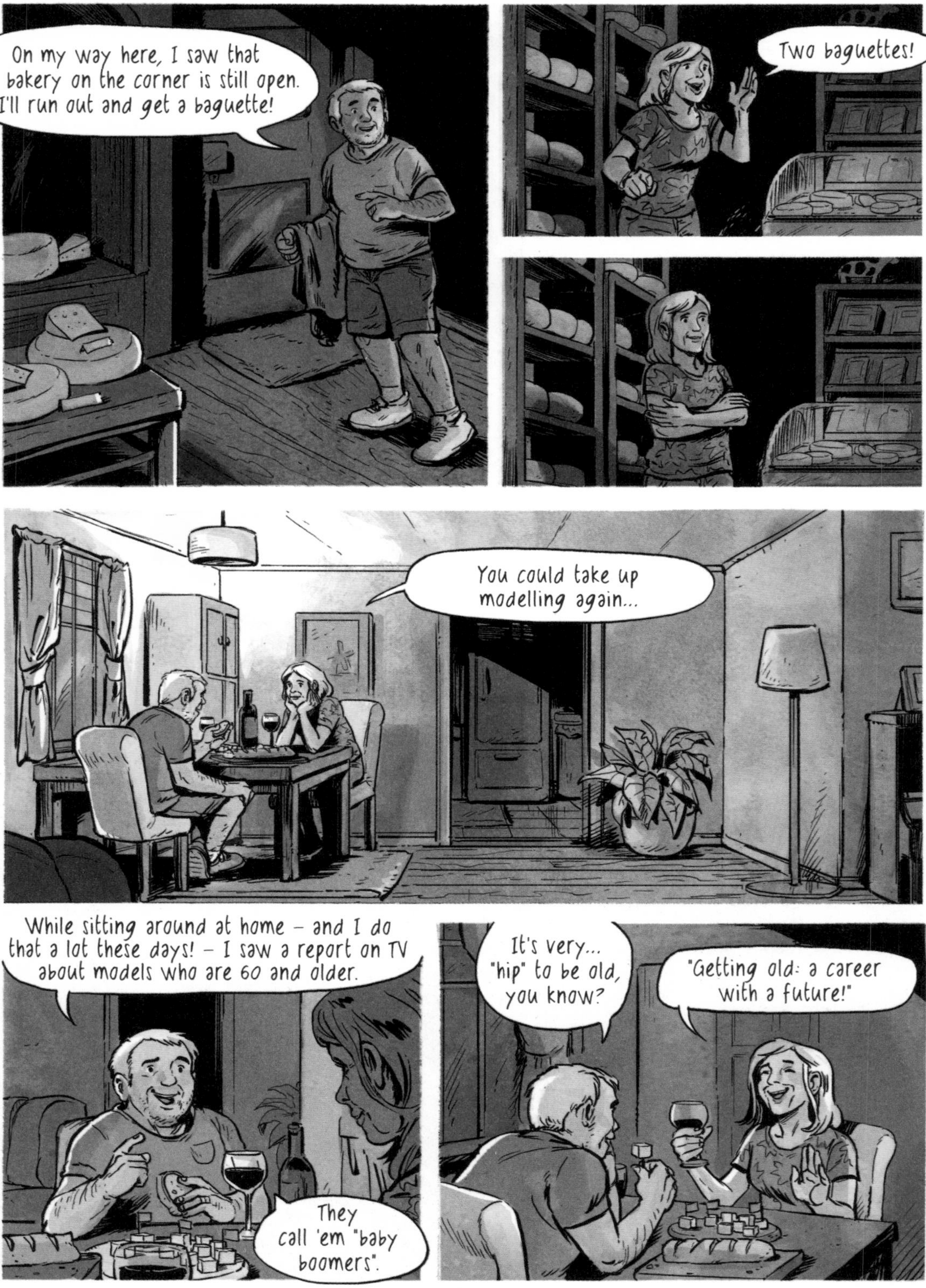
On my way here, I saw that the bakery on the corner is still open. I'll run out and get a baguette!
Two baguettes!
You could take up modelling again...
While sitting around at home – and I do that a lot these days! – I saw a report on TV about models who are 60 and older.
They call 'em "baby boomers".
It's very... "hip" to be old, you know?
"Getting old: a career with a future!"

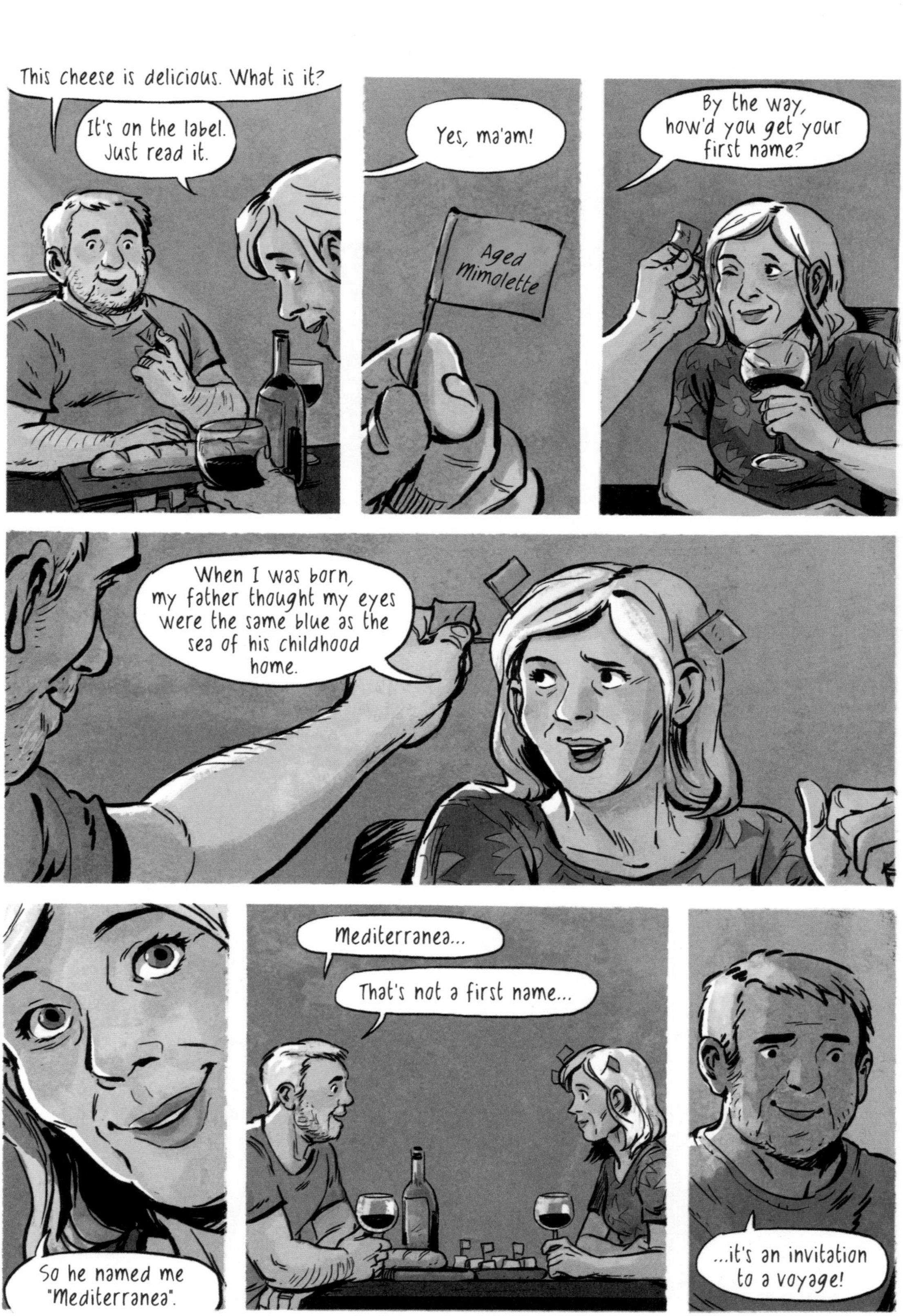
This cheese is delicious. What is it?
It's on the label. Just read it.
Yes, ma'am!
Aged Mimolette
By the way, how'd you get your first name?
When I was born, my father thought my eyes were the same blue as the sea of his childhood home.
So he named me "Mediterranea".
Mediterranea...
That's not a first name...
...it's an invitation to a voyage!

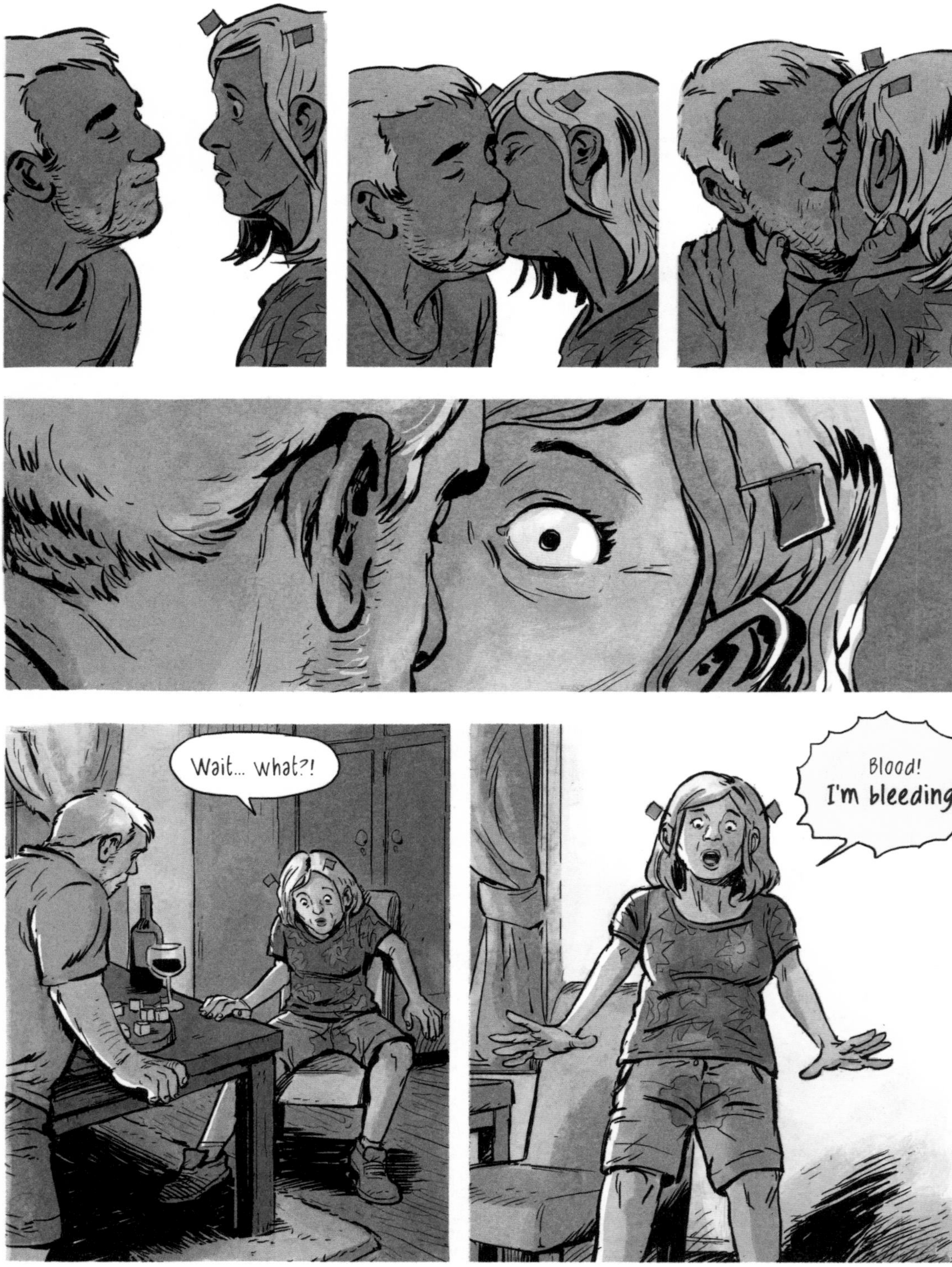
Wait... what?!
Blood!
I'm bleeding!

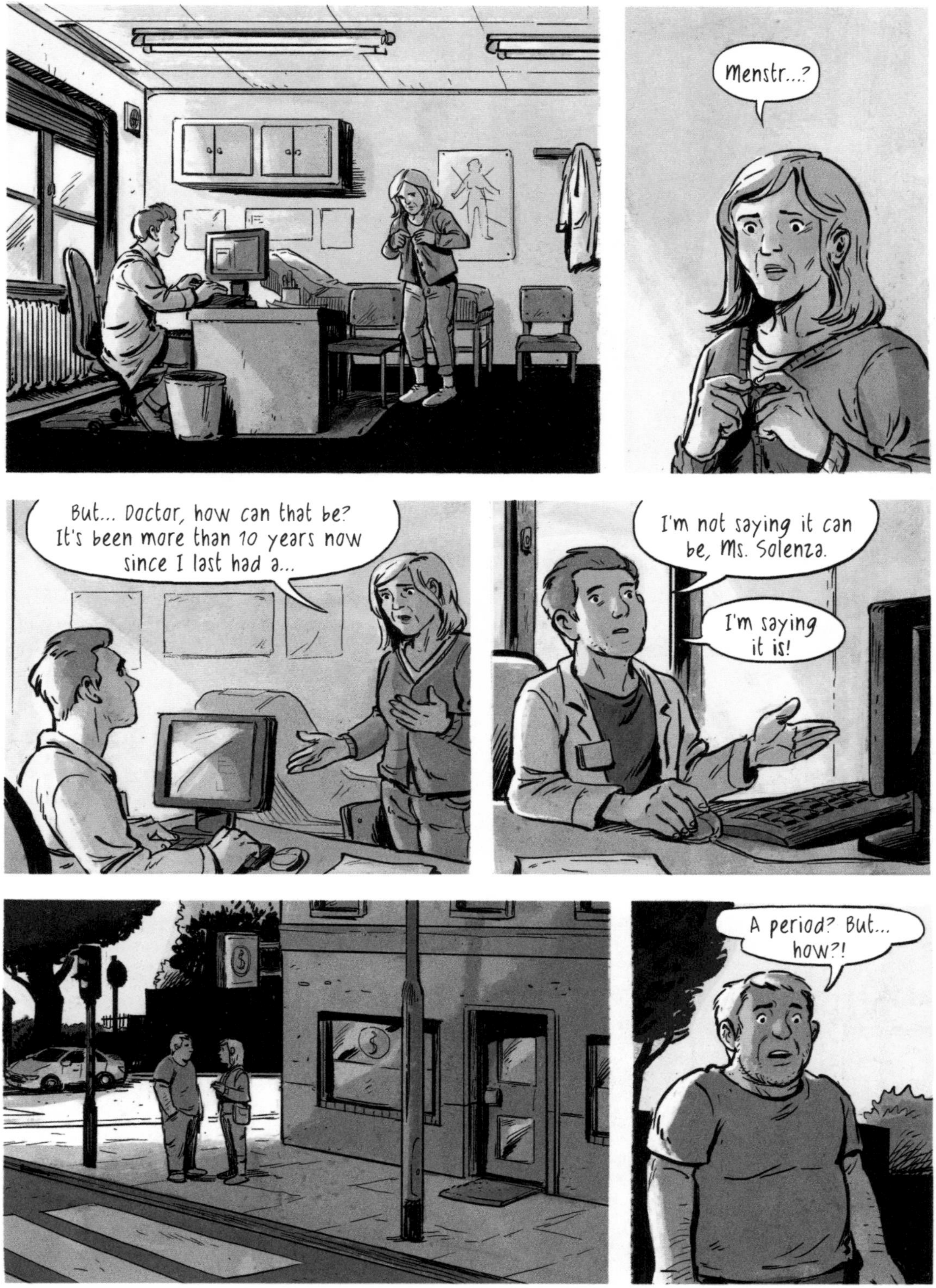
Menstr...?
But... Doctor, how can that be? It's been more than 10 years now since I last had a...
I'm not saying it can be, Ms. Solenza.
I'm saying it is!
A period? But... how?!

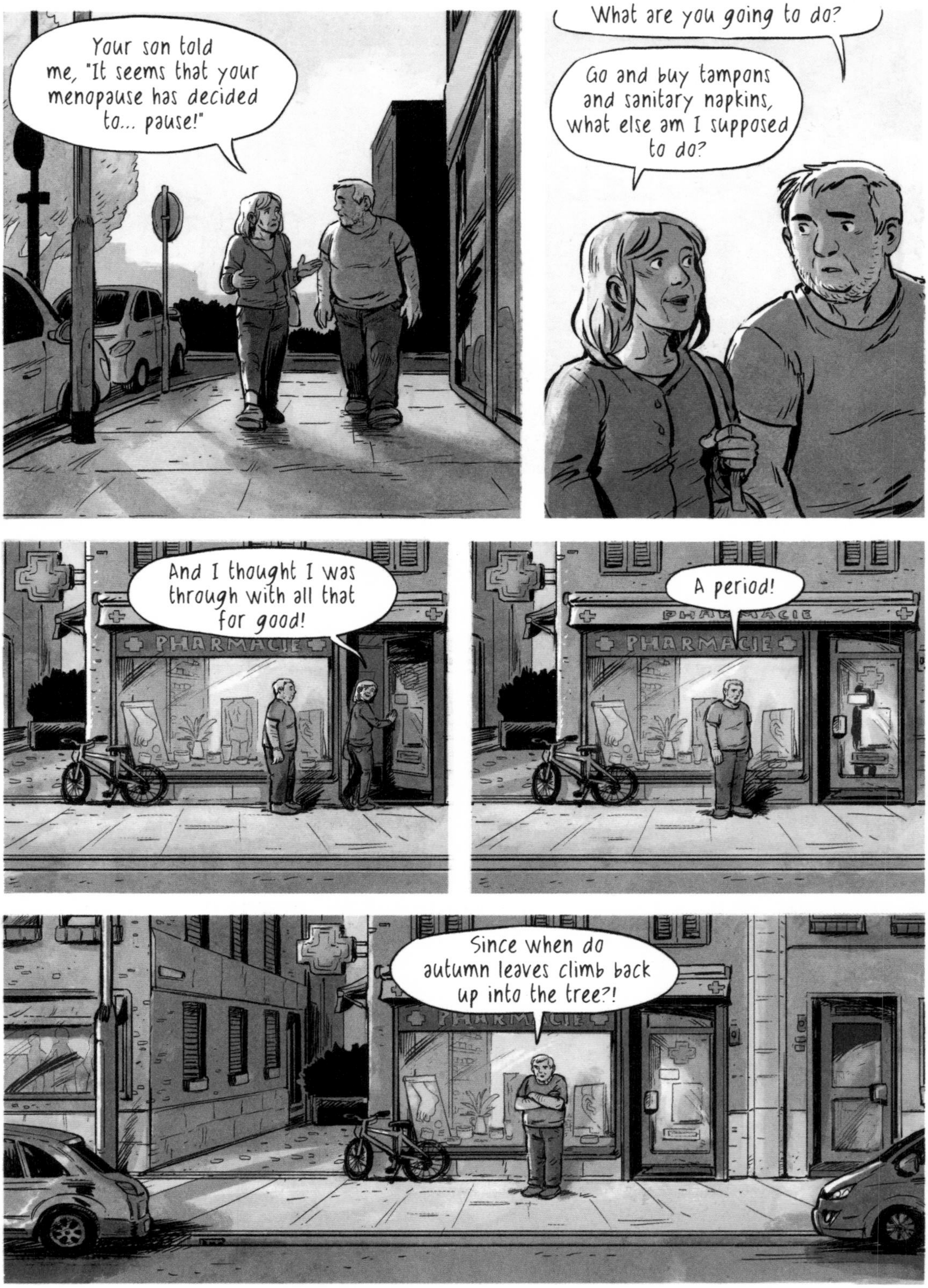
Your son told me, "It seems that your menopause has decided to... pause!"
What are you going to do?
Go and buy tampons and sanitary napkins, what else am I supposed to do?
And I thought I was through with all that for good!
PHARMACIE
A period!
PHARMACIE
Since when do autumn leaves climb back up into the tree?!

5.

The comfort woman

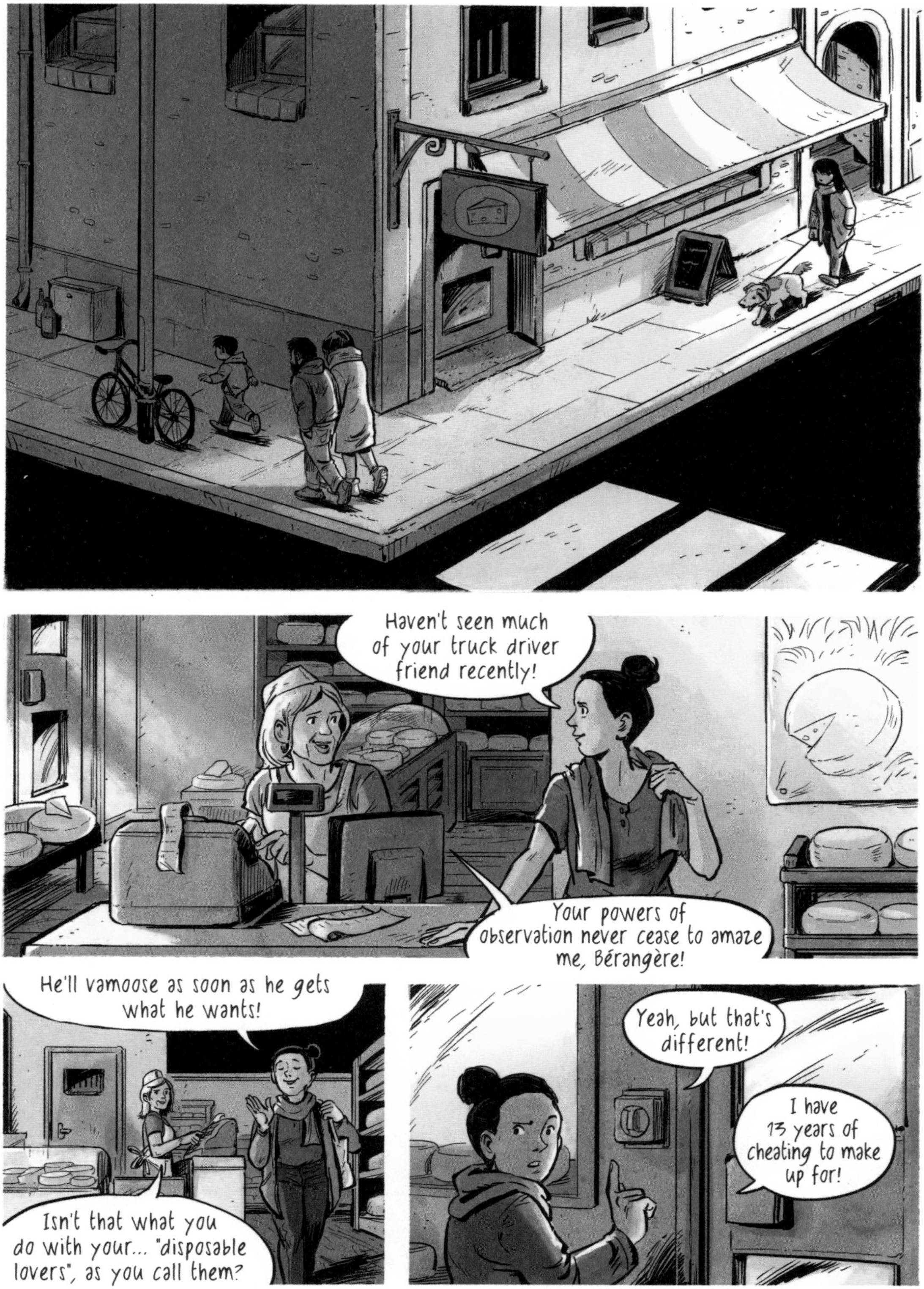

Haven't seen much of your truck driver friend recently!
Your powers of observation never cease to amaze me, Bérangère!
He'll vamoose as soon as he gets what he wants!
Isn't that what you do with your... "disposable lovers", as you call them?
Yeah, but that's different!
I have 13 years of cheating to make up for!

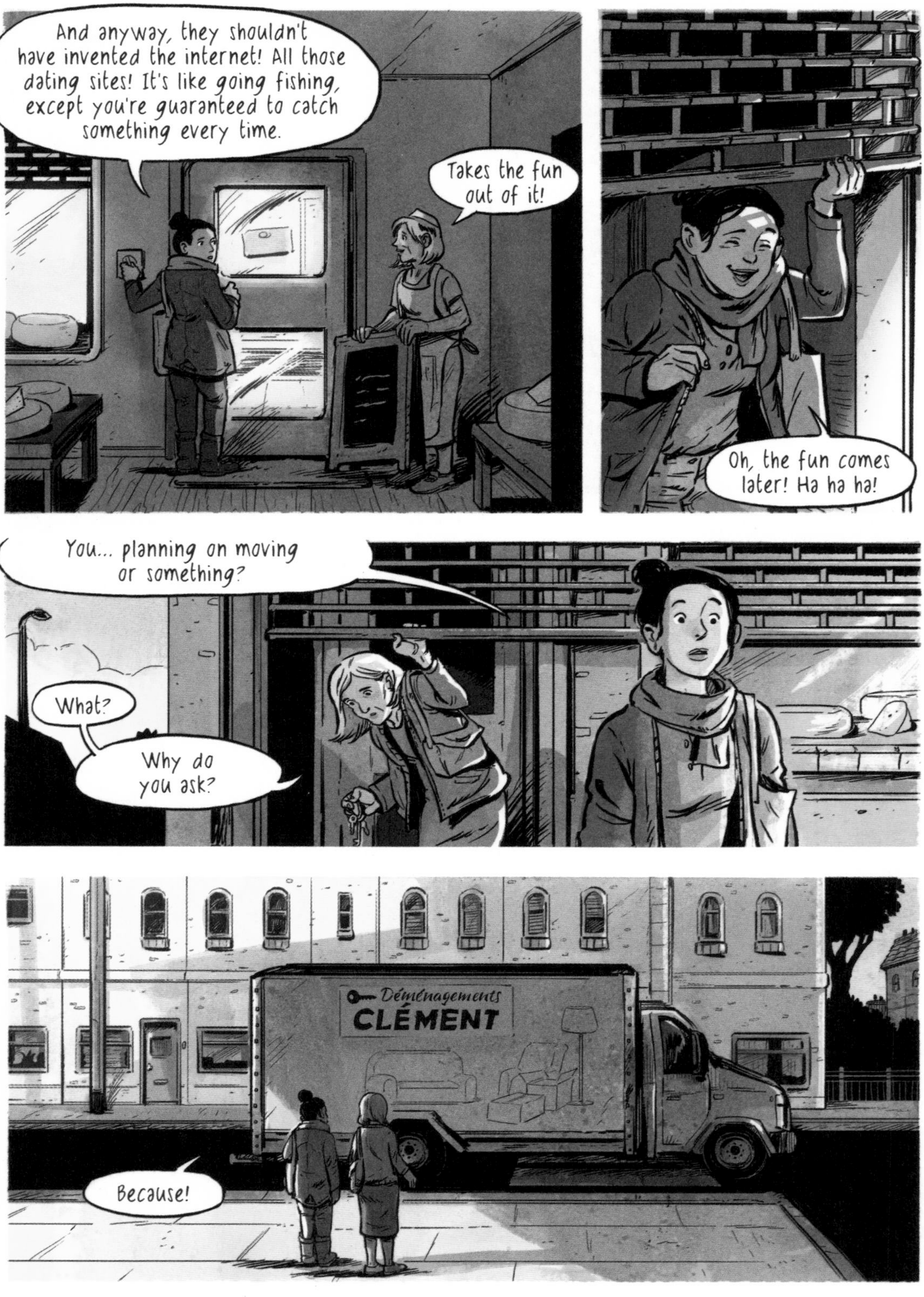
And anyway, they shouldn't have invented the internet! All those dating sites! It's like going fishing, except you're guaranteed to catch something every time.
Takes the fun out of it!
Oh, the fun comes later! Ha ha ha!
You... planning on moving or something?
What?
Why do you ask?
Déménagements CLÉMENT
Because!

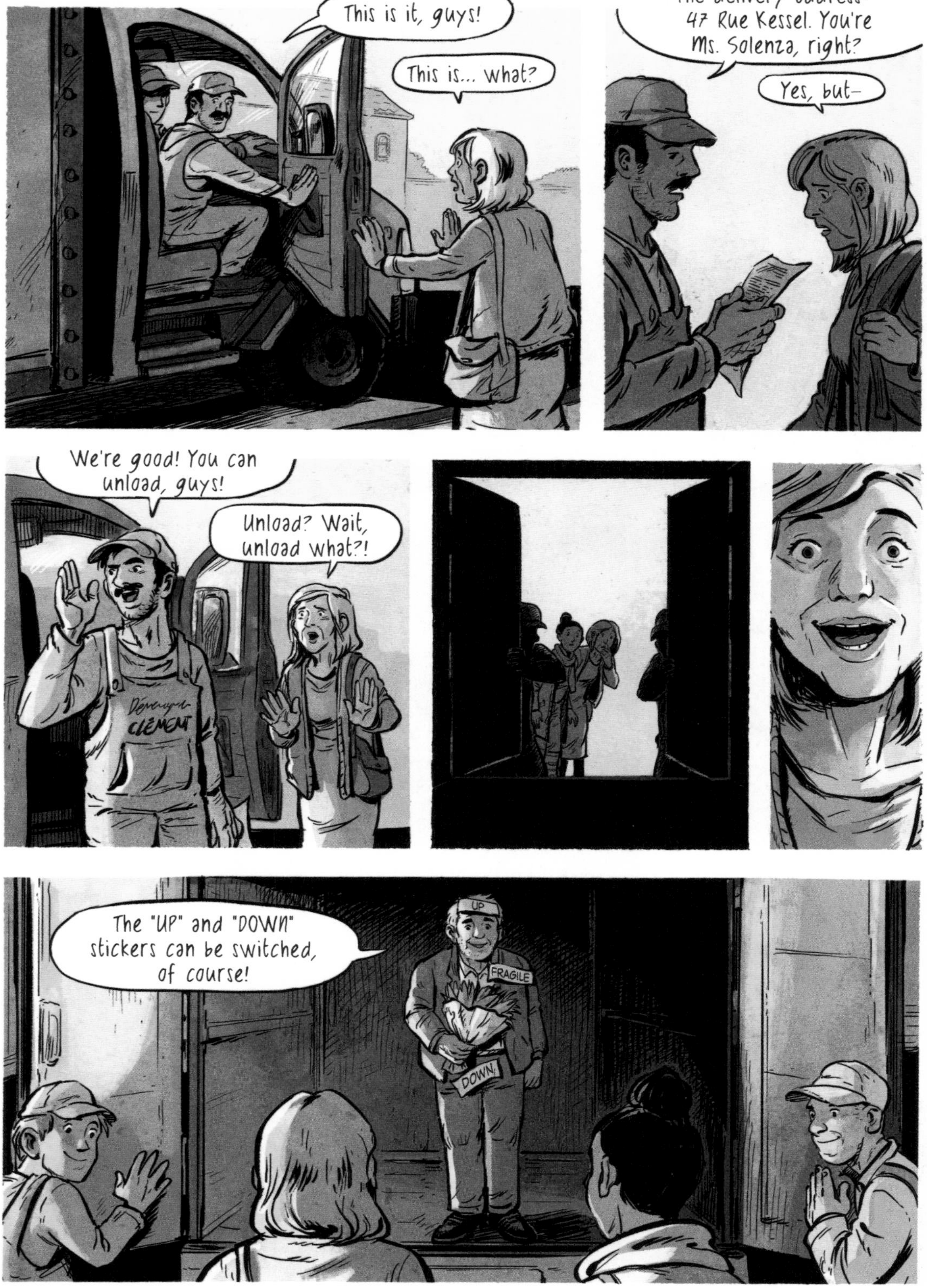
This is it, guys!
This is... what?
The delivery address: 47 Rue Kessel. You're Ms. Solenza, right?
Yes, but–
We're good! You can unload, guys!
Unload? Wait, unload what?!
CLÉMENT
The "UP" and "DOWN" stickers can be switched, of course!
UP
FRAGILE
DOWN

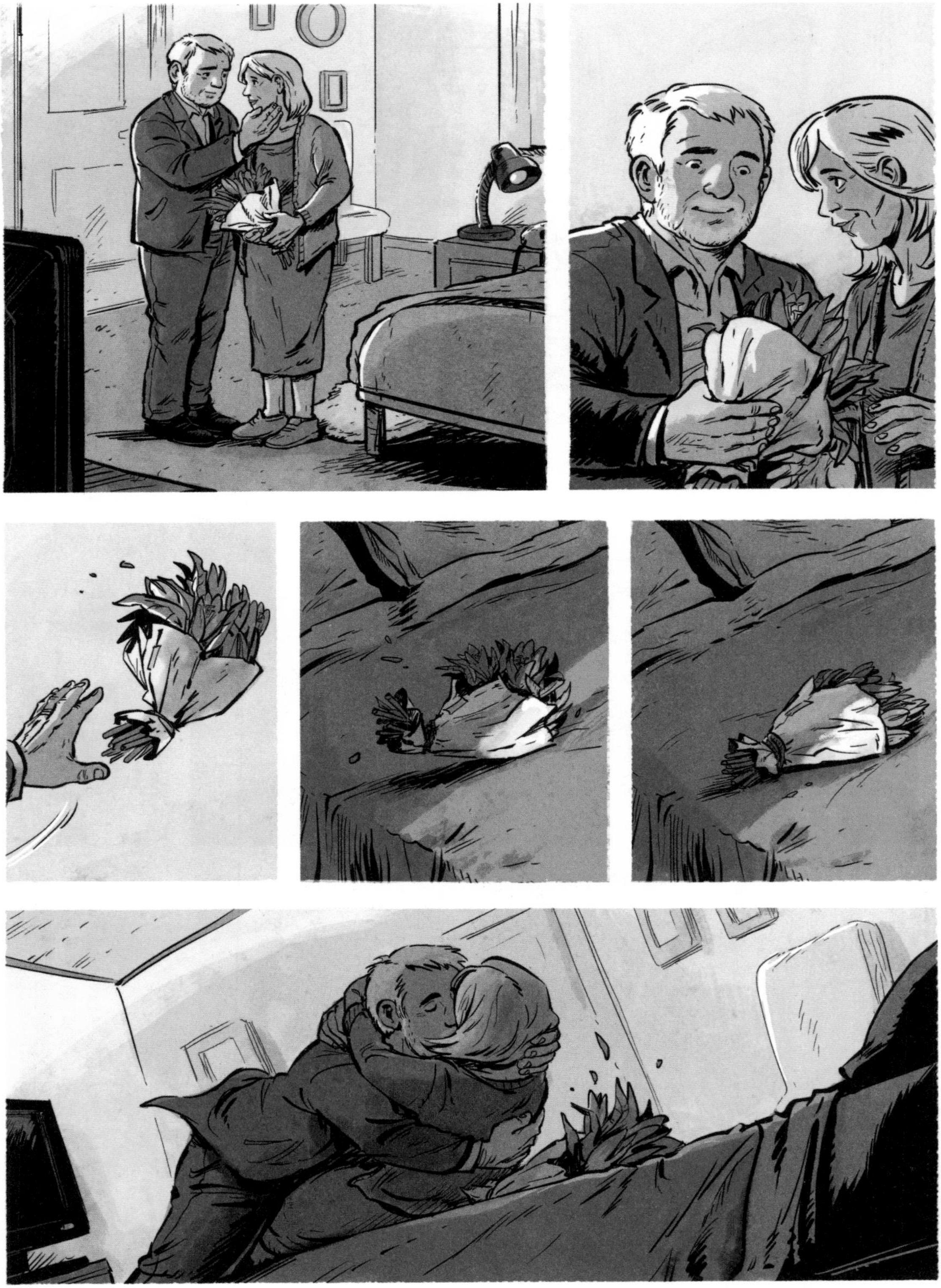

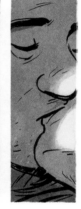

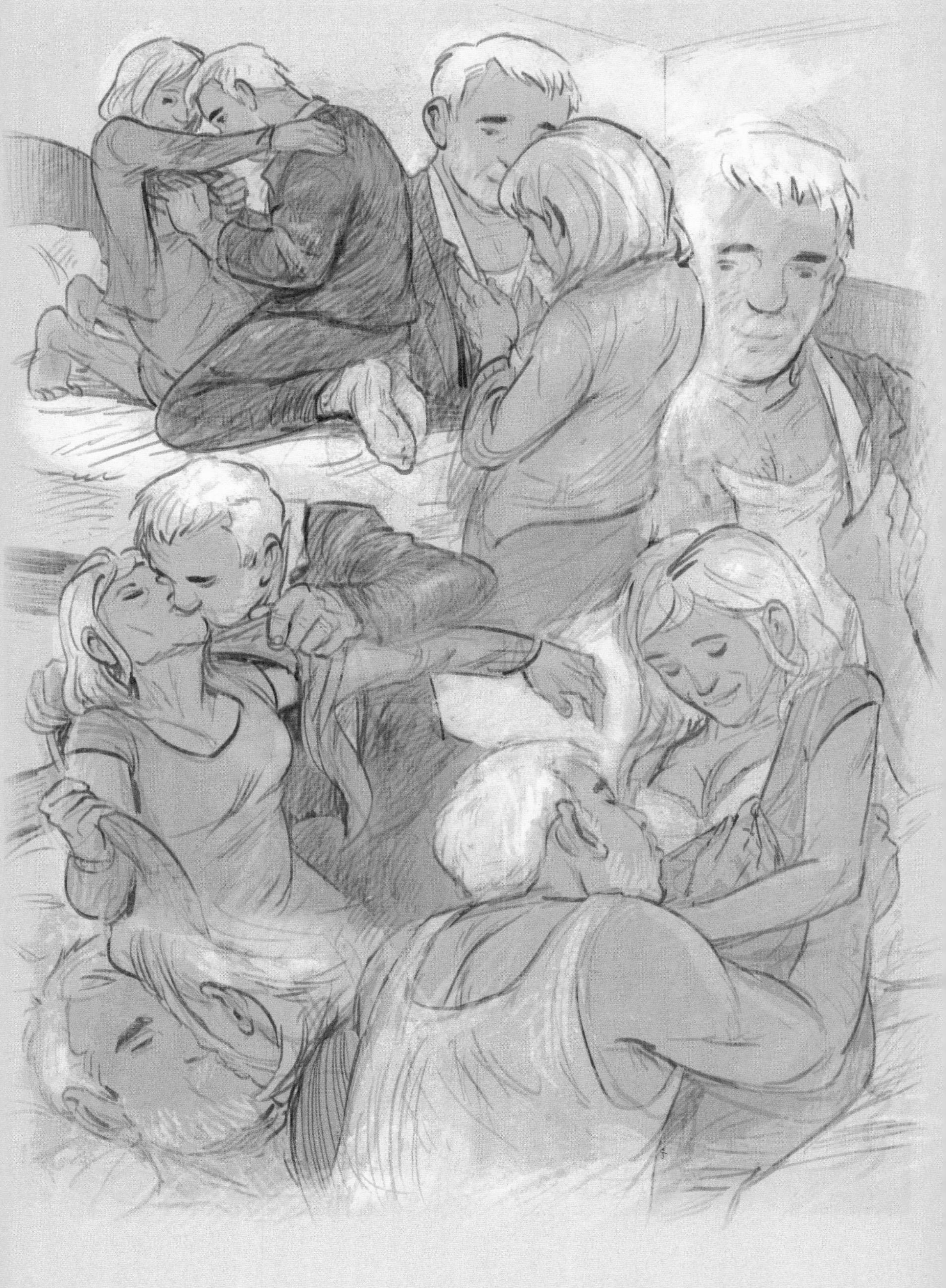

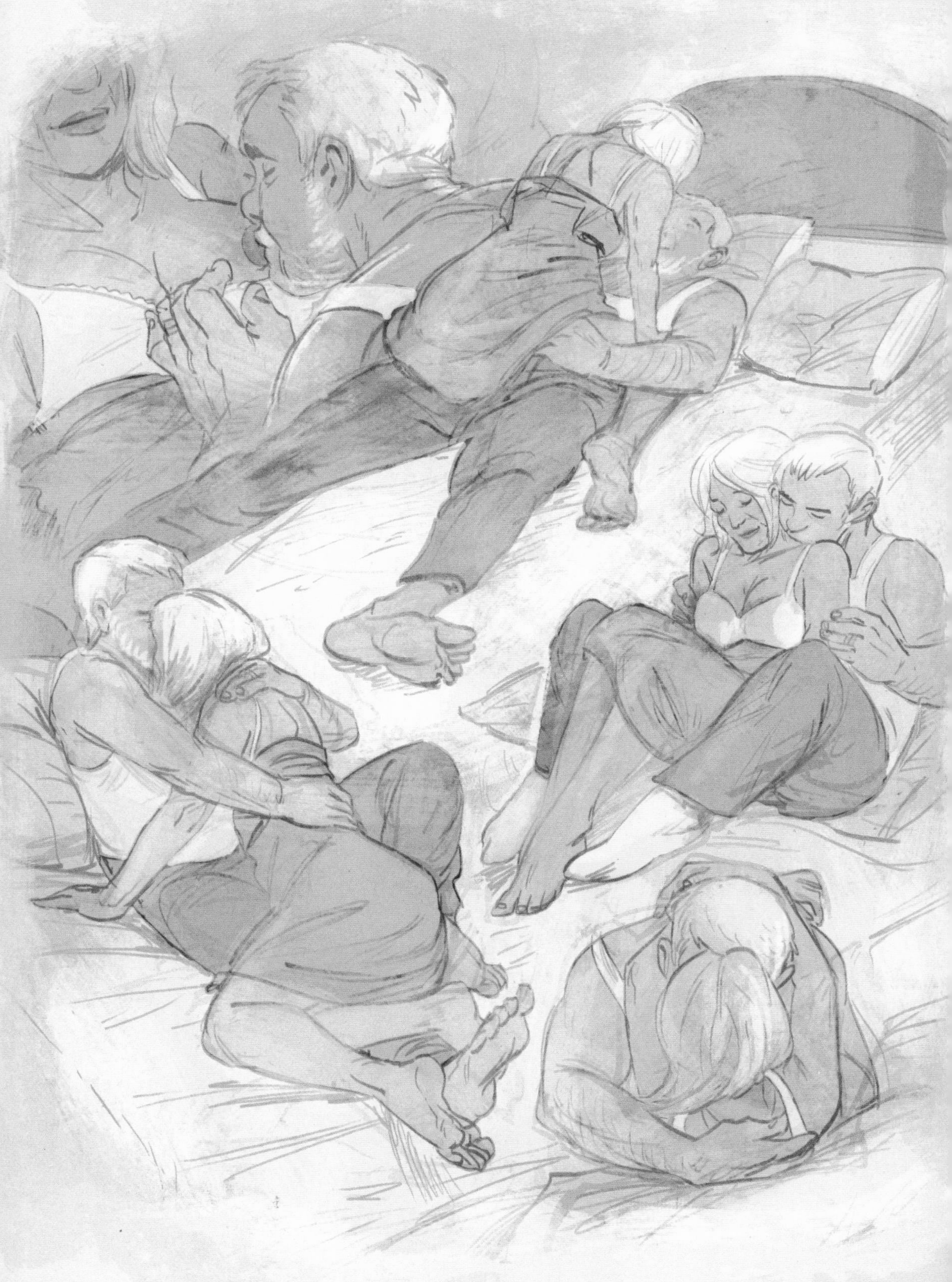

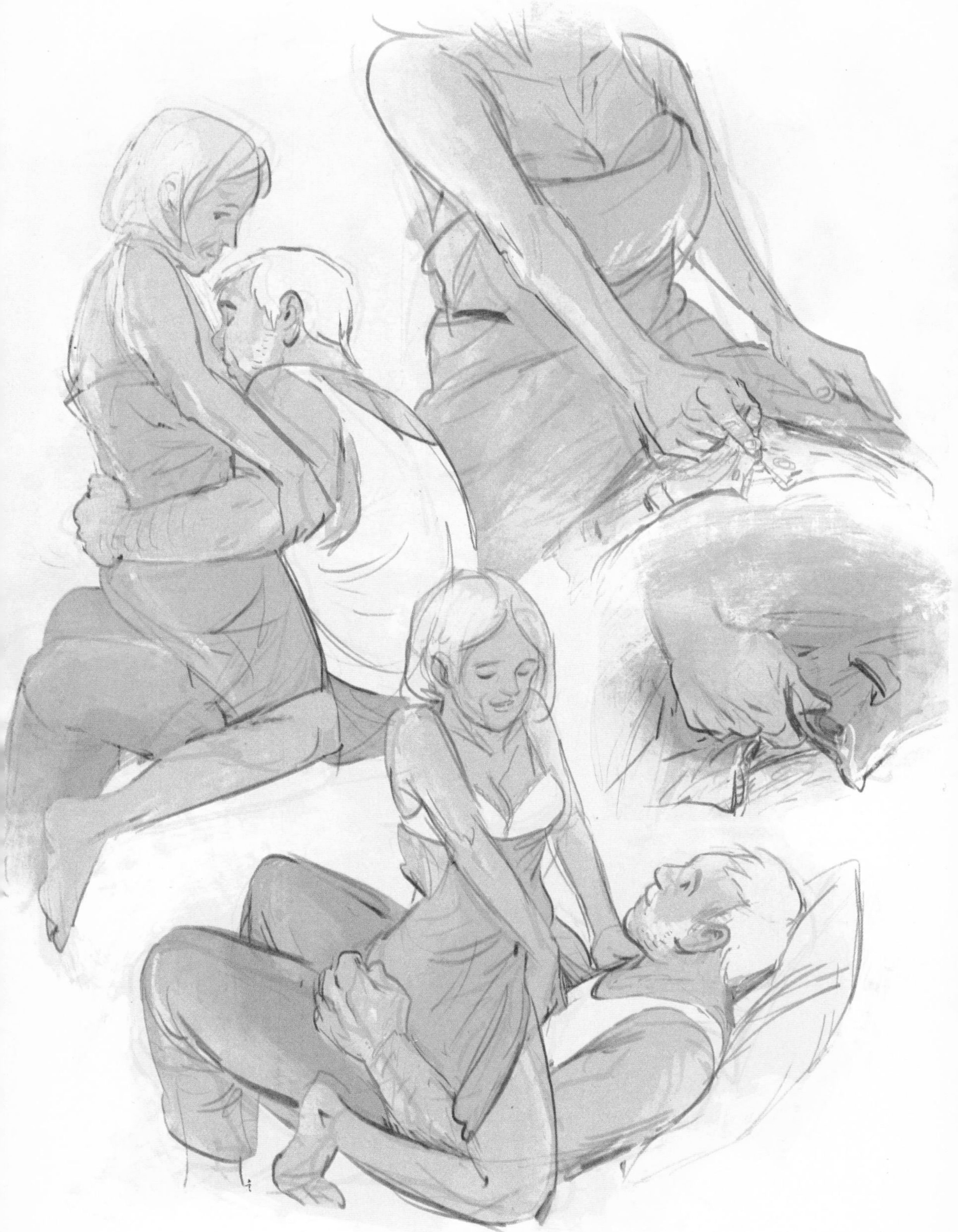

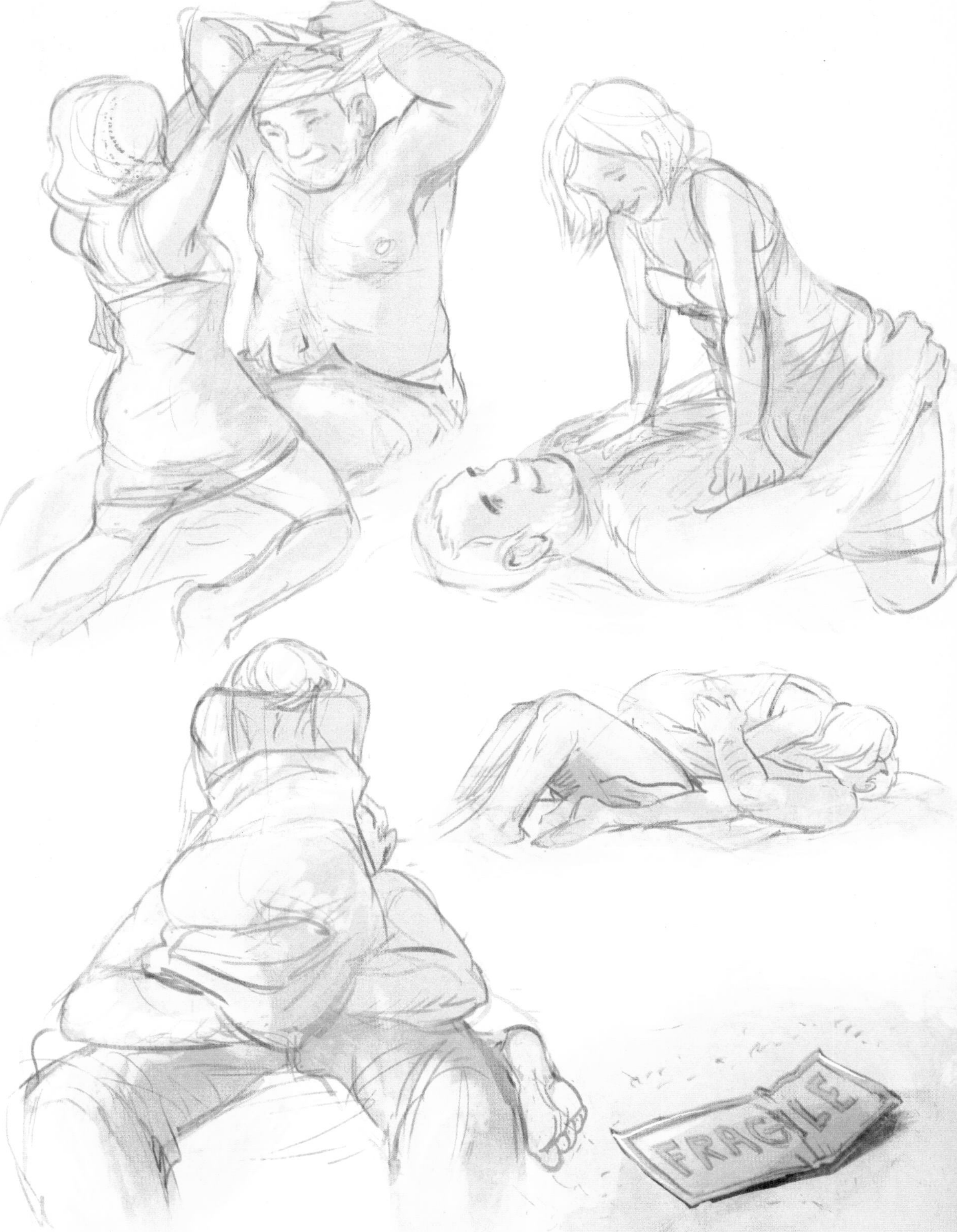
FRAGILE

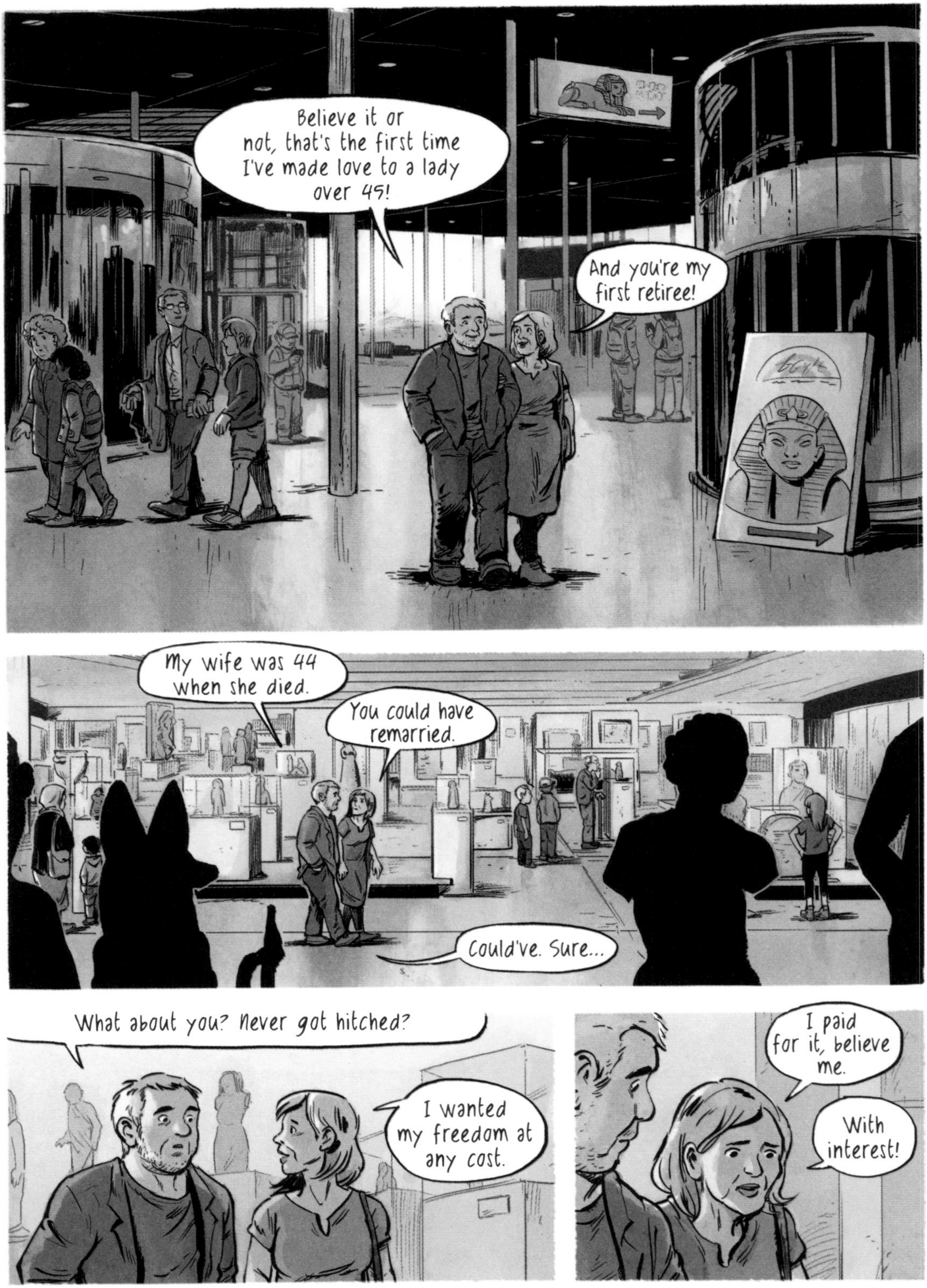
Believe it or not, that's the first time I've made love to a lady over 45!
And you're my first retiree!
My wife was 44 when she died.
You could have remarried.
Could've. Sure...
What about you? Never got hitched?
I wanted my freedom at any cost.
I paid for it, believe me.
With interest!

No children?
No children.
No regrets?
All the time.
...
...
...
And you? How many kids do you have?
Two.
Well... one.

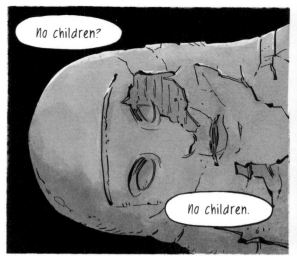

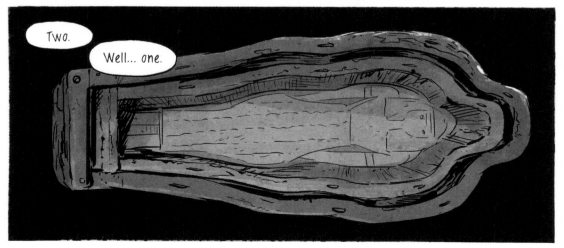

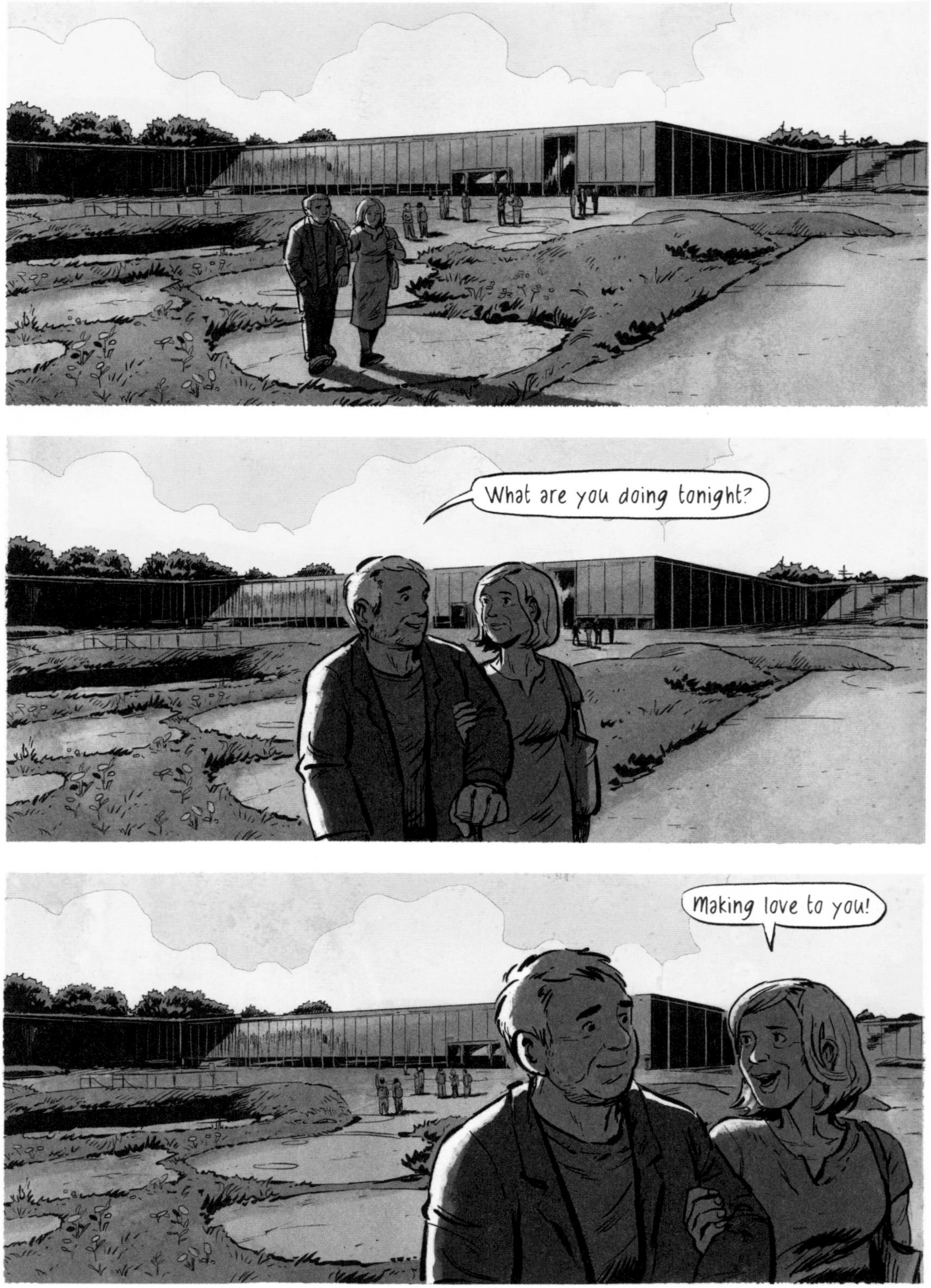
What are you doing tonight?
Making love to you!

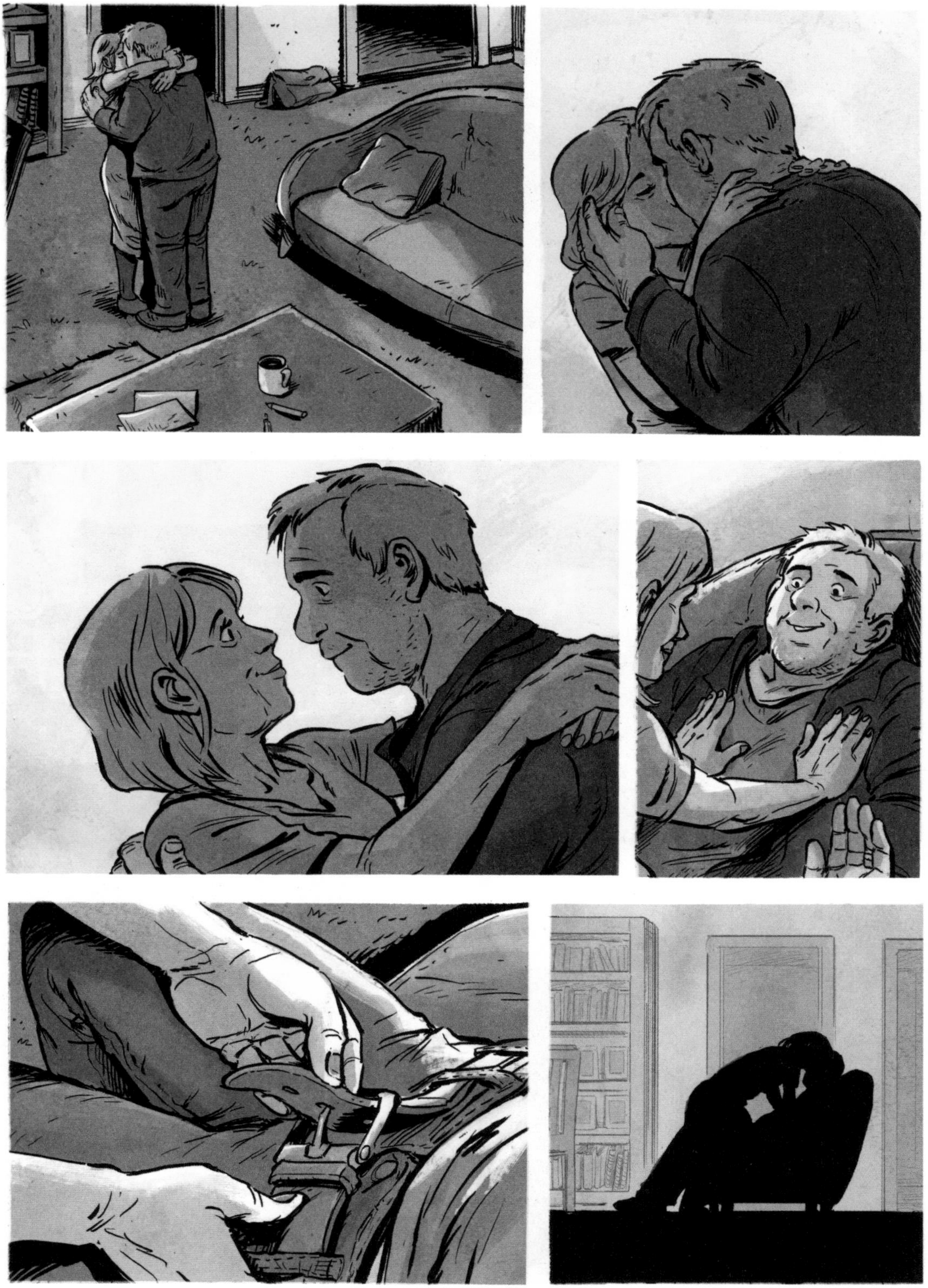

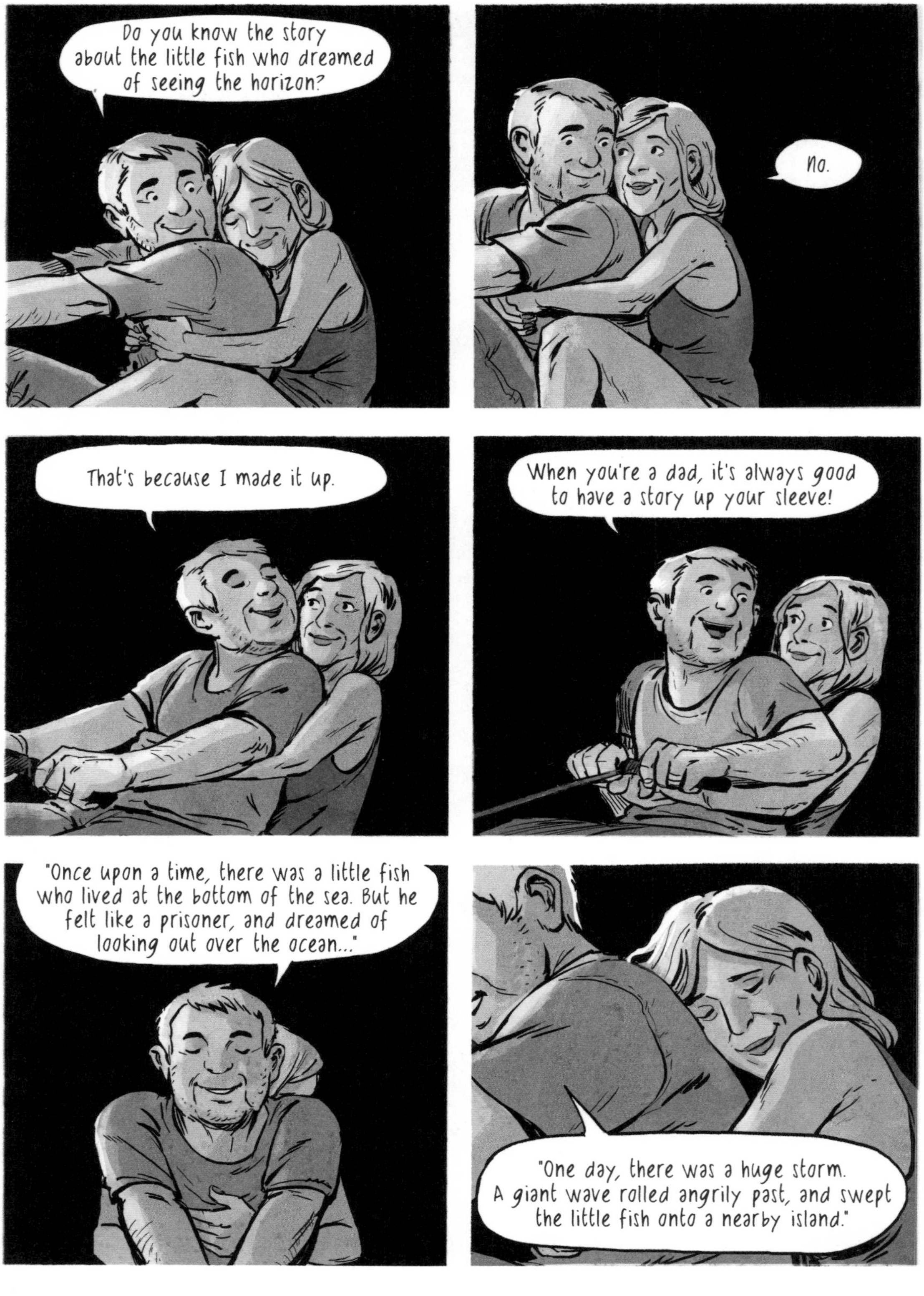

Do you know the story about the little fish who dreamed of seeing the horizon?
No.
That's because I made it up.
When you're a dad, it's always good to have a story up your sleeve!
"Once upon a time, there was a little fish who lived at the bottom of the sea. But he felt like a prisoner, and dreamed of looking out over the ocean..."
"One day, there was a huge storm. A giant wave rolled angrily past, and swept the little fish onto a nearby island."

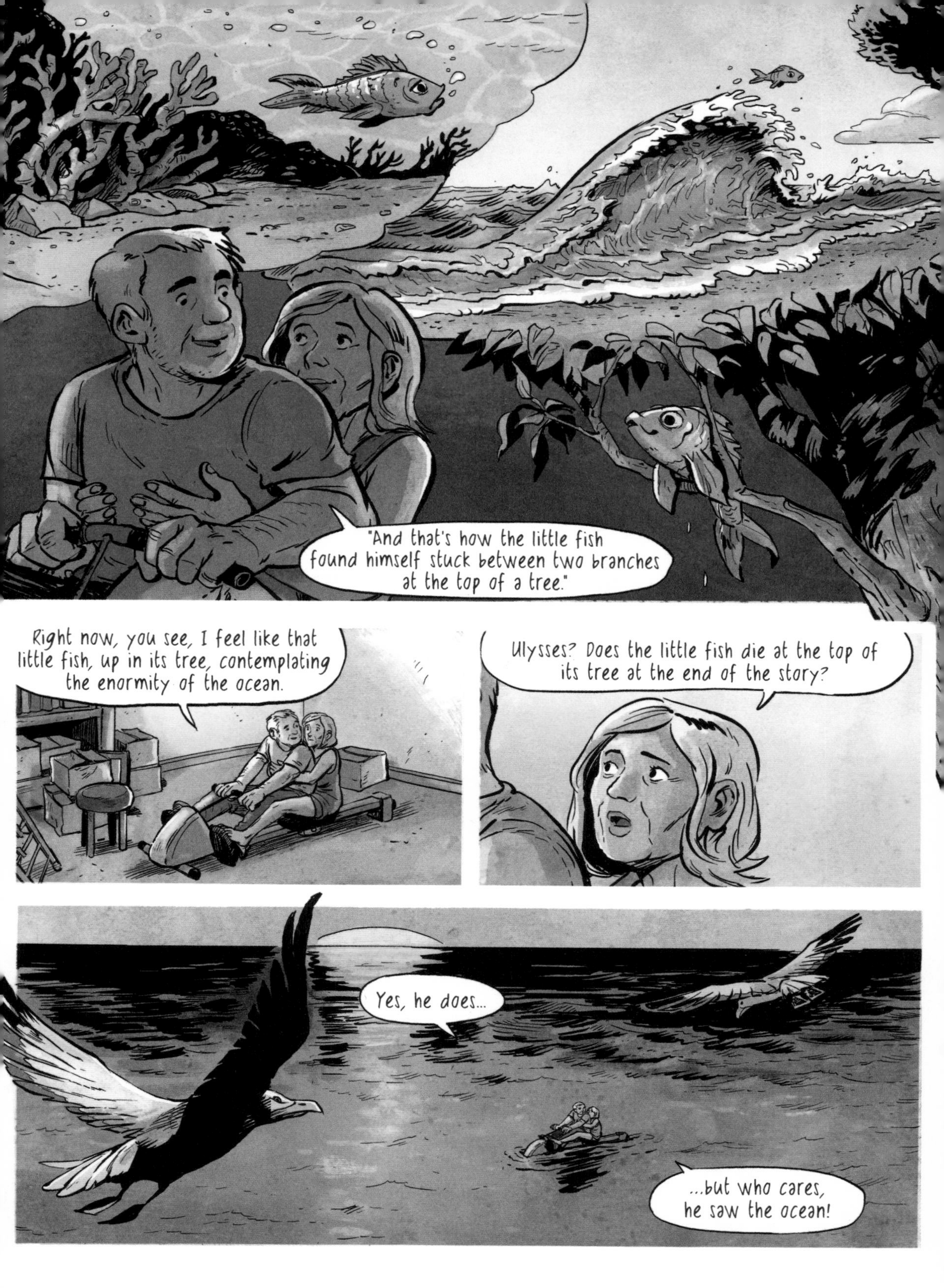
"And that's how the little fish found himself stuck between two branches at the top of a tree."
Right now, you see, I feel like that little fish, up in its tree, contemplating the enormity of the ocean.
Ulysses? Does the little fish die at the top of its tree at the end of the story?
Yes, he does...
...but who cares, he saw the ocean!

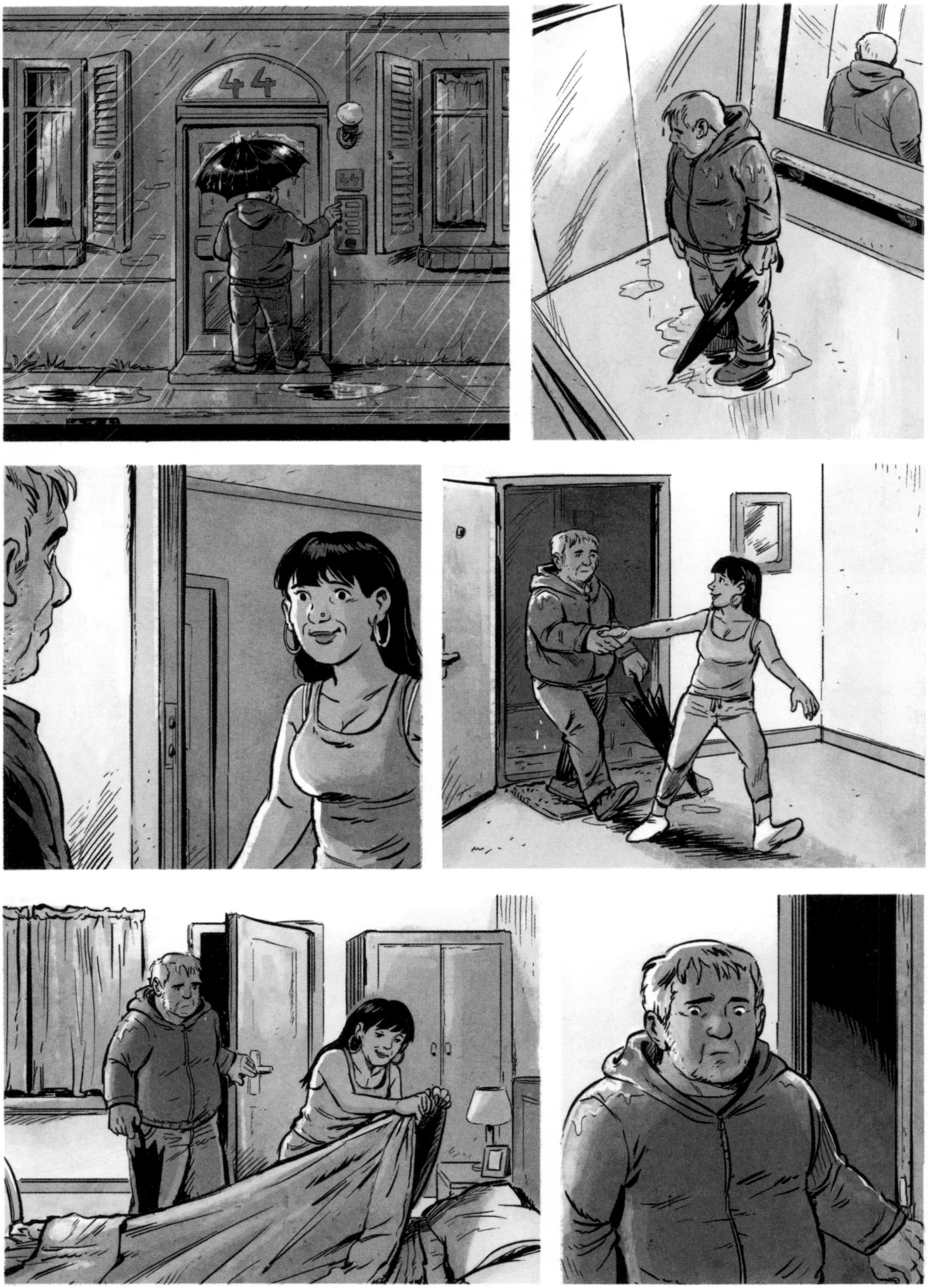
44

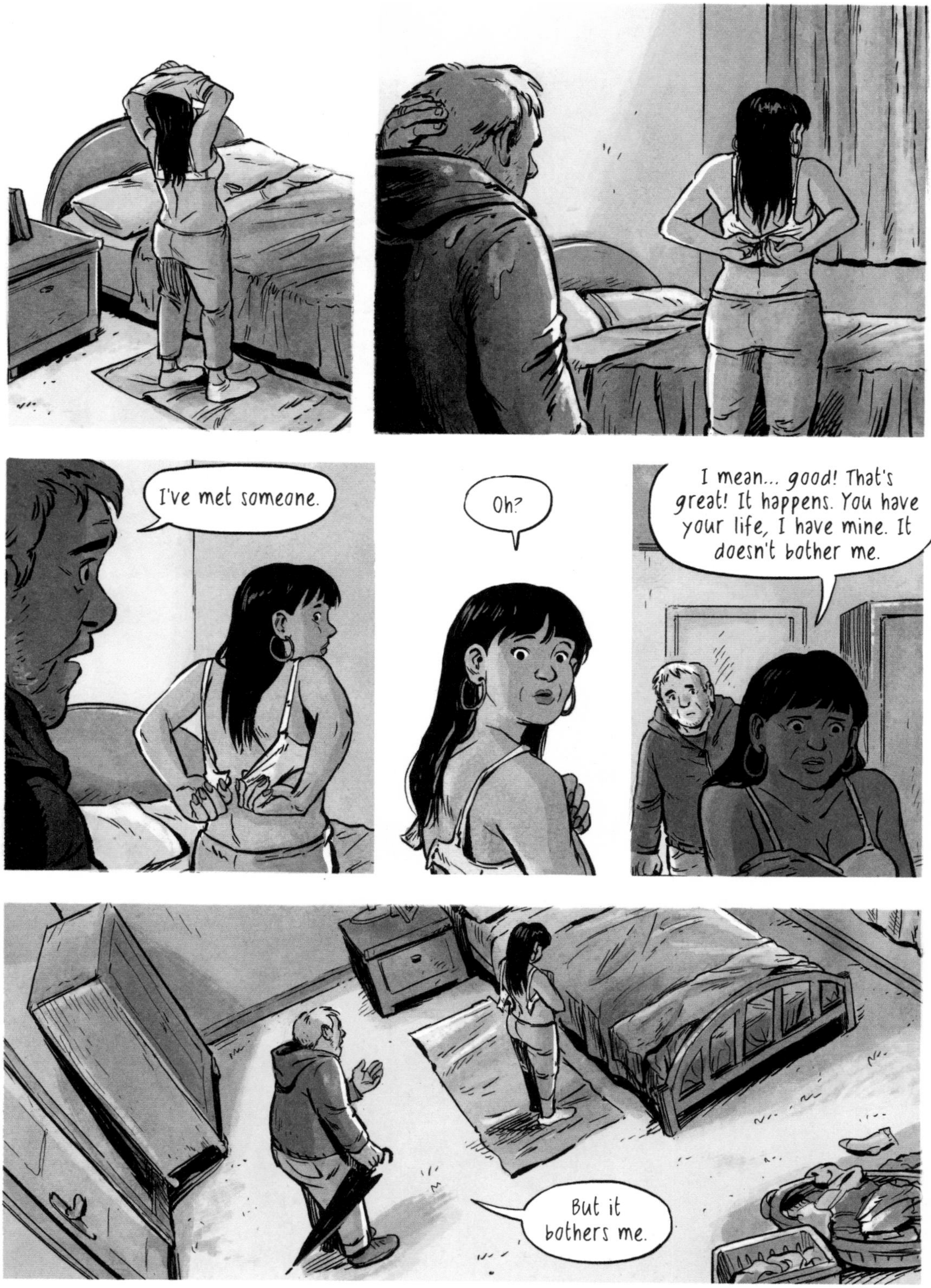
I've met someone.
Oh?
I mean... good! That's great! It happens. You have your life, I have mine. It doesn't bother me.
But it bothers me.

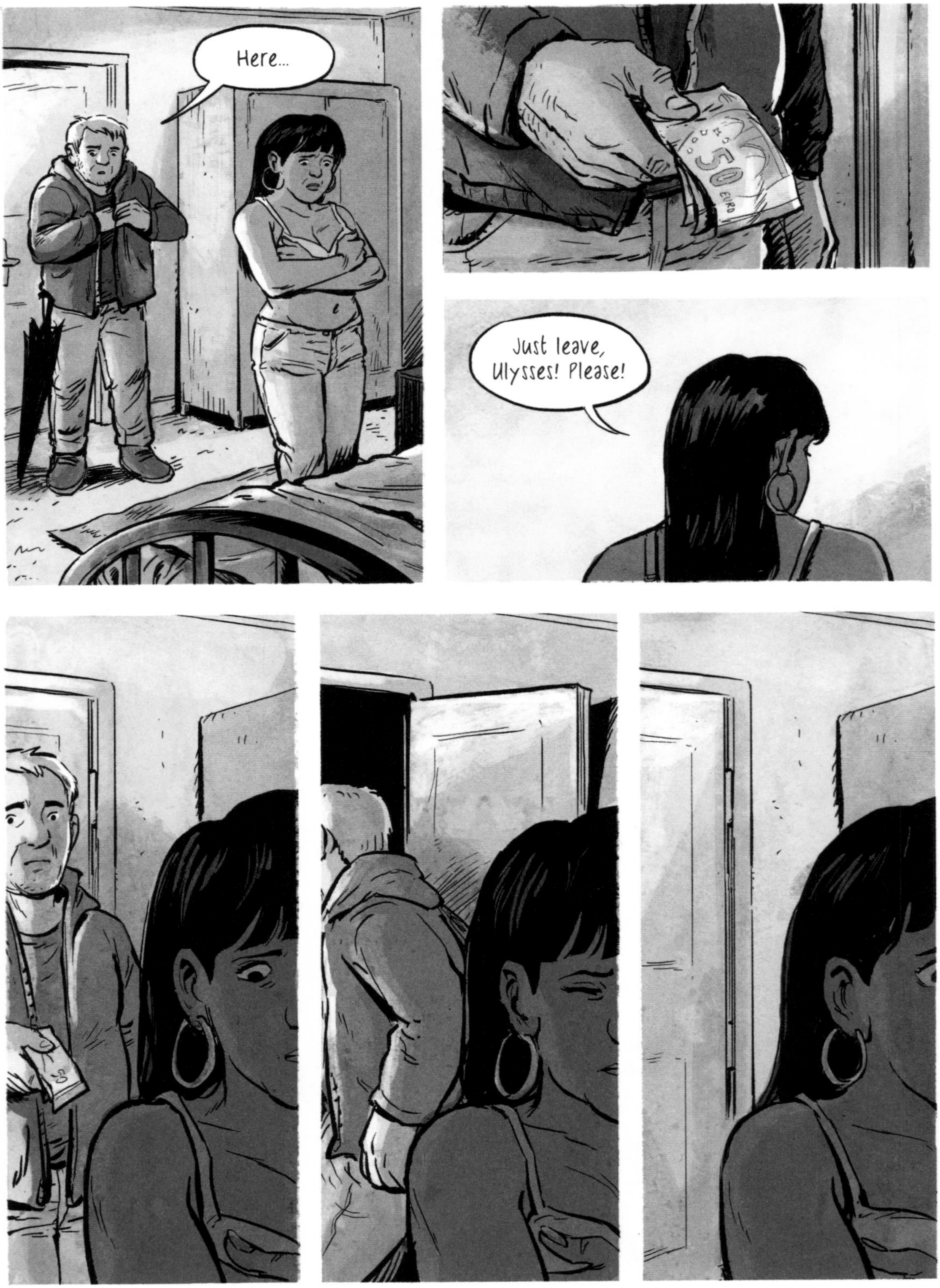
Here...
50 EURO
Just leave, Ulysses! Please!

6.

The best devilled eggs this side of the border

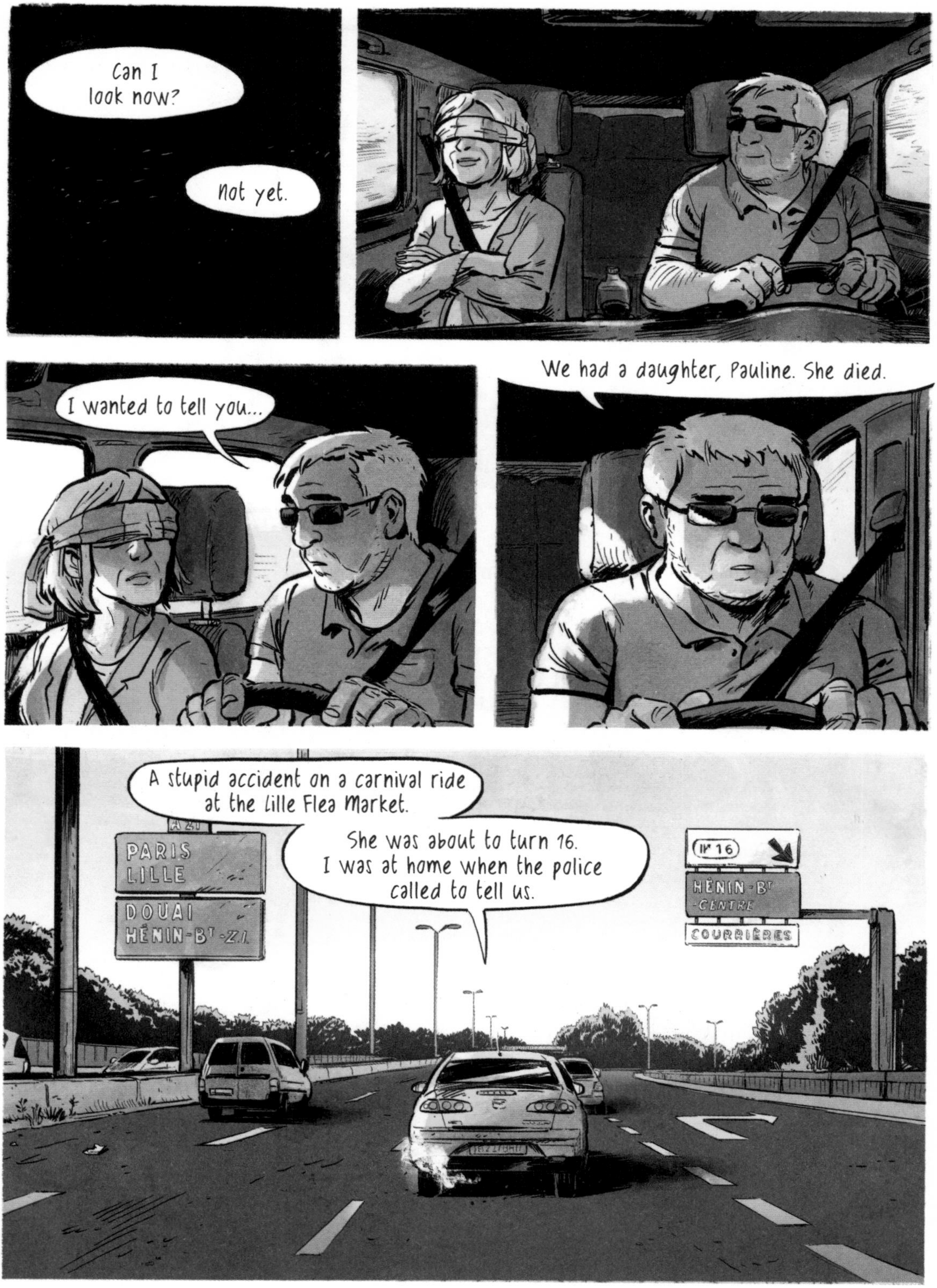

Can I look now?
Not yet.
I wanted to tell you...
We had a daughter, Pauline. She died.
A stupid accident on a carnival ride at the Lille Flea Market.
She was about to turn 16. I was at home when the police called to tell us.
A 21
PARIS LILLE
DOUAI HÉNIN-BT -Z.I.
Nº 16
HÉNIN-BT -CENTRE
COURRIÈRES

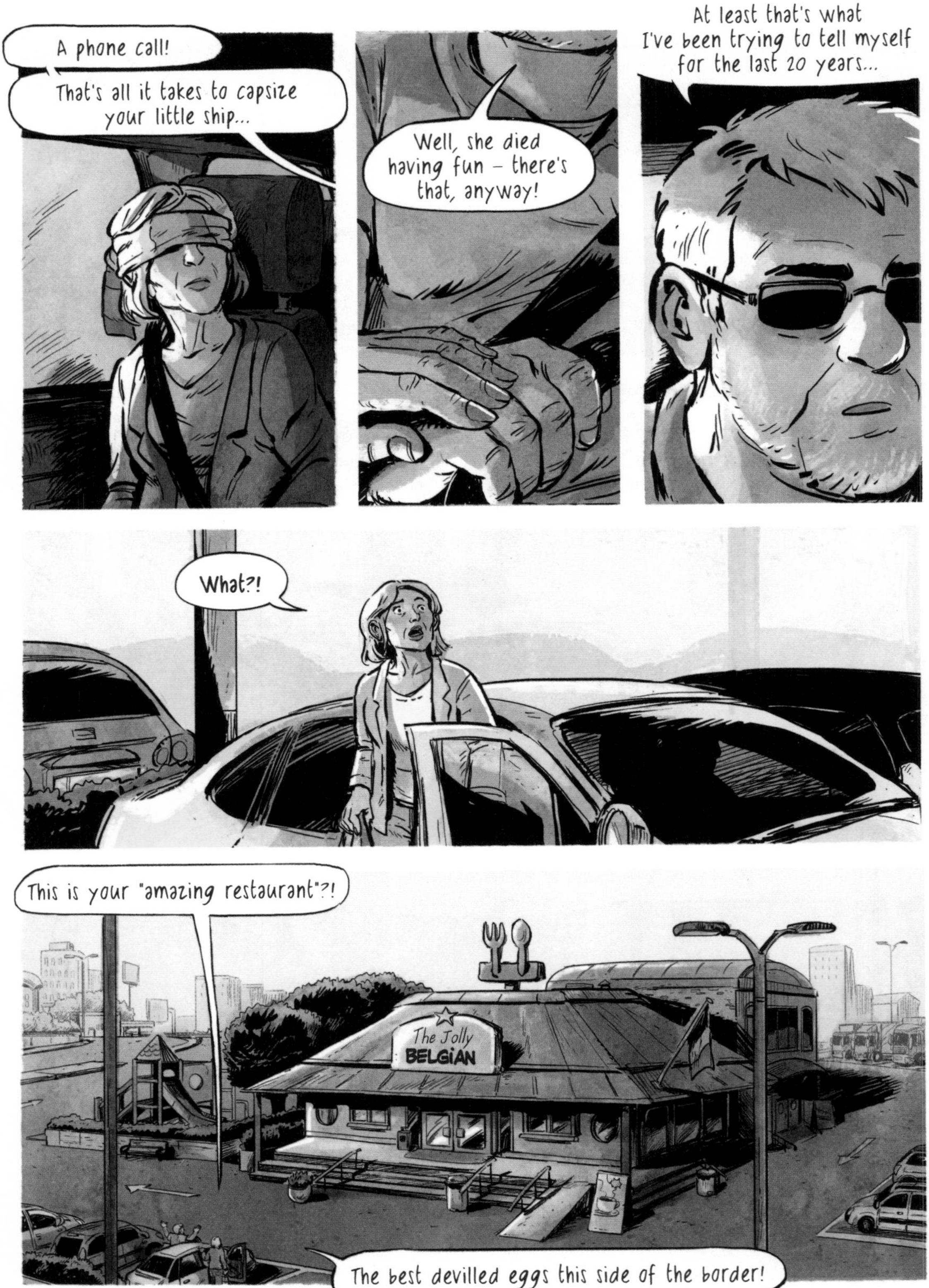
A phone call!
That's all it takes to capsize your little ship...
Well, she died having fun – there's that, anyway!
At least that's what I've been trying to tell myself for the last 20 years...
What?!
This is your "amazing restaurant"?!
The Jolly BELGIAN
The best devilled eggs this side of the border!

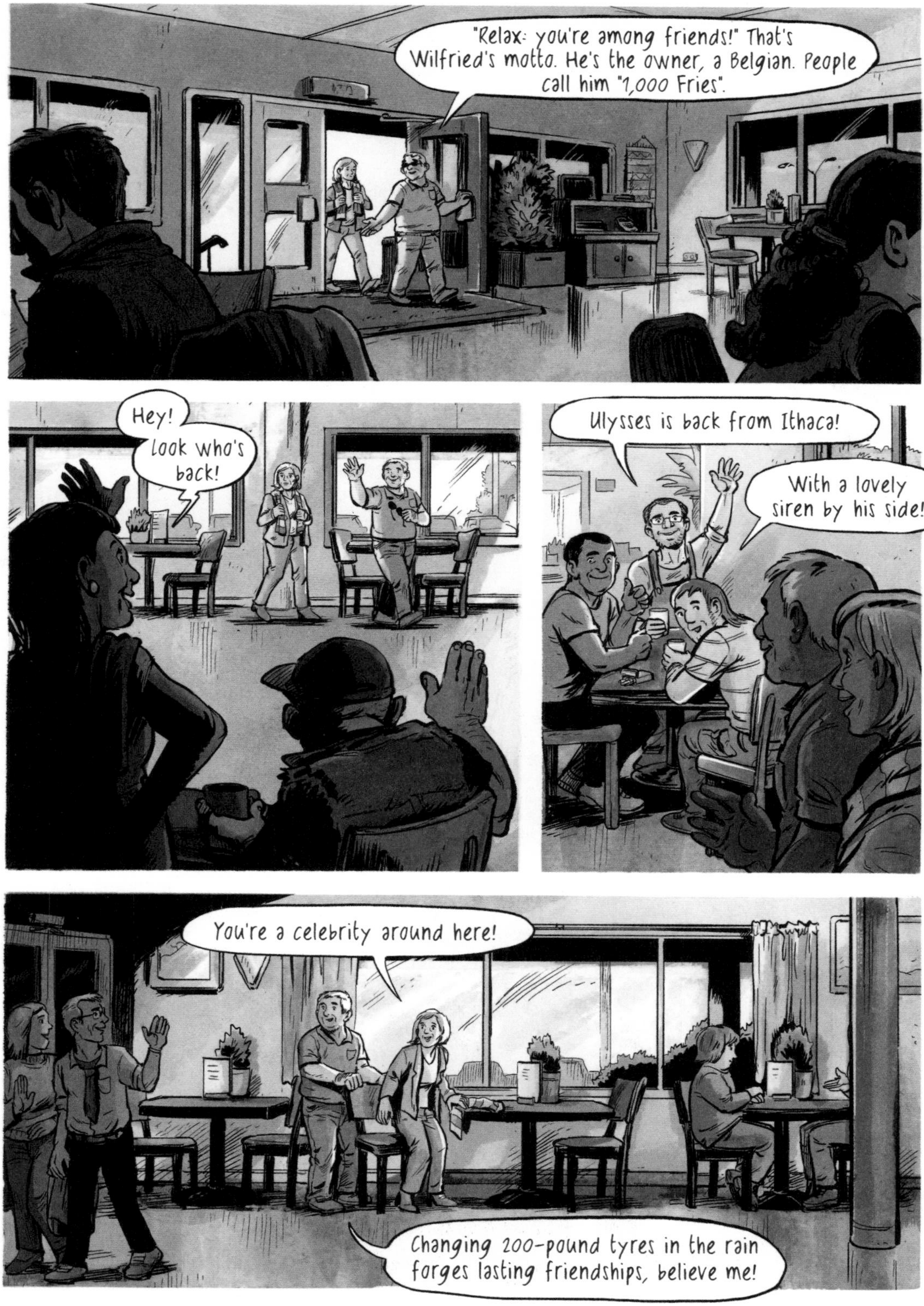
"Relax: you're among friends!" That's Wilfried's motto. He's the owner, a Belgian. People call him "1,000 Fries".
Hey! Look who's back!
Ulysses is back from Ithaca!
With a lovely siren by his side!
You're a celebrity around here!
Changing 200-pound tyres in the rain forges lasting friendships, believe me!

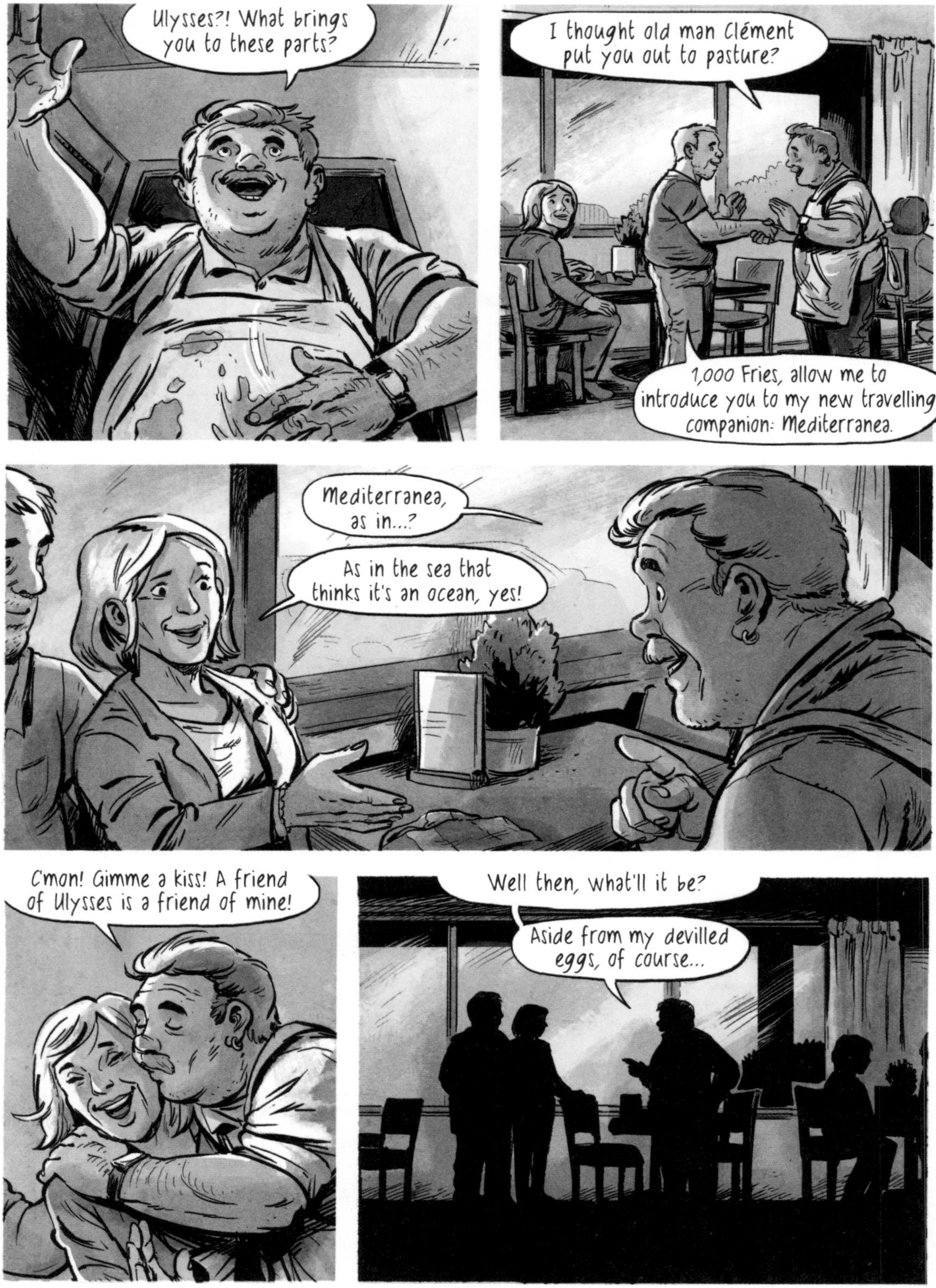
Ulysses?! What brings you to these parts?
I thought old man Clément put you out to pasture?
1,000 Fries, allow me to introduce you to my new travelling companion: Mediterranea.
Mediterranea, as in...?
As in the sea that thinks it's an ocean, yes!
C'mon! Gimme a kiss! A friend of Ulysses is a friend of mine!
Well then, what'll it be?
Aside from my devilled eggs, of course...

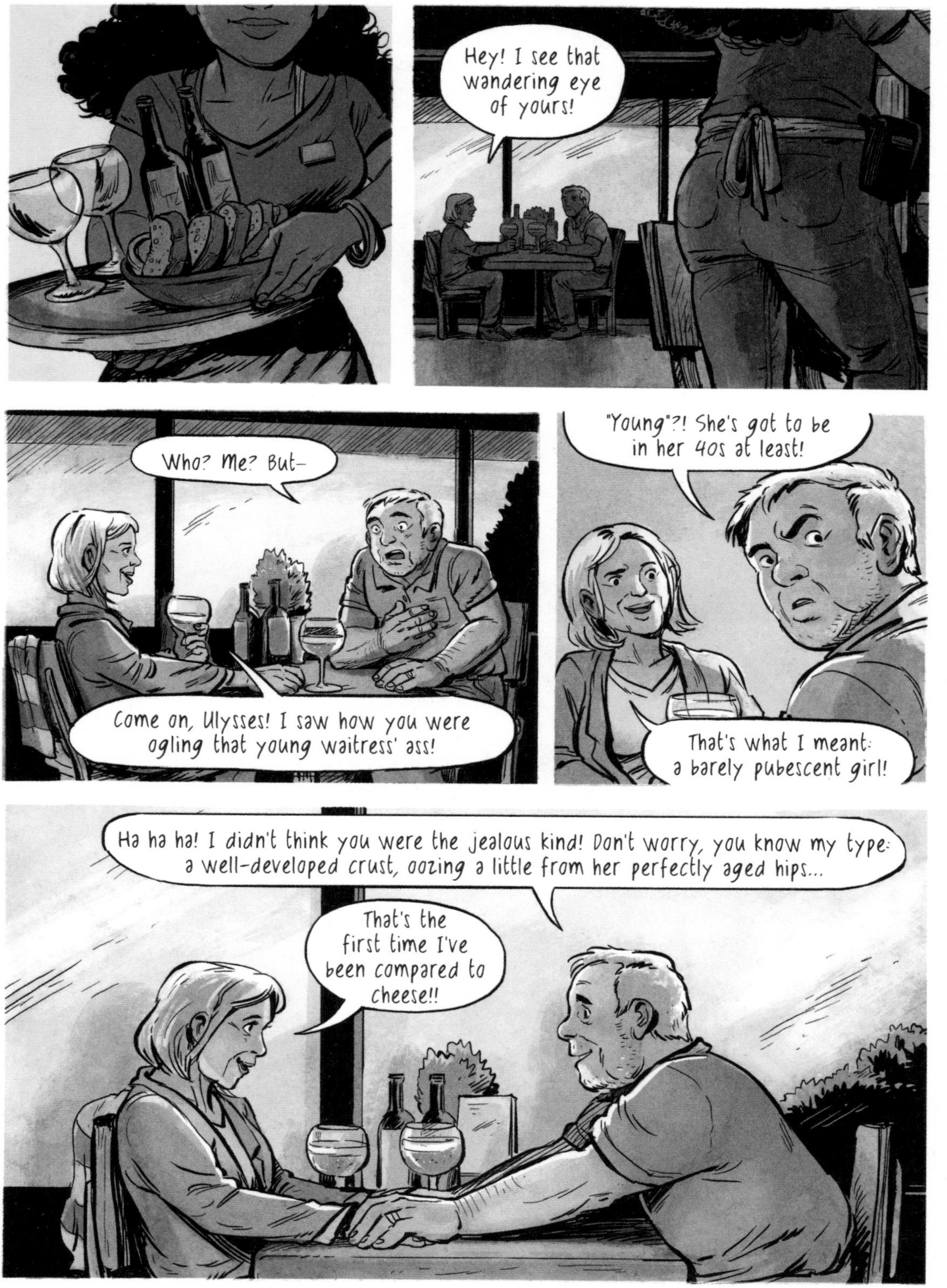
Hey! I see that wandering eye of yours!
Who? Me? But–
Come on, Ulysses! I saw how you were ogling that young waitress' ass!
"Young"?! She's got to be in her 40s at least!
That's what I meant: a barely pubescent girl!
Ha ha ha! I didn't think you were the jealous kind! Don't worry, you know my type: a well-developed crust, oozing a little from her perfectly aged hips...
That's the first time I've been compared to cheese!!

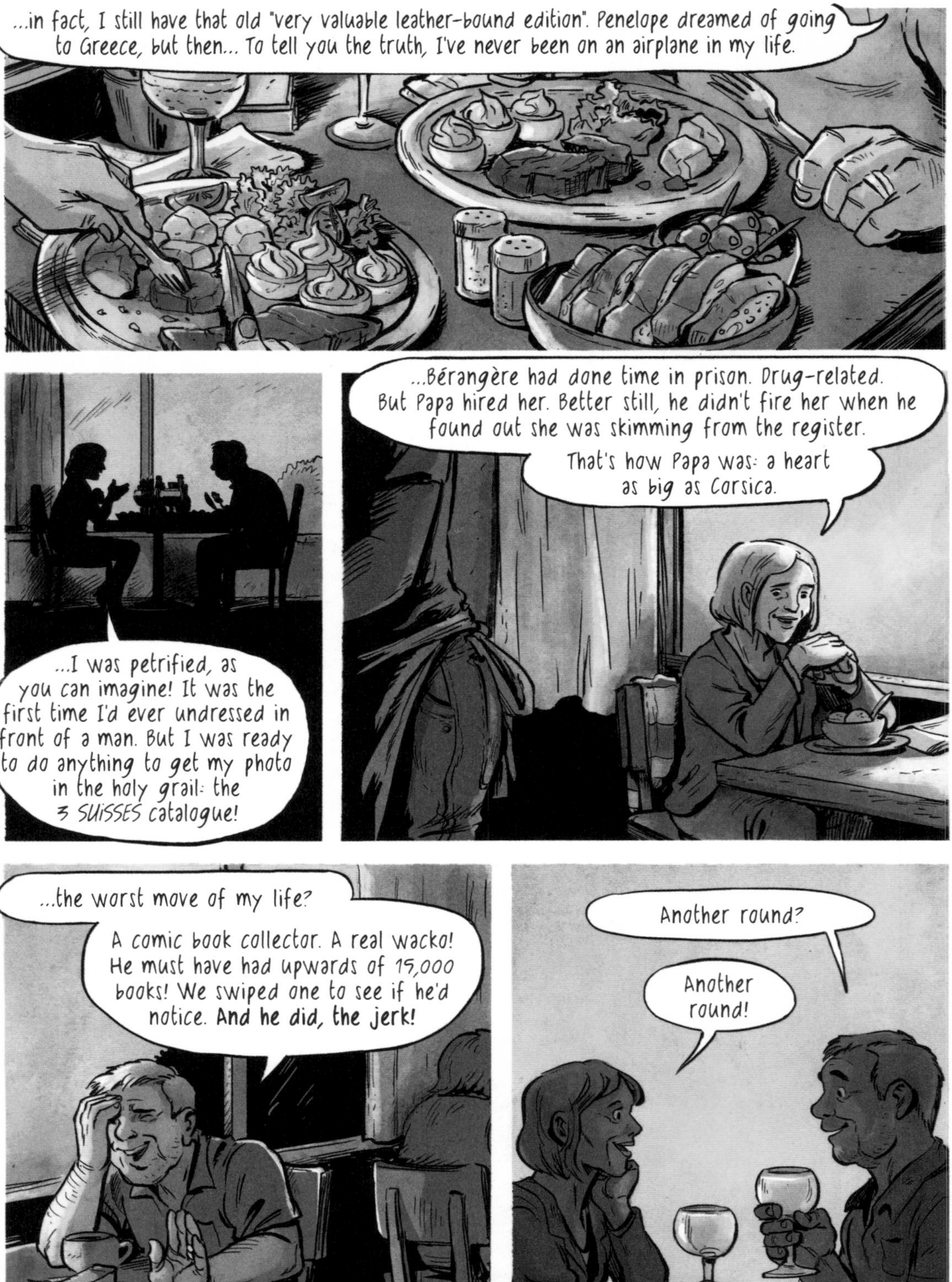

...in fact, I still have that old "very valuable leather-bound edition". Penelope dreamed of going to Greece, but then... To tell you the truth, I've never been on an airplane in my life.
...I was petrified, as you can imagine! It was the first time I'd ever undressed in front of a man. But I was ready to do anything to get my photo in the holy grail: the 3 SUISSES catalogue!
...Bérangère had done time in prison. Drug-related. But Papa hired her. Better still, he didn't fire her when he found out she was skimming from the register.
That's how Papa was: a heart as big as Corsica.
...the worst move of my life?
A comic book collector. A real wacko! He must have had upwards of 15,000 books! We swiped one to see if he'd notice. **And he did, the jerk!**
Another round?
Another round!

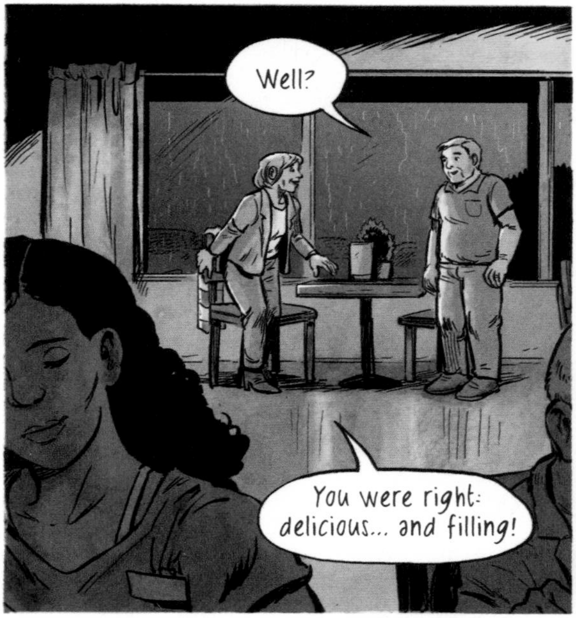
Well?
You were right: delicious... and filling!

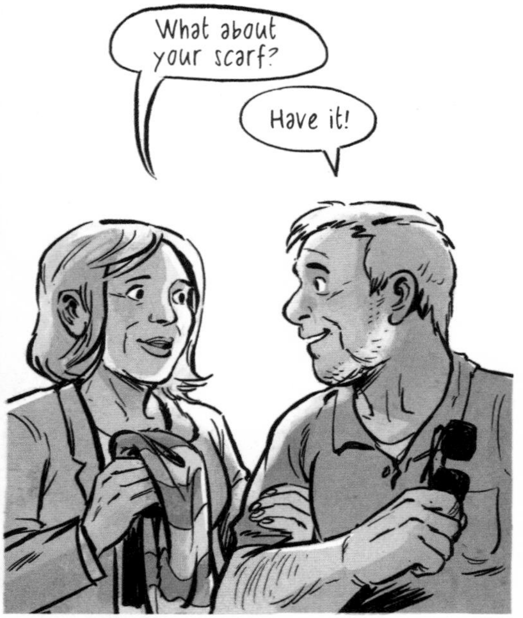
What about your scarf?
Have it!

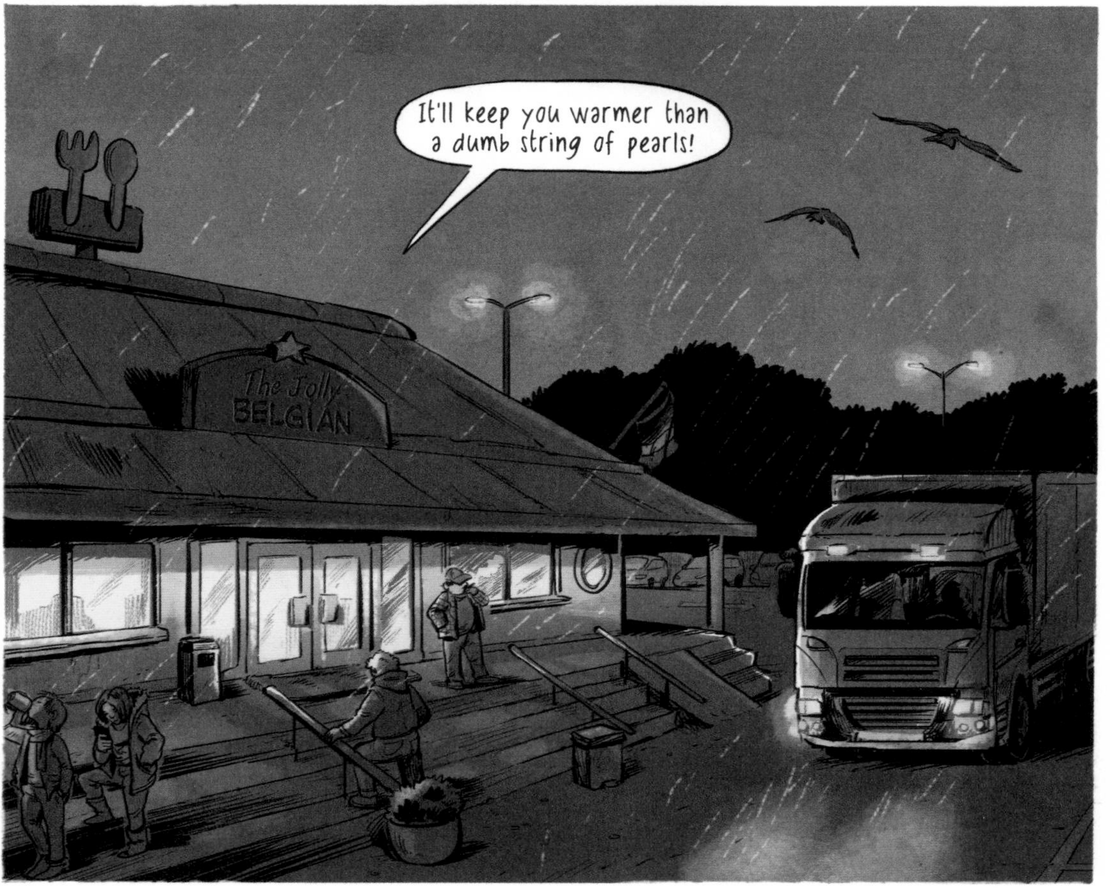
It'll keep you warmer than a dumb string of pearls!
The Jolly BELGIAN

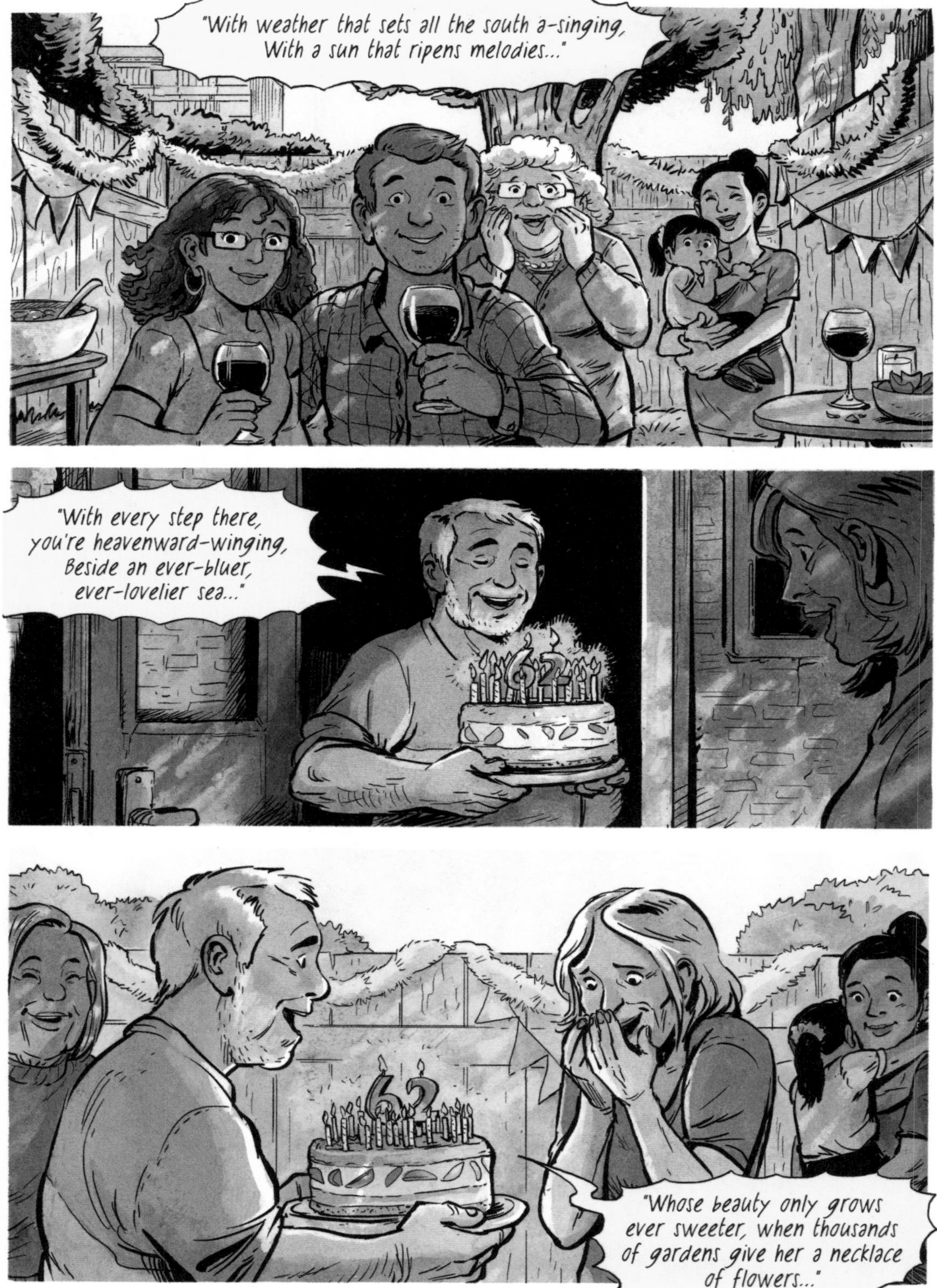
"With weather that sets all the south a-singing, With a sun that ripens melodies..."
"With every step there, you're heavenward-winging, Beside an ever-bluer, ever-lovelier sea..."
"Whose beauty only grows ever sweeter, when thousands of gardens give her a necklace of flowers..."

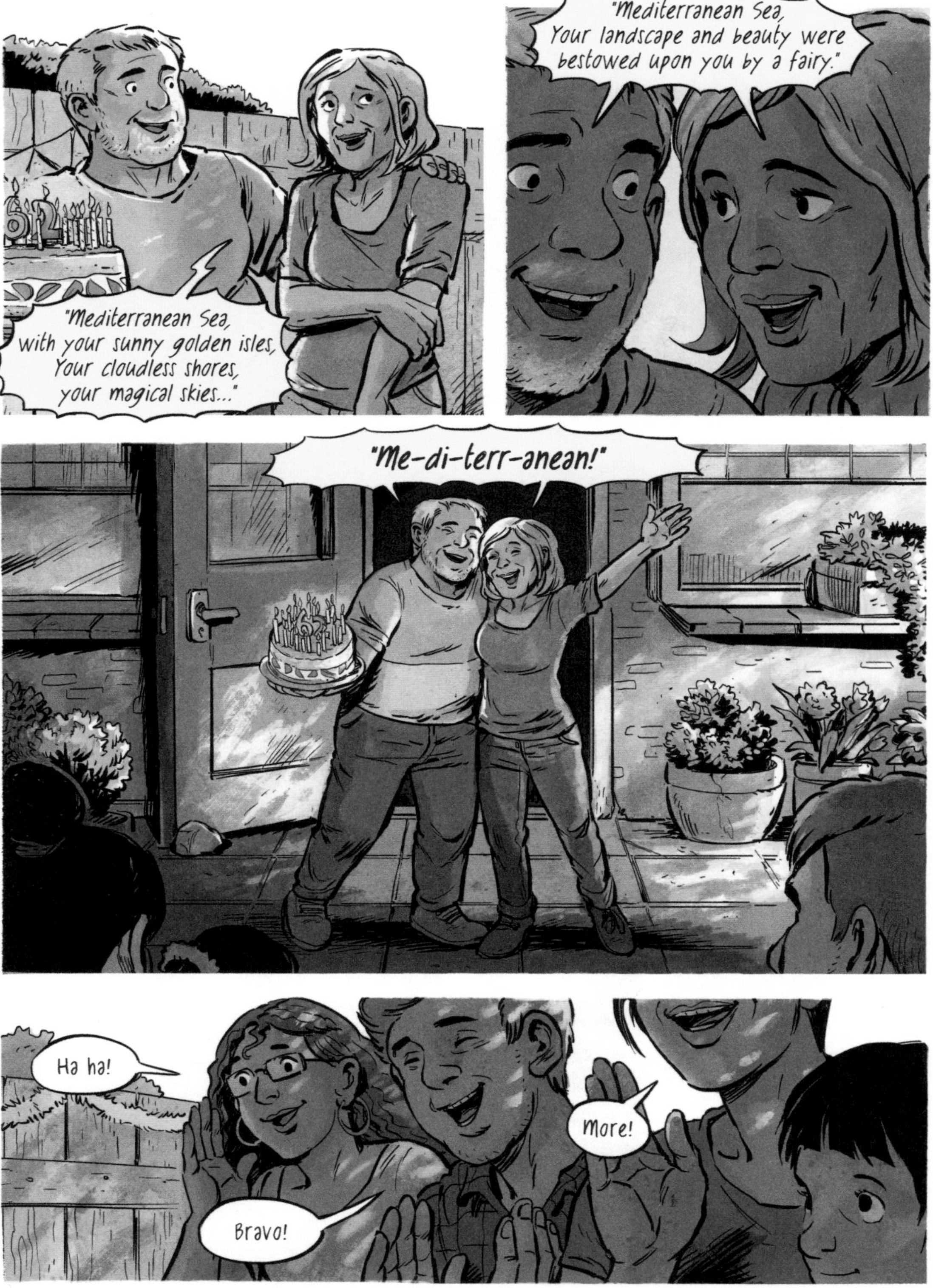
"Mediterranean Sea,
with your sunny golden isles,
Your cloudless shores,
your magical skies..."
"Mediterranean Sea,
Your landscape and beauty were
bestowed upon you by a fairy."
"Me-di-terr-anean!"
Ha ha!
More!
Bravo!

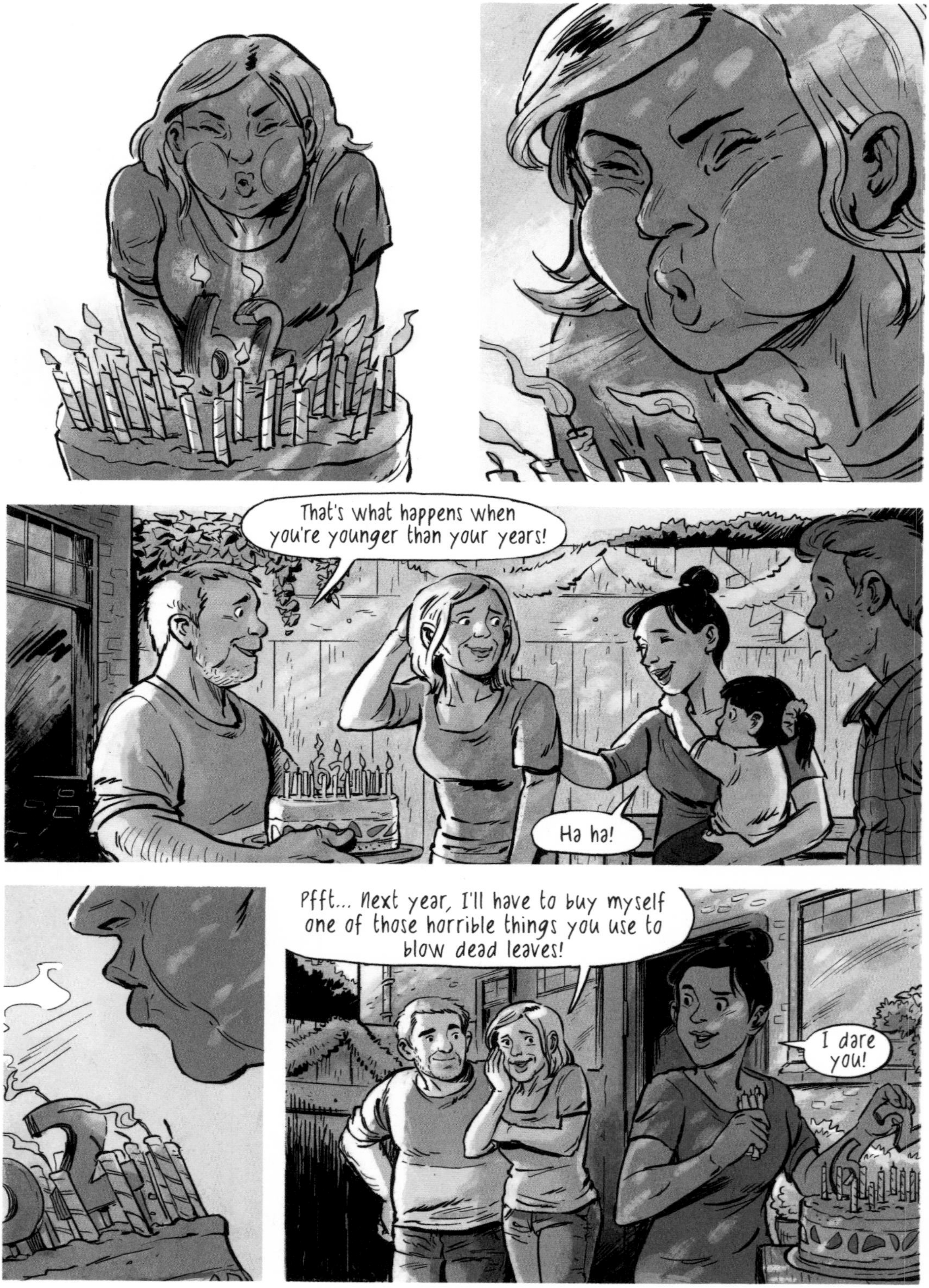
That's what happens when you're younger than your years!
Ha ha!
Pfft... Next year, I'll have to buy myself one of those horrible things you use to blow dead leaves!
I dare you!

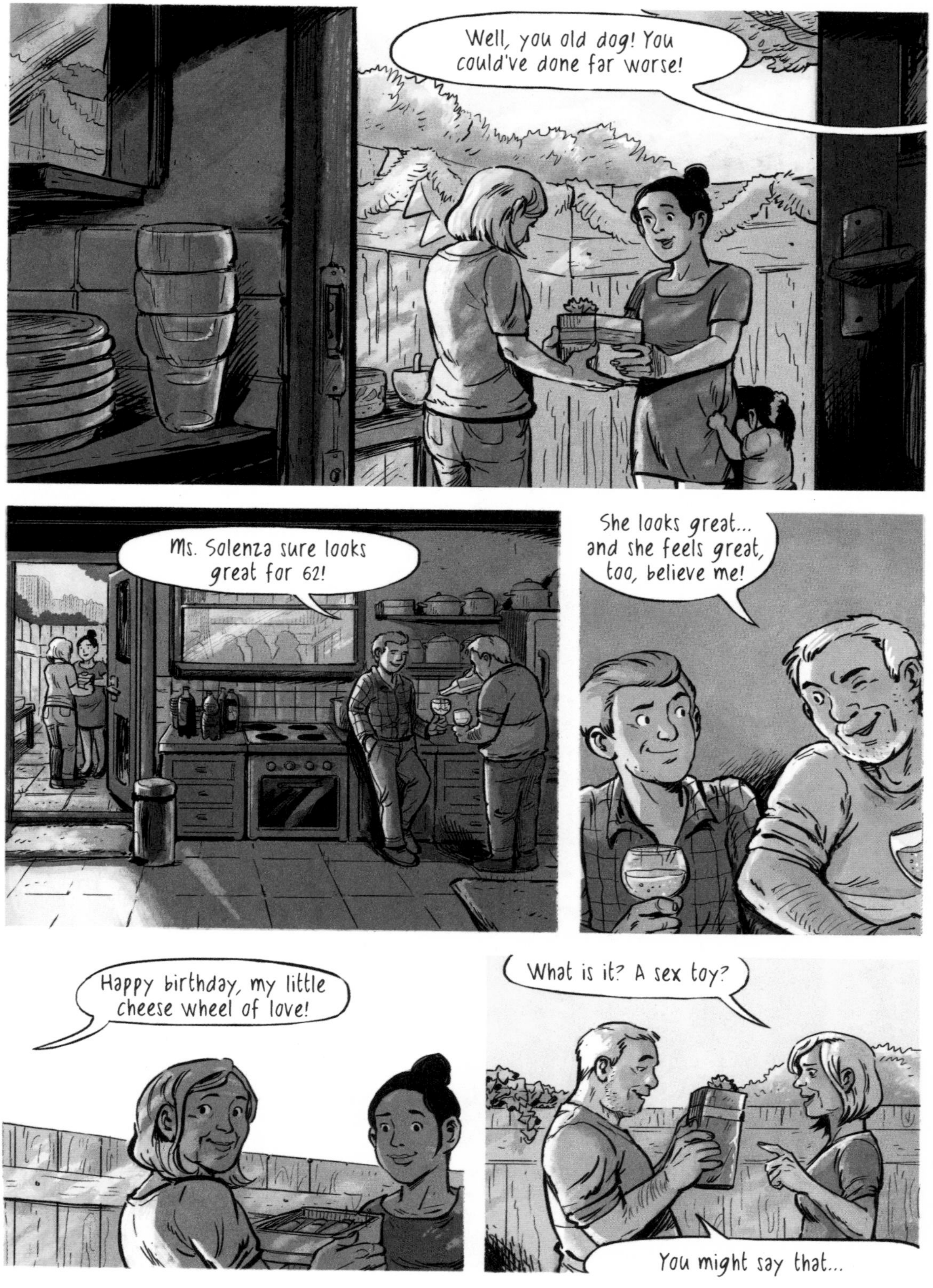

Well, you old dog! You could've done far worse!
Ms. Solenza sure looks great for 62!
She looks great... and she feels great, too, believe me!
Happy birthday, my little cheese wheel of love!
What is it? A sex toy?
You might say that...

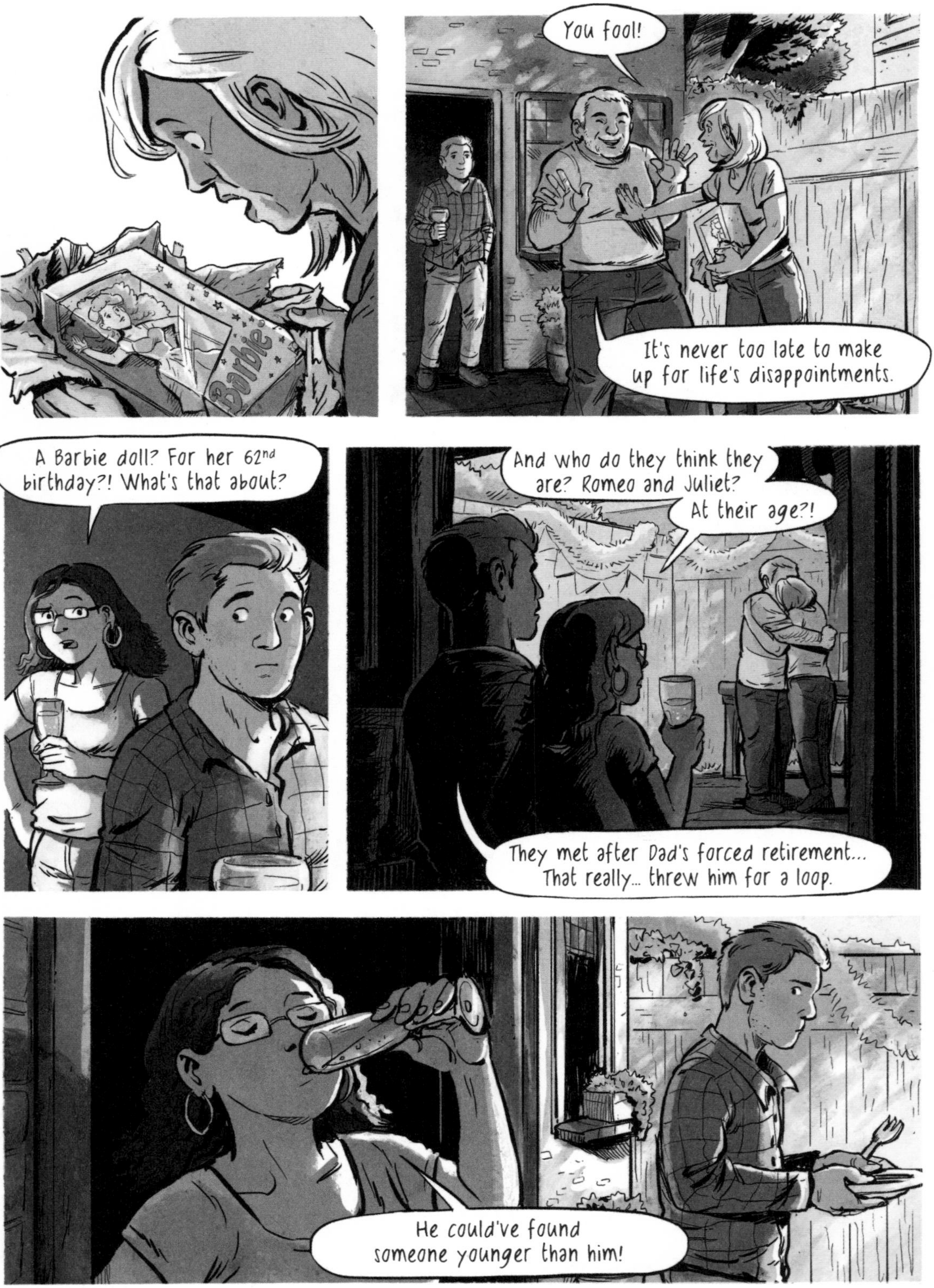

You fool!
It's never too late to make up for life's disappointments.
A Barbie doll? For her 62nd birthday?! What's that about?
And who do they think they are? Romeo and Juliet?
At their age?!
They met after Dad's forced retirement... That really... threw him for a loop.
He could've found someone younger than him!

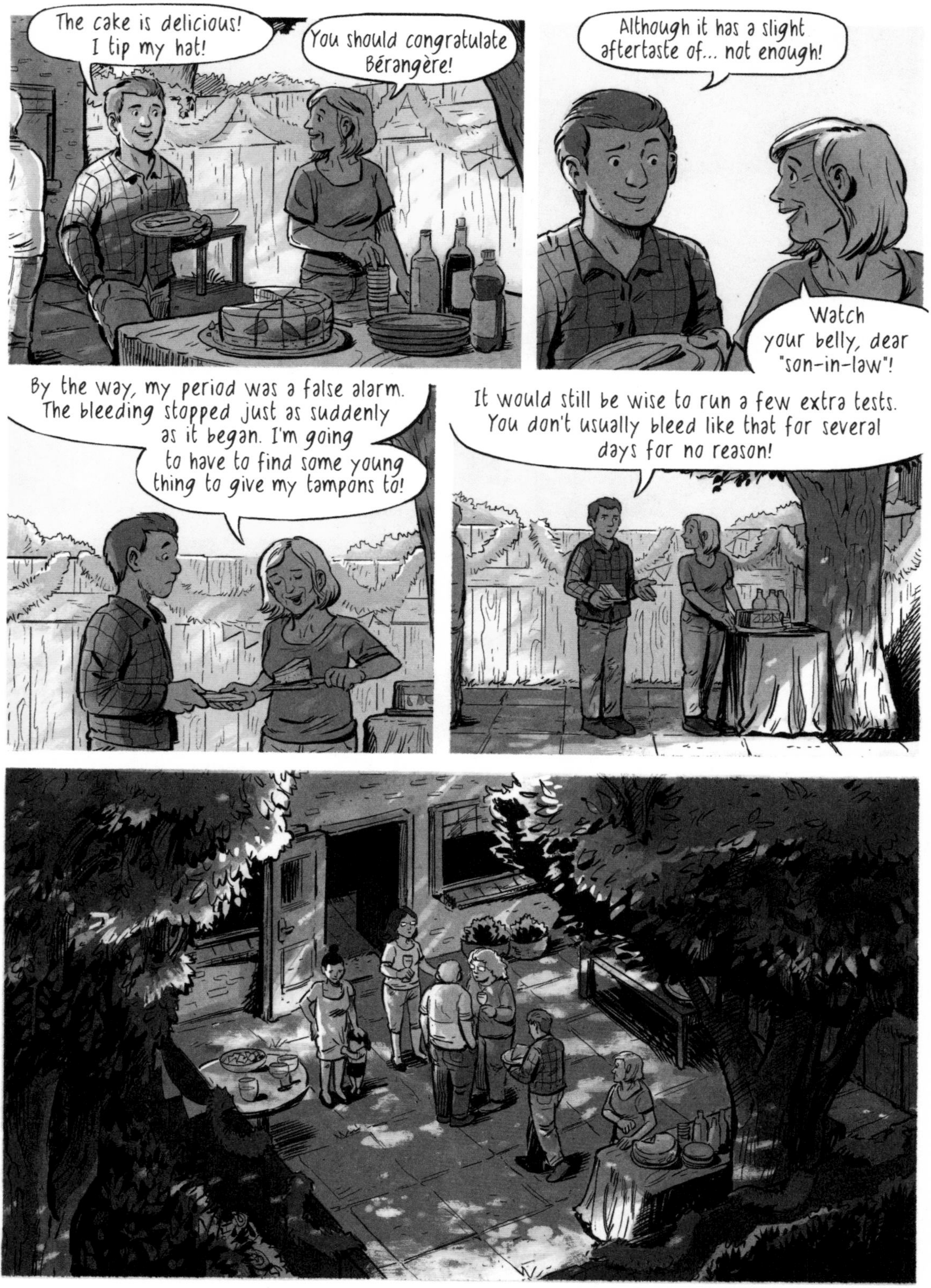
The cake is delicious! I tip my hat!
You should congratulate Bérangère!
Although it has a slight aftertaste of... not enough!
Watch your belly, dear "son-in-law"!
By the way, my period was a false alarm. The bleeding stopped just as suddenly as it began. I'm going to have to find some young thing to give my tampons to!
It would still be wise to run a few extra tests. You don't usually bleed like that for several days for no reason!

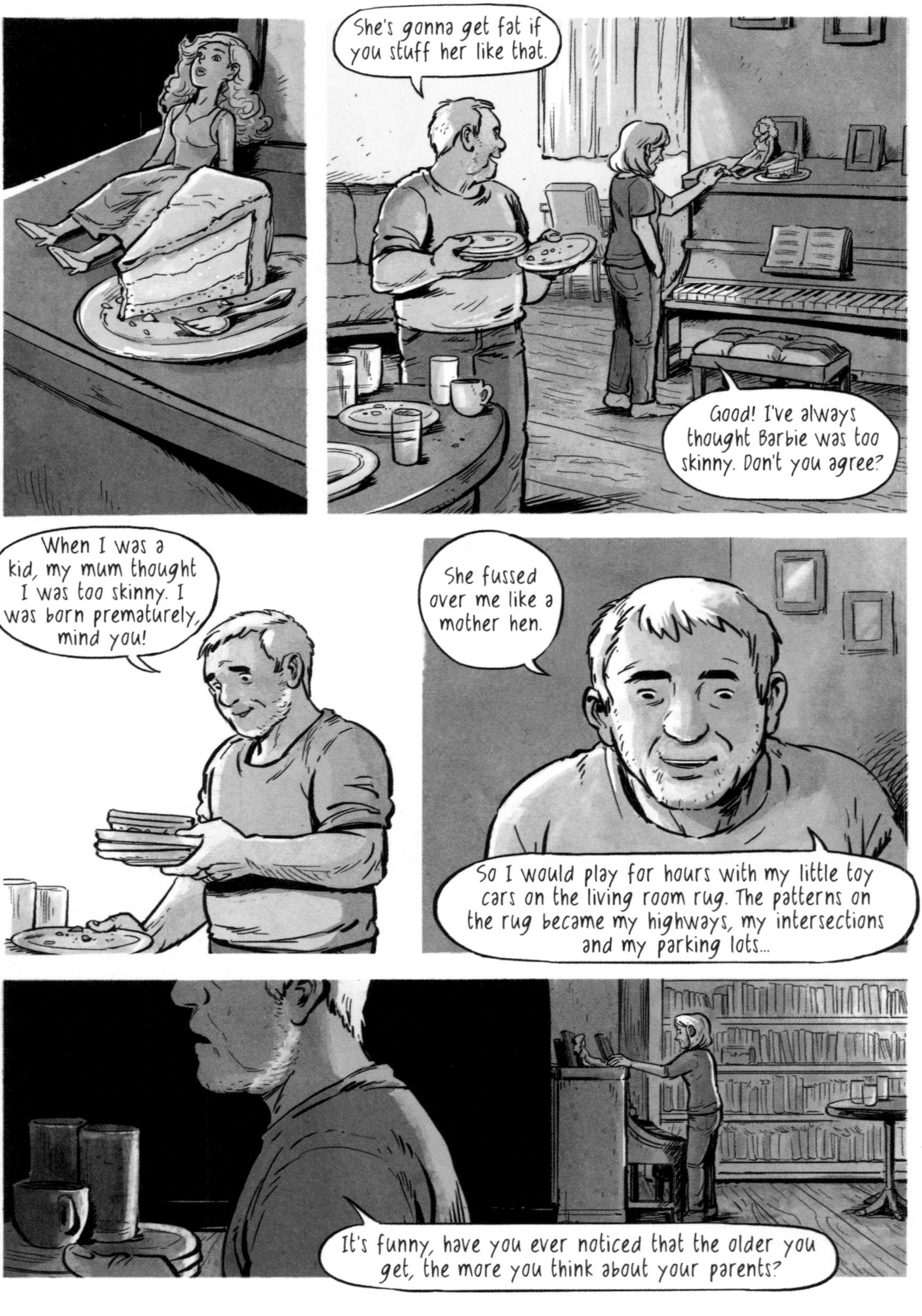
She's gonna get fat if you stuff her like that.
Good! I've always thought Barbie was too skinny. Don't you agree?
When I was a kid, my mum thought I was too skinny. I was born prematurely, mind you!
She fussed over me like a mother hen.
So I would play for hours with my little toy cars on the living room rug. The patterns on the rug became my highways, my intersections and my parking lots...
It's funny, have you ever noticed that the older you get, the more you think about your parents?

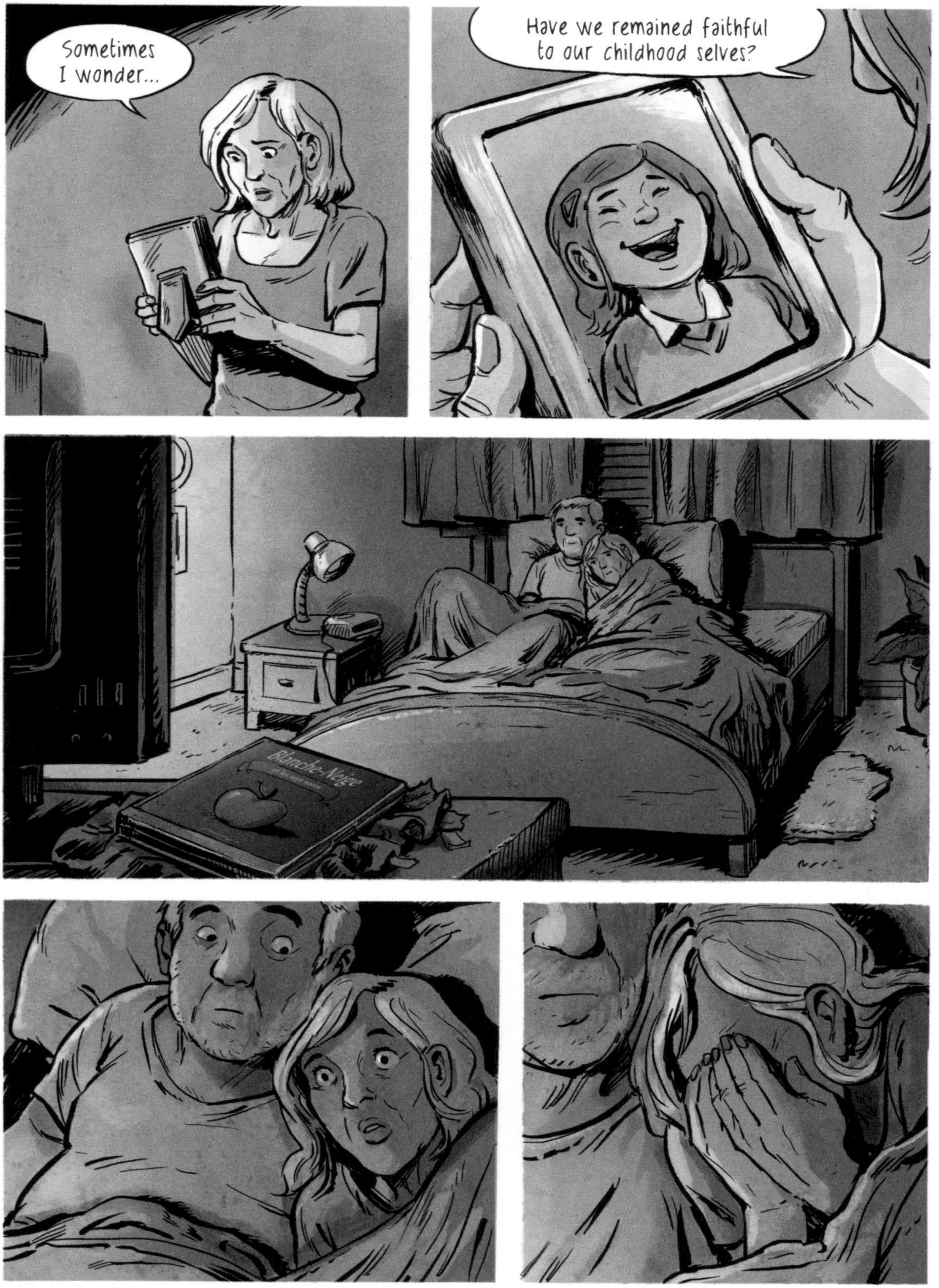
Sometimes I wonder...
Have we remained faithful to our childhood selves?
Blanche-Neige

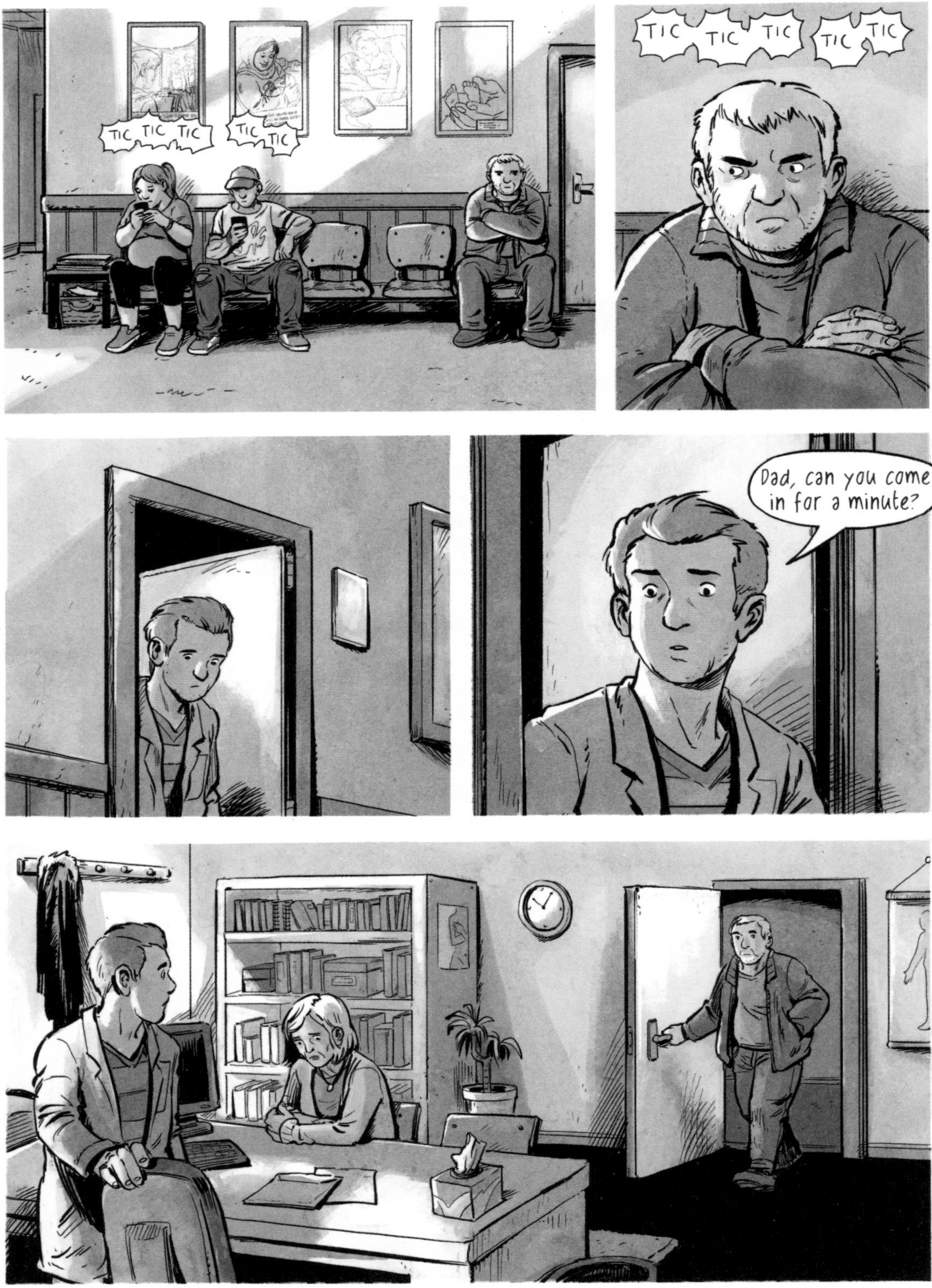
TIC TIC TIC
TIC TIC
TIC TIC TIC TIC TIC
Dad, can you come in for a minute?

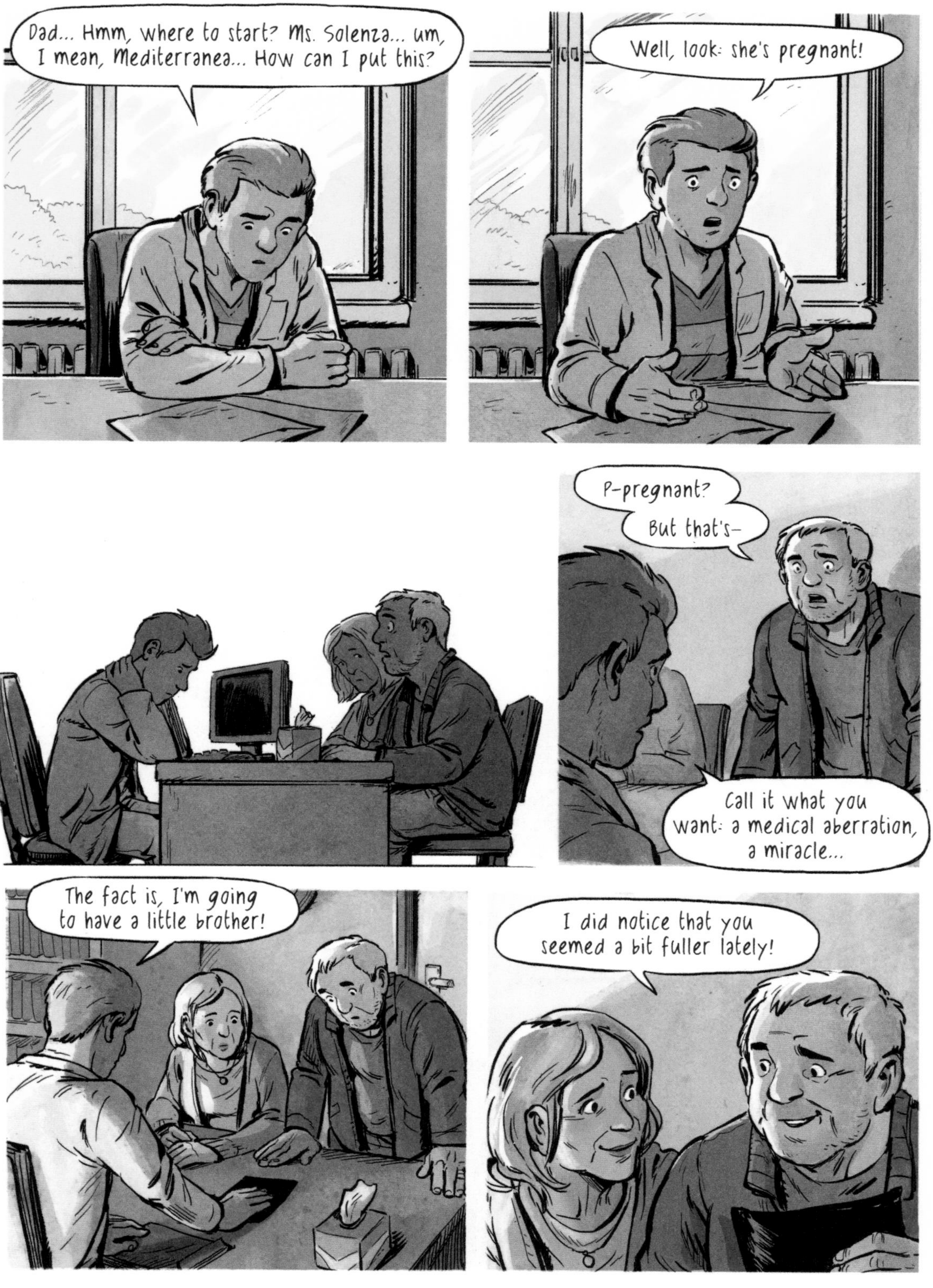
Dad... Hmm, where to start? Ms. Solenza... um, I mean, Mediterranea... How can I put this?
Well, look: she's pregnant!
P-pregnant?
But that's—
Call it what you want: a medical aberration, a miracle...
The fact is, I'm going to have a little brother!
I did notice that you seemed a bit fuller lately!

Well, that is, if you decide to keep it, of course.

Mediterranea is 18 weeks pregnant.

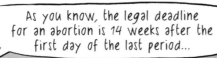

As you know, the legal deadline for an abortion is 14 weeks after the first day of the last period...

But given the... let's say, **unusual** circumstances, I could... fudge the dates a bit.

Julien, we're talking about the most important event since the RC Lens title in '98...

...and you're talking about legality?!

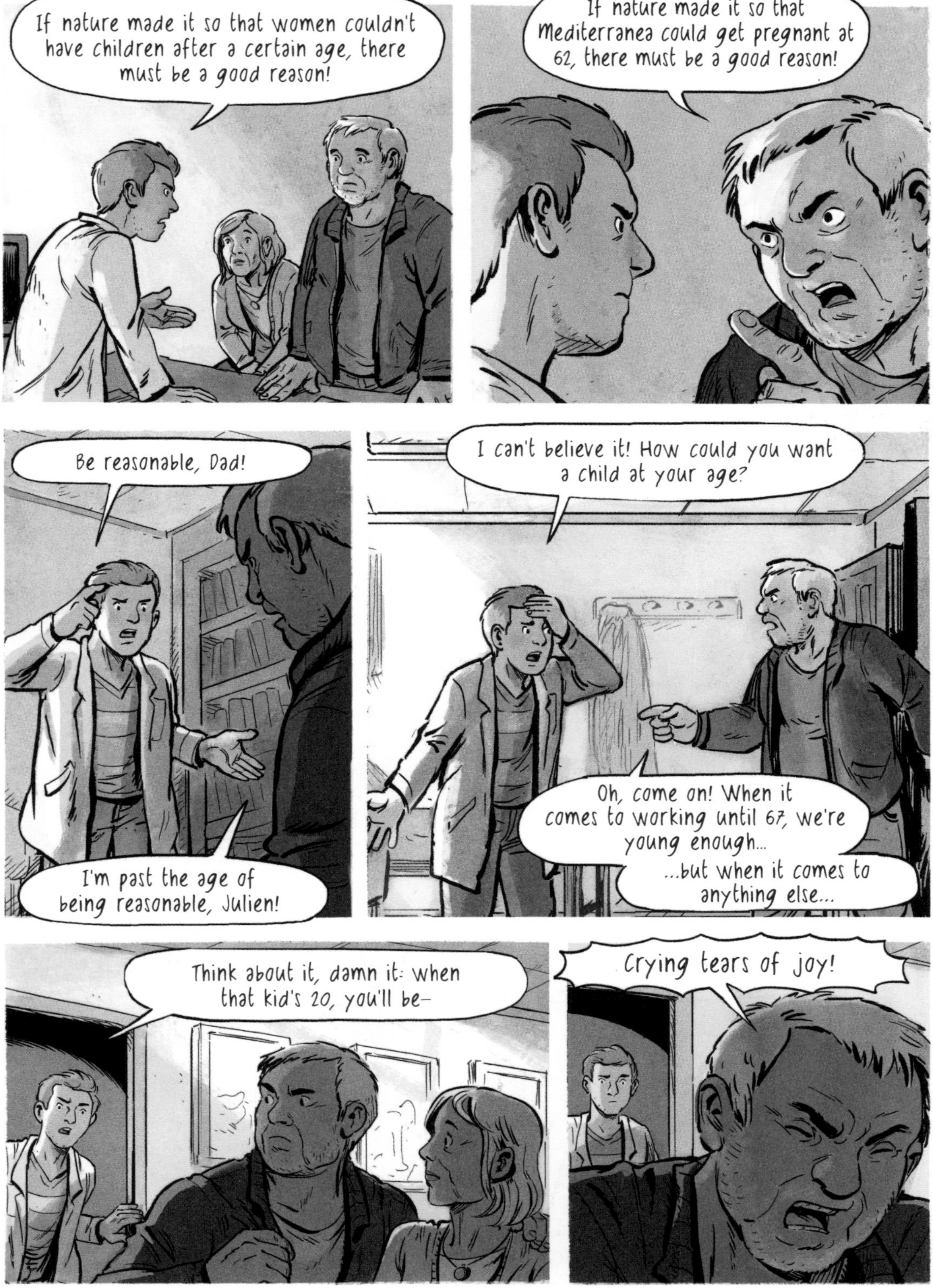
If nature made it so that women couldn't have children after a certain age, there must be a good reason!
If nature made it so that Mediterranea could get pregnant at 62, there must be a good reason!
Be reasonable, Dad!
I'm past the age of being reasonable, Julien!
I can't believe it! How could you want a child at your age?
Oh, come on! When it comes to working until 67, we're young enough...
...but when it comes to anything else...
Think about it, damn it: when that kid's 20, you'll be–
Crying tears of joy!

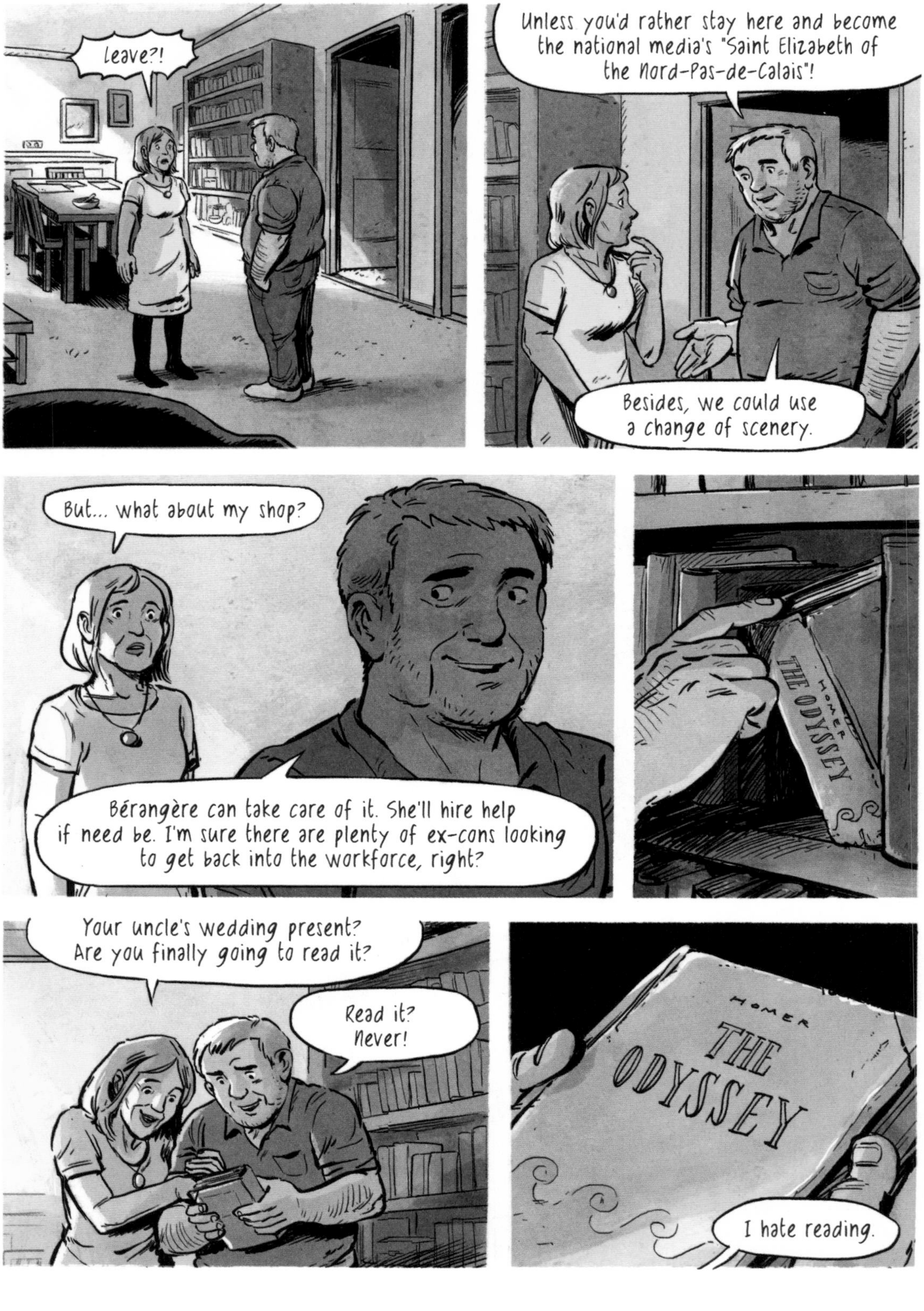
Leave?!
Unless you'd rather stay here and become the national media's "Saint Elizabeth of the Nord-Pas-de-Calais"!
Besides, we could use a change of scenery.
But... what about my shop?
Bérangère can take care of it. She'll hire help if need be. I'm sure there are plenty of ex-cons looking to get back into the workforce, right?
HOMER
THE ODYSSEY
Your uncle's wedding present? Are you finally going to read it?
Read it? Never!
HOMER
THE ODYSSEY
I hate reading.

7.

The Odyssey

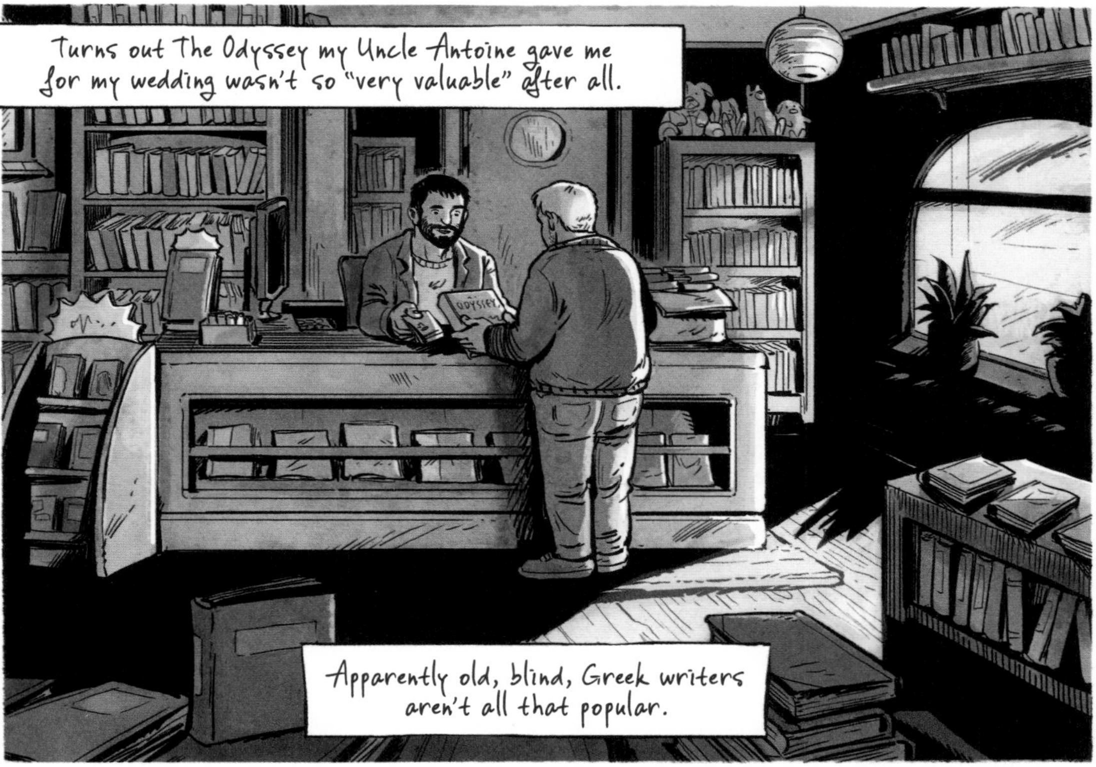
Turns out The Odyssey my Uncle Antoine gave me for my wedding wasn't so "very valuable" after all.
ODYSSEY
Apparently old, blind, Greek writers aren't all that popular.

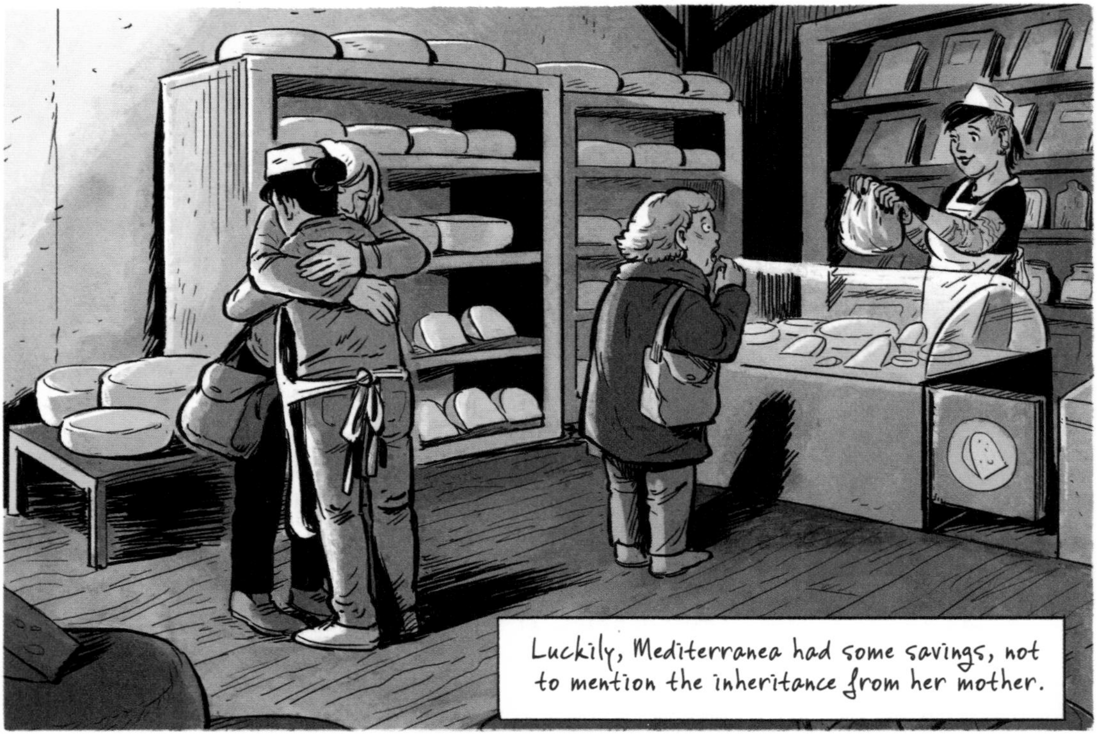
Luckily, Mediterranea had some savings, not to mention the inheritance from her mother.

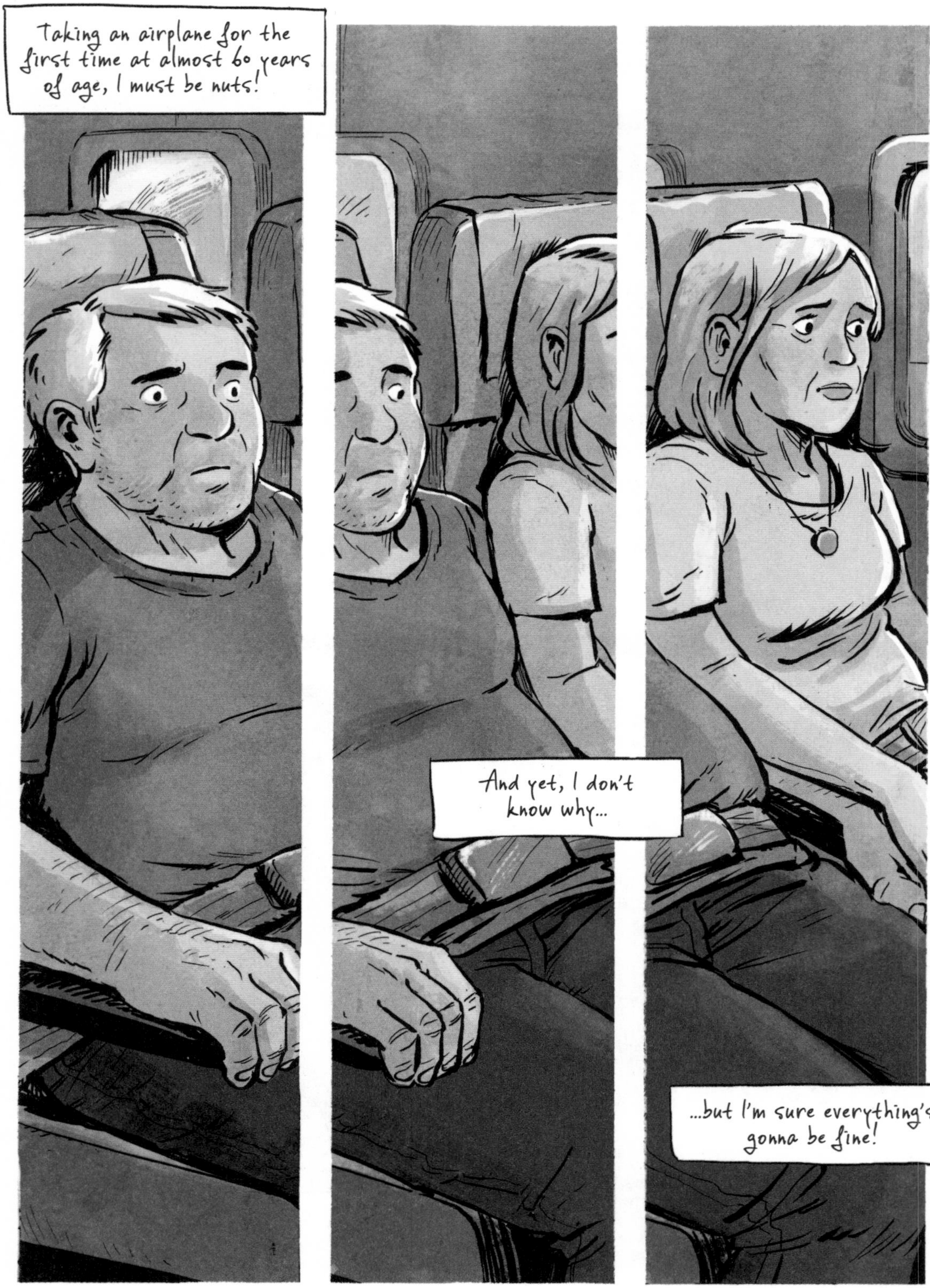
Taking an airplane for the first time at almost 60 years of age, I must be nuts!
And yet, I don't know why...
...but I'm sure everything's gonna be fine!

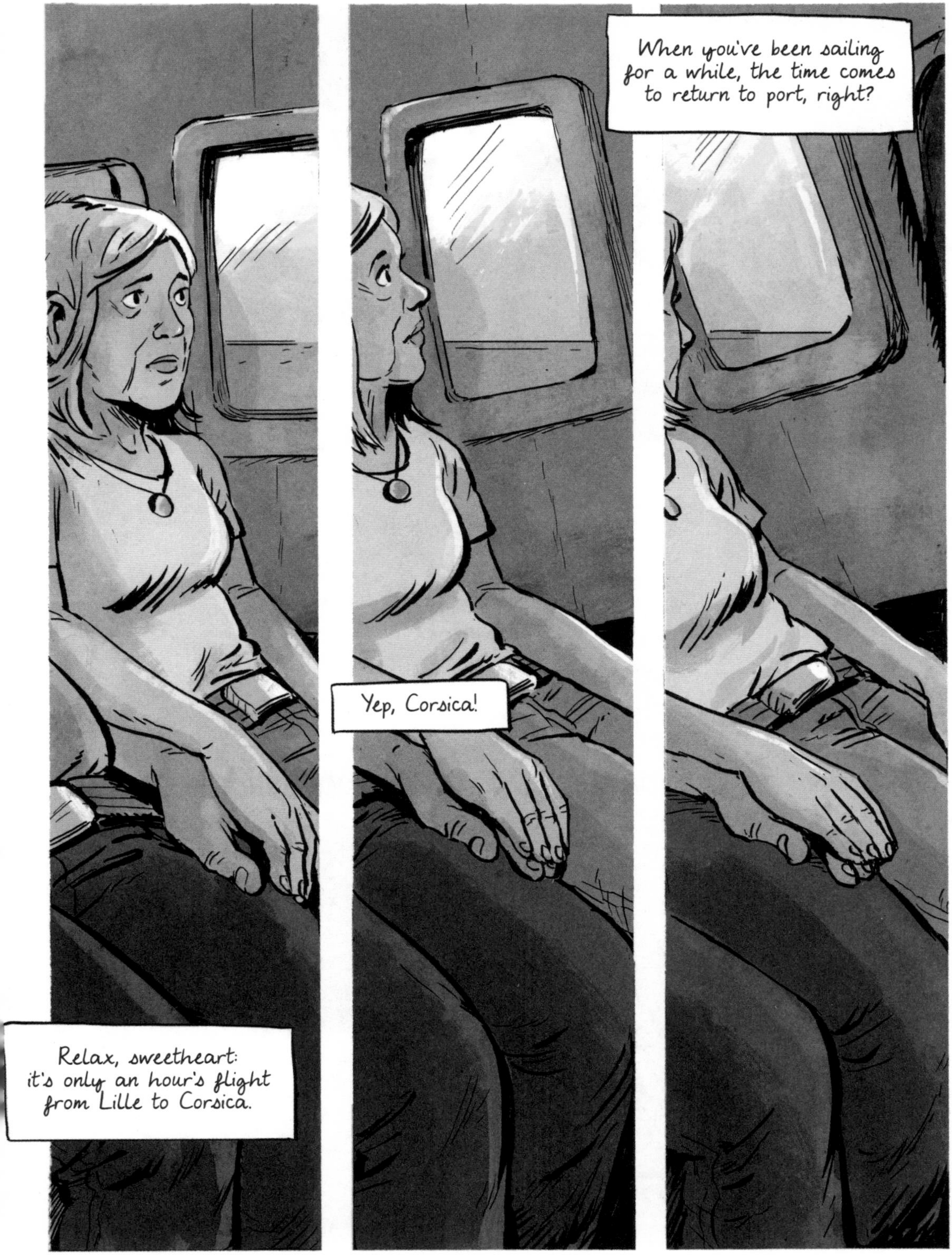
Relax, sweetheart: it's only an hour's flight from Lille to Corsica.
Yep, Corsica!
When you've been sailing for a while, the time comes to return to port, right?

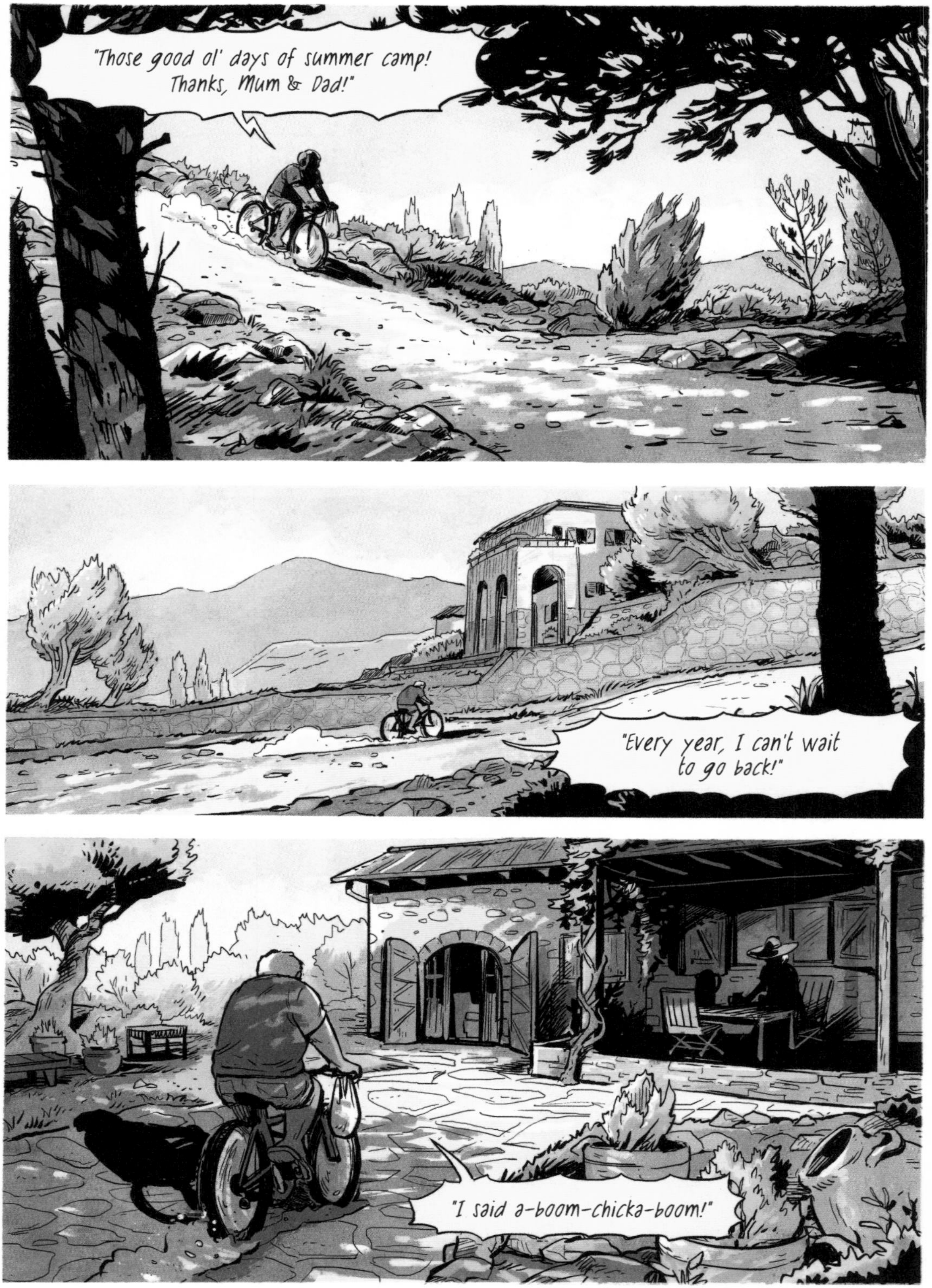
"Those good ol' days of summer camp! Thanks, Mum & Dad!"
"Every year, I can't wait to go back!"
"I said a-boom-chicka-boom!"

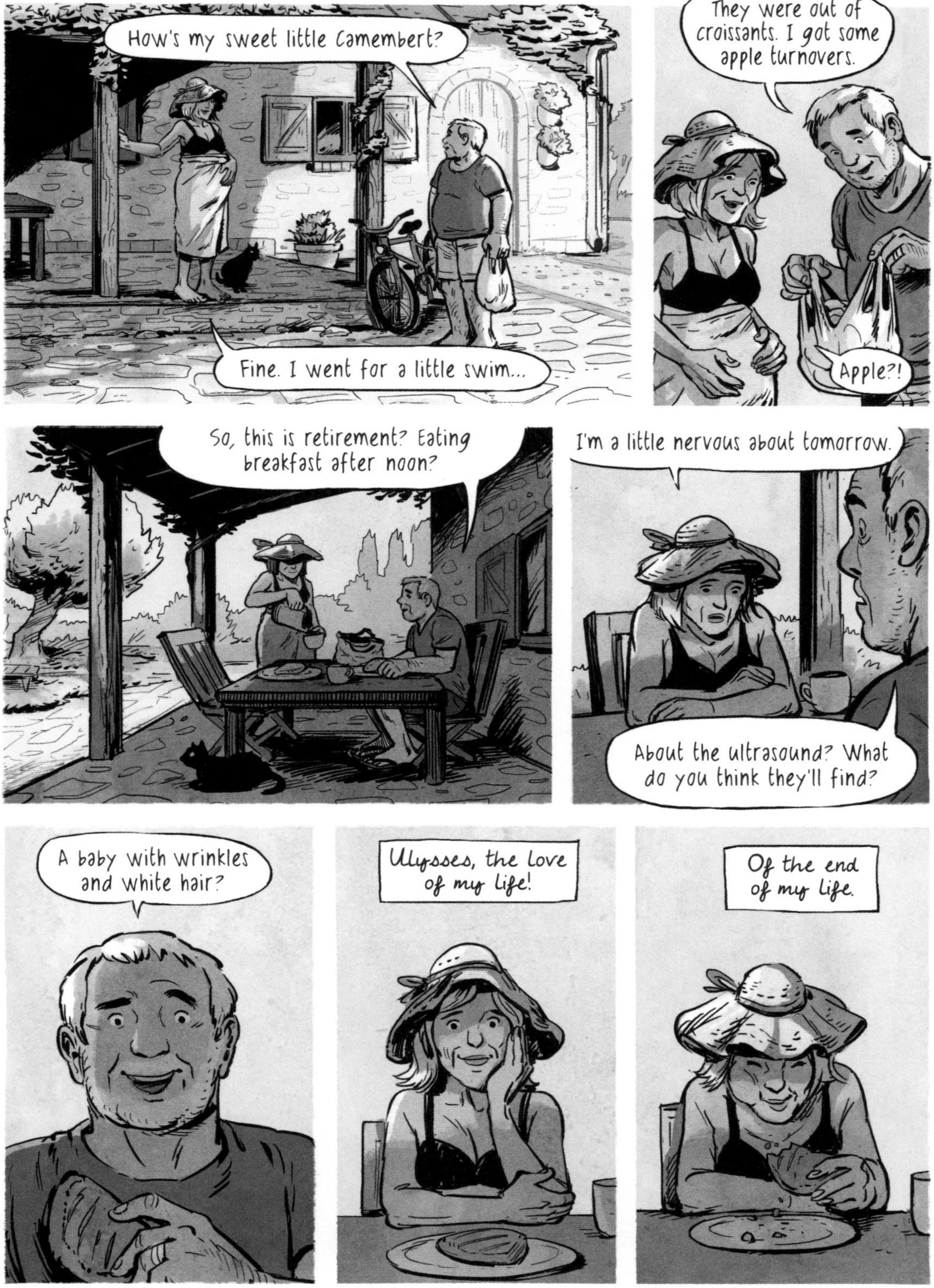
How's my sweet little Camembert?
Fine. I went for a little swim...
They were out of croissants. I got some apple turnovers.
Apple?!
So, this is retirement? Eating breakfast after noon?
I'm a little nervous about tomorrow.
About the ultrasound? What do you think they'll find?
A baby with wrinkles and white hair?
Ulysses, the love of my life!
Of the end of my life.

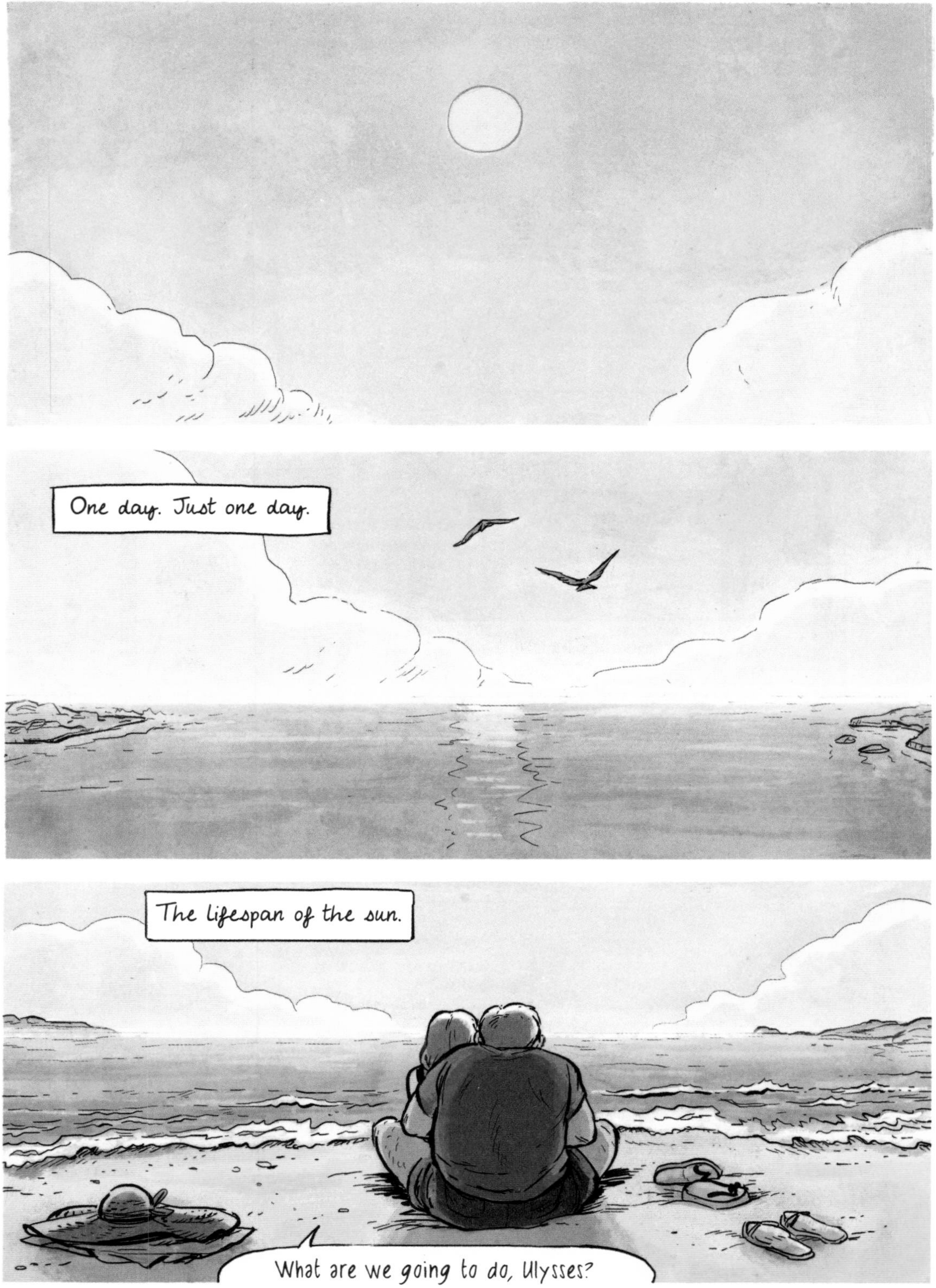
One day. Just one day.
The lifespan of the sun.
What are we going to do, Ulysses?

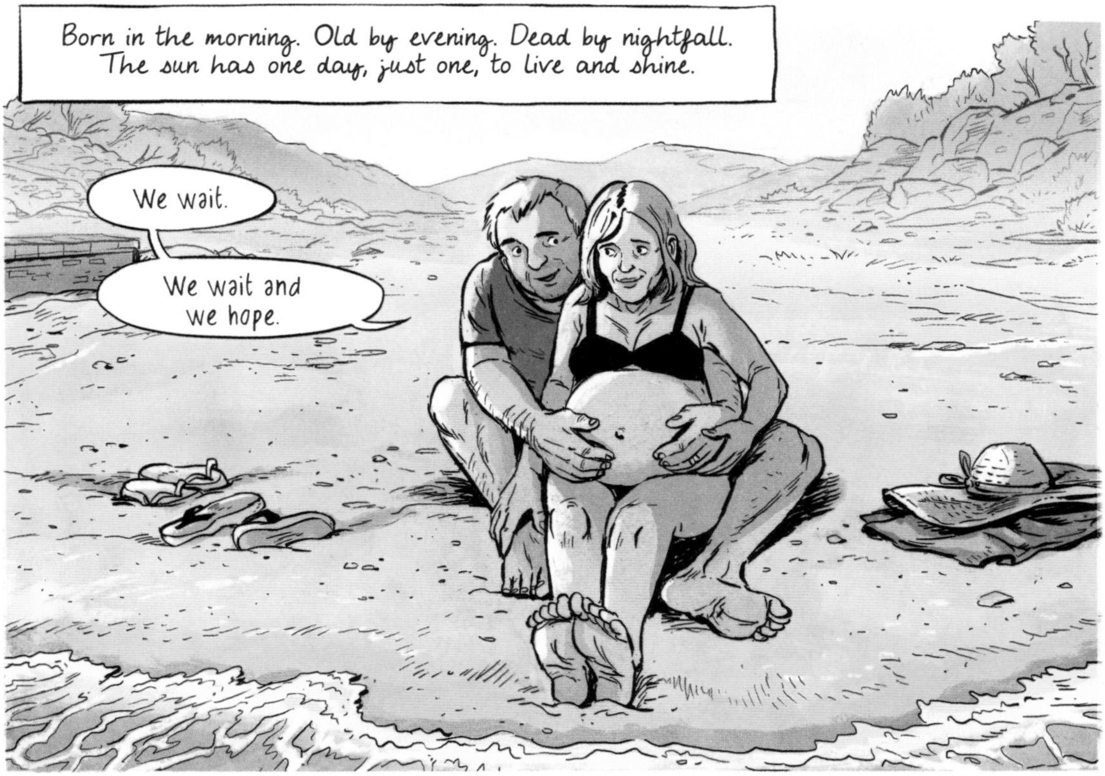
Born in the morning. Old by evening. Dead by nightfall.
The sun has one day, just one, to live and shine.
We wait.
We wait and we hope.

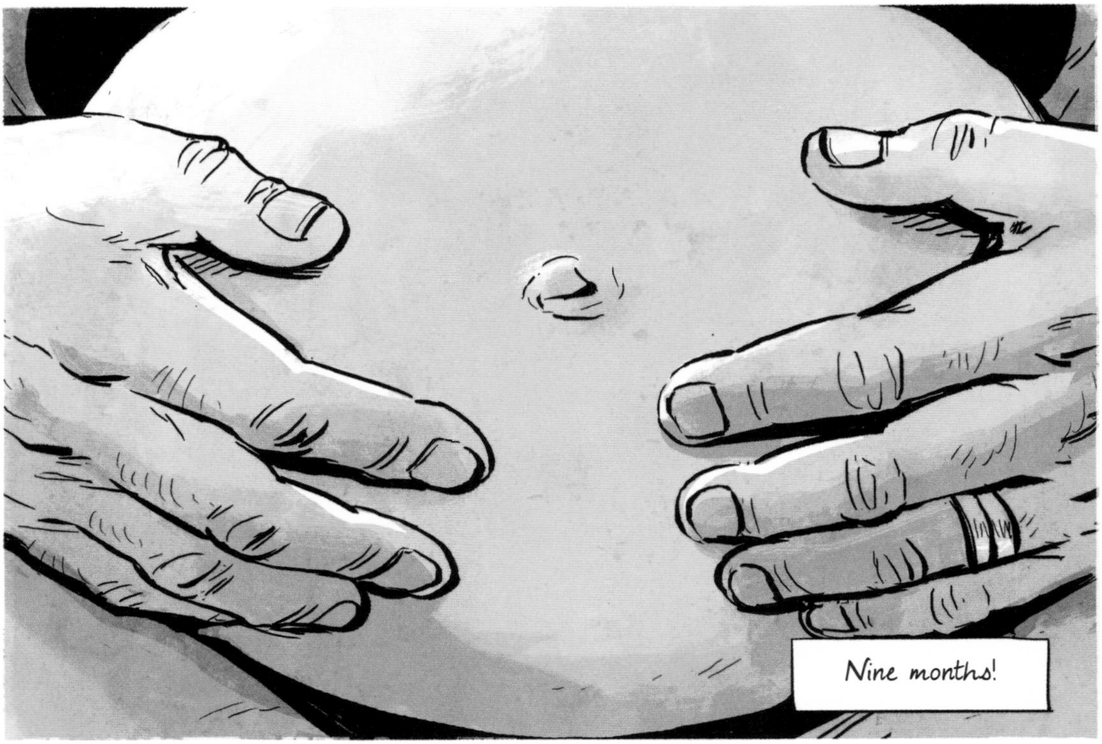
Nine months!

THE END

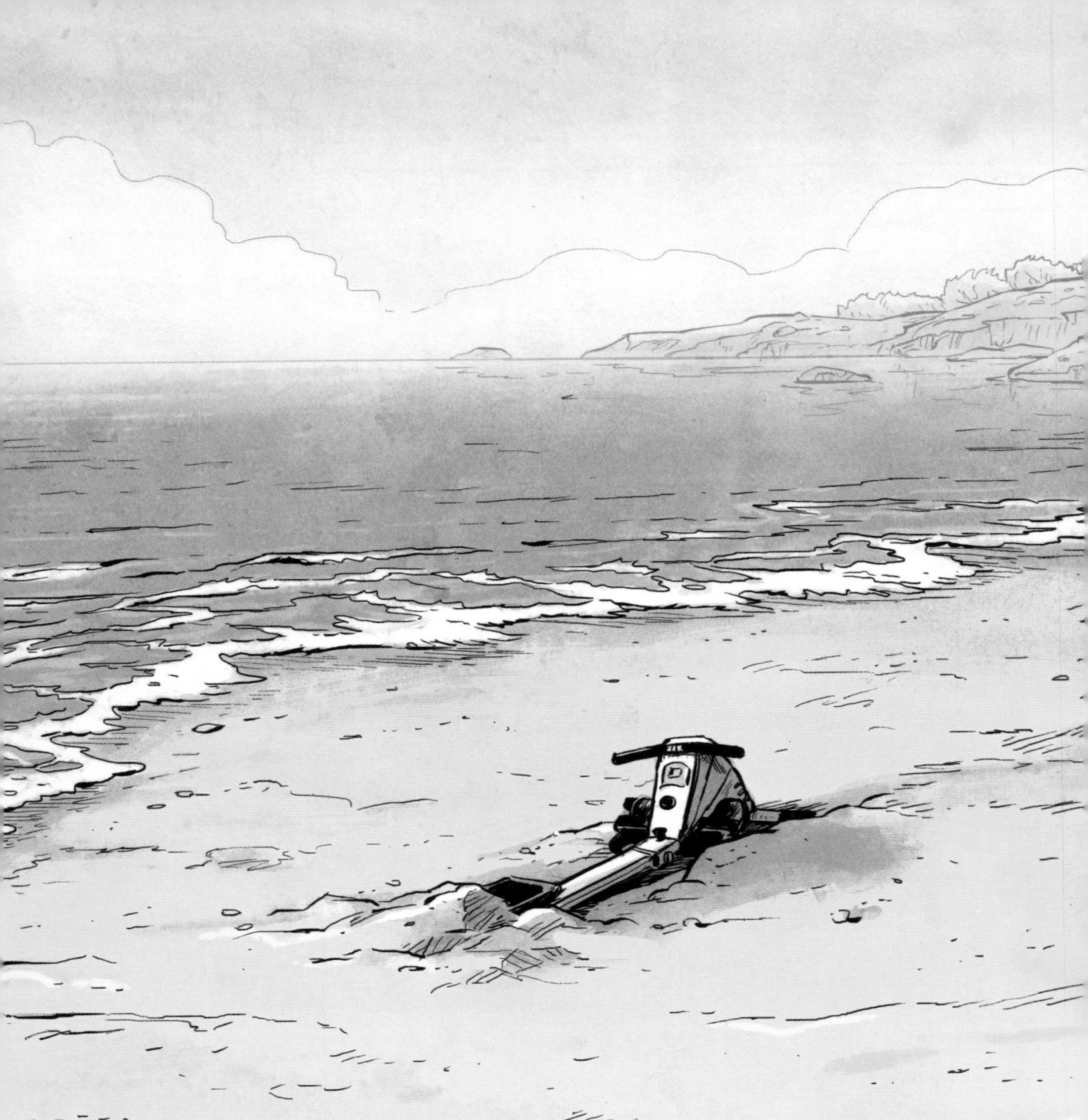

To all fish, big and small.

May a wave carry you to the top of a tree some day. And from that height, may you contemplate the immensity of the ocean.

– Aimée de Jongh and Zidrou

Thank you to my body for putting up with me for a little while longer, if possible. After all, I've been making do with you for 56 years now!

- Zidrou

I'd like to dedicate this book to my father, who will never be older than 50. To my mother, who looks younger by the day. And to my sister, who shares my age, but is light years ahead of me.
Thank you from the bottom of my heart.

- Aimée

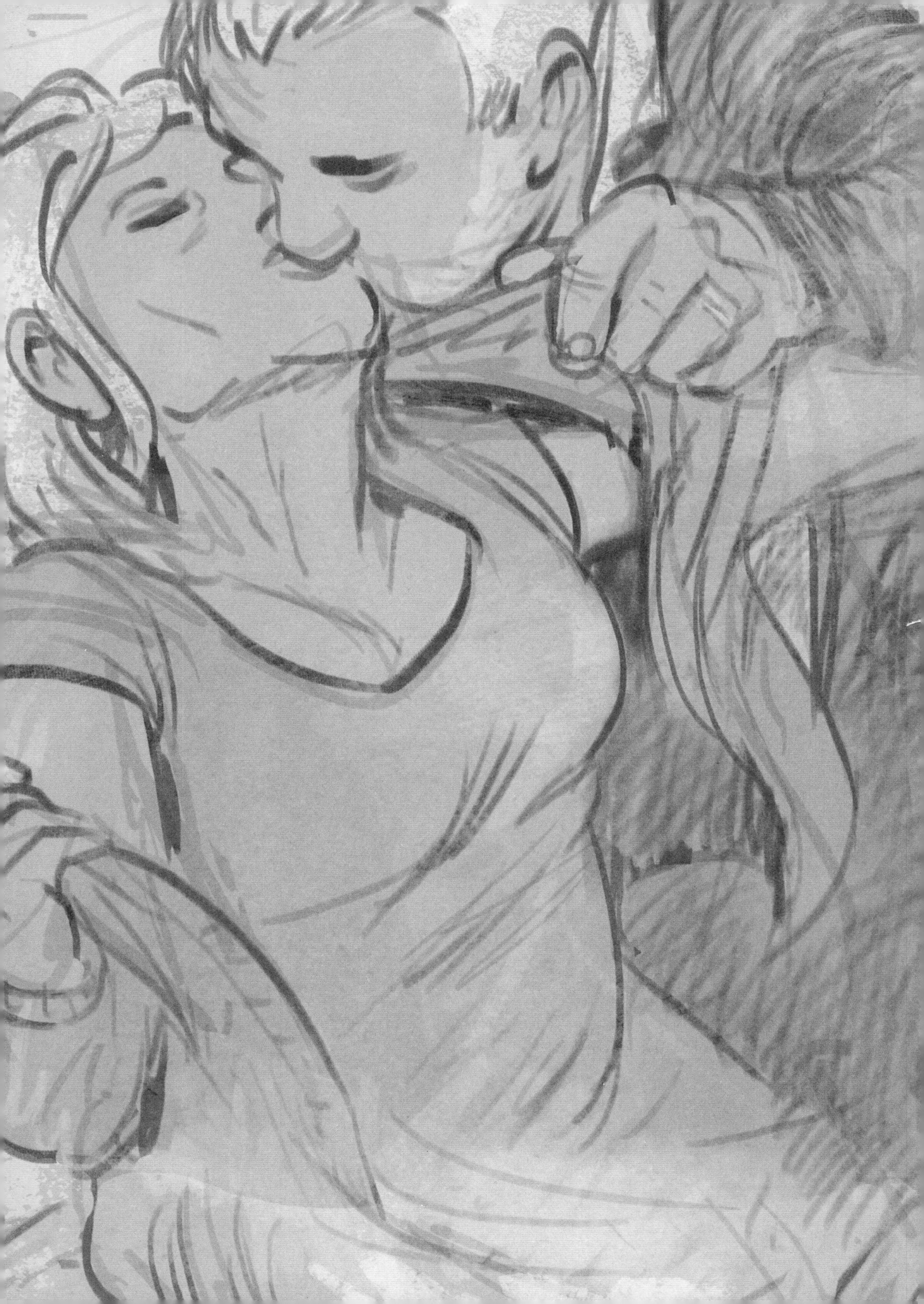

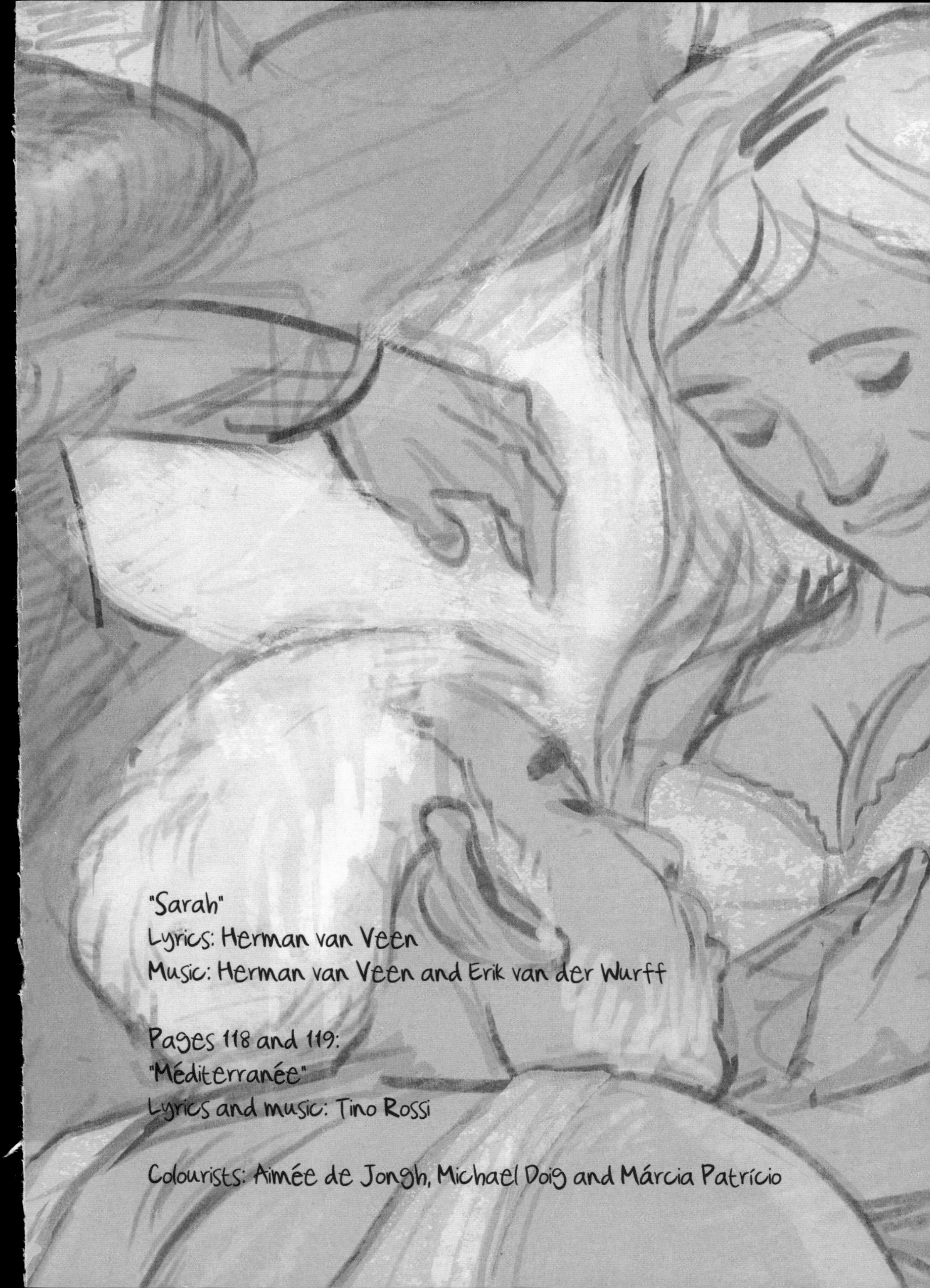

"Sarah"
Lyrics: Herman van Veen
Music: Herman van Veen and Erik van der Wurff

Pages 118 and 119:
"Méditerranée"
Lyrics and music: Tino Rossi

Colourists: Aimée de Jongh, Michael Doig and Márcia Patrício

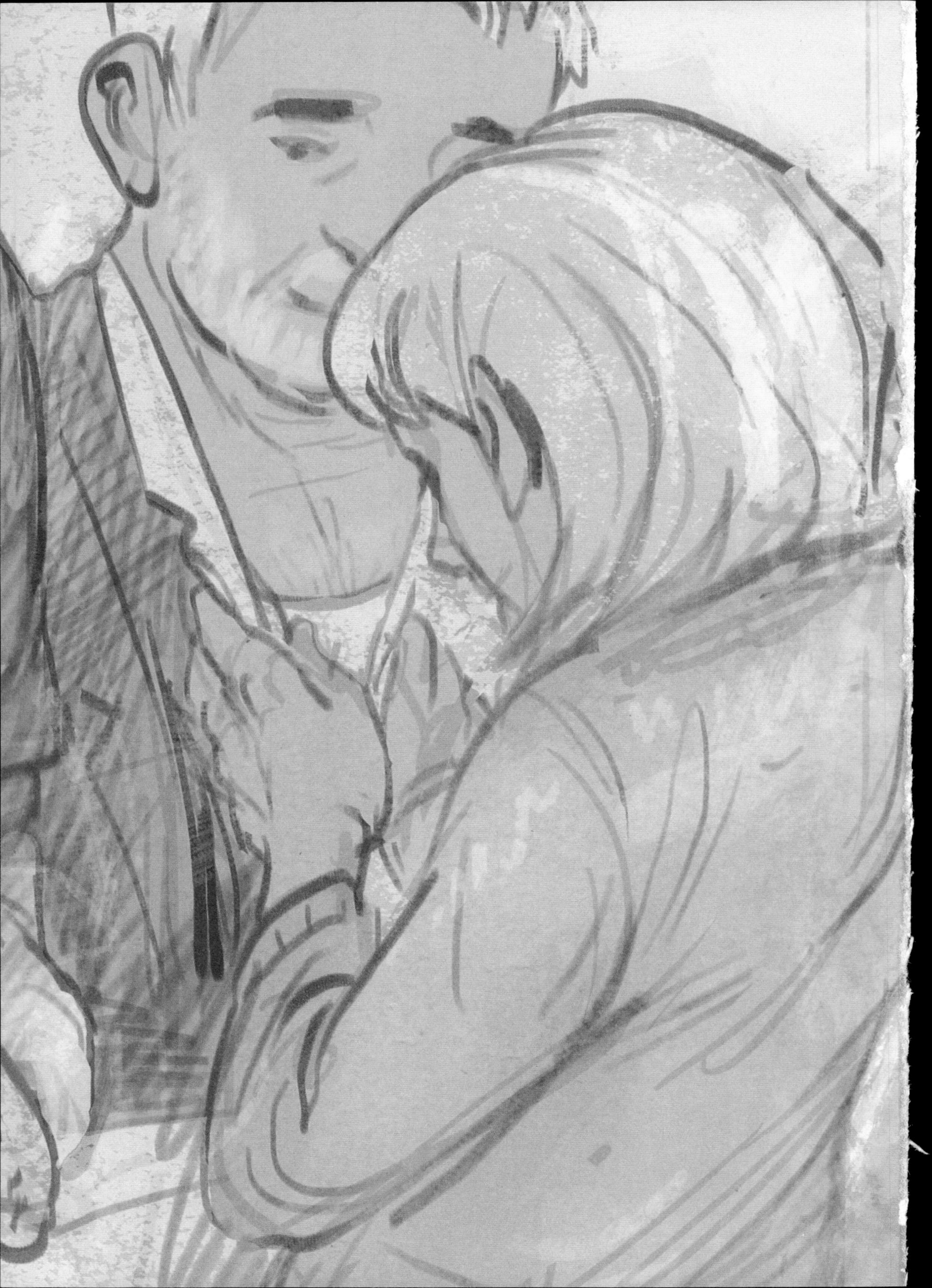

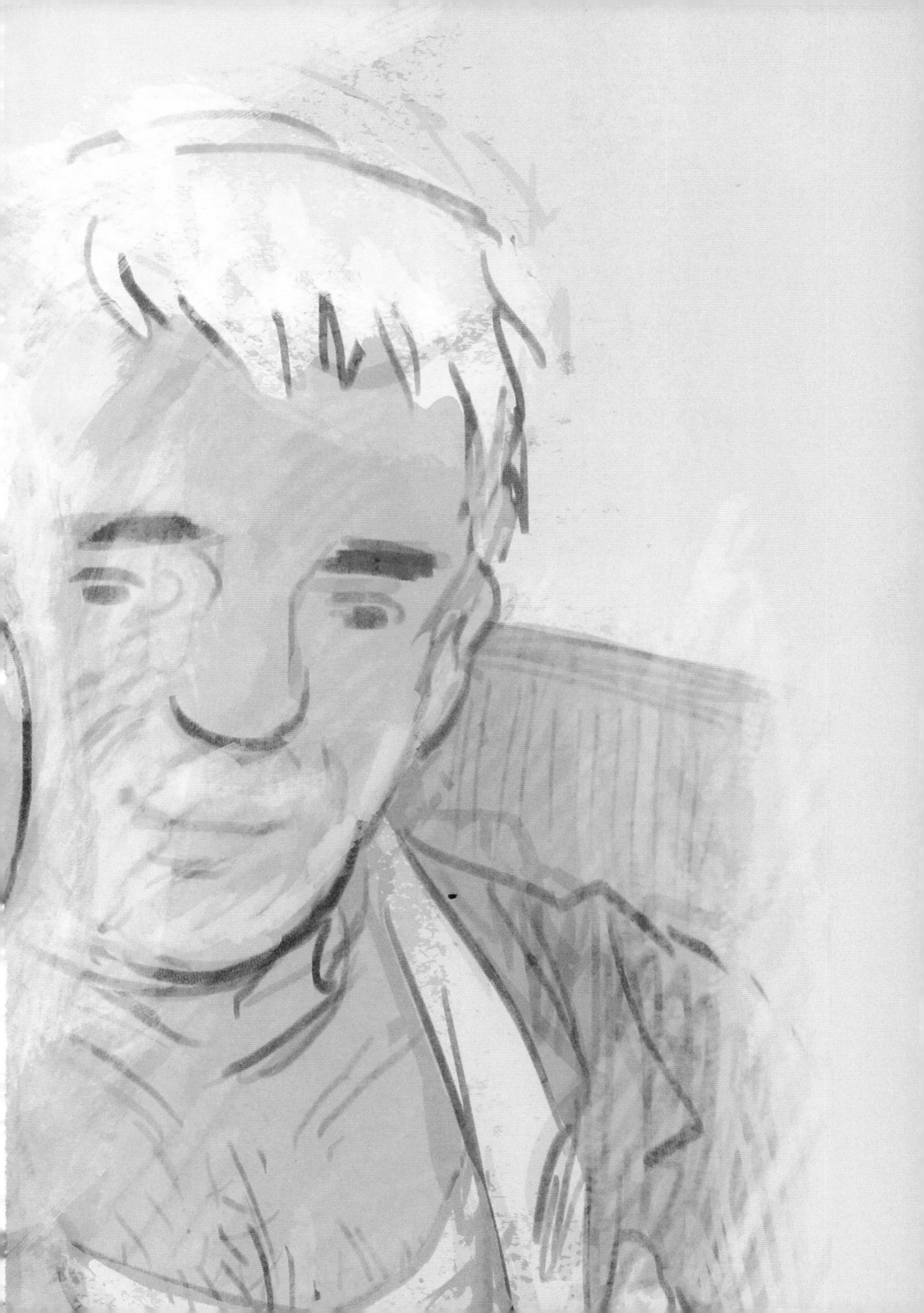